Hill-Fort Studies

Hill-Fort Studies

Essays for A. H. A. Hogg

Edited by Graeme Guilbert

Leicester University Press   1981

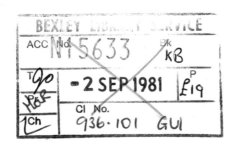
First published in 1981 by Leicester University Press
Distributed in North America by Humanities Press Inc, New Jersey

Designed by Arthur Lockwood
Typeset in Linotron Palatino, printed and bound in Great Britain by
Redwood Burn Limited
Trowbridge and Esher

British Library Cataloguing in Publication Data
Hill-fort studies.
  1. Fortification, Primitives – Great Britain
  I. Hogg, A. H. A.   II. Guilbert, Graeme
  936.1   GN805

ISBN 0–7185–1200–6

Contents

Illustrations

Abbreviations

Note In abbreviating titles of less frequently cited periodicals, the commonly accepted usage of, for example, *Soc.* for *Society*, *Arch.* for *Archaeological*, *J.* for *Journal* etc. has been followed. Other abbreviations are listed below.

Ant. J.	*Antiquaries Journal*
Arch. Ael.	*Archaeologia Aeliana*
Arch. Camb.	*Archaeologia Cambrensis*
Arch. Cant.	*Archaeologia Cantiana*
Arch. J.	*Archaeological Journal*
BA	*Bulletin archéologique*
BAR	British Archaeological Reports
BSPF	*Bulletin de la Société Préhistorique Française*
CBA	Council for British Archaeology
PDNHAS	*Proceedings of the Dorset Natural History and Archaeological Society*
PHFCAS	*Proceedings of the Hampshire Field Club and Archaeological Society*
PPS	*Proceedings of the Prehistoric Society*
PSAS	*Proceedings of the Society of Antiquaries of Scotland*
RA	*Revue archéologique*
RAECE	*Revue archéologique de l'Est et du Centre-Est* (Dijon)
RCAHME	Royal Commission on Ancient and Historical Monuments in England
RCAHMS	Royal Commission on Ancient and Historical Monuments in Scotland
RCAHMW	Royal Commission on Ancient and Historical Monuments in Wales
SAC	*Sussex Archaeological Collections*
SyAC	*Surrey Archaeological Collections*
WAM	*Wiltshire Archaeological and Natural History Magazine*

Preface

The study of hill-forts embraces a great variety of sites, totalling more than 3300 in Britain alone, and a wide range of types of evidence. This collection of essays, each a synthesis of some facet of hill-fort studies, illustrates something of that scope, chronologically, methodologically and, to a lesser extent, geographically. As the recognized chronology of hill-forts and kindred enclosures lengthens, their study broadens to include scholars from a widening sector of the archaeological sphere, so that the topics reviewed in this volume can draw matter from a gross span of over 3000 years, stretching from the neolithic to the early historic centuries, with an appropriate peak in the last millennium BC, the heyday of hill-forts in Britain and Europe. The diversity of approaches and attitudes seen in these papers, exploring evidence derived from excavation, surface fieldwork, historical sources and artifacts, plus some theoretical possibilities, is equally representative of the increasing breadth of hill-fort research. Many of the sites discussed here lie in southern England, but Wales and Scotland too are featured, and French *enceintes* introduce a Continental flavour. This book is not intended to provide the final word on any aspect of hill-forts, nor could it pretend to do so, for the pace of discovery is too hot to allow of such conceit; indeed, it is now almost inevitable that new and relevant information will become available to any writer in this field before his own words have reached the bookshelves. What *Hill-Fort Studies* does offer, then, is debate and comment to a healthy and expansive discipline.

Each contributor is a member of the Hill-Fort Study Group, putting pen to paper with affection and gratitude for the many contributions to hill-fort studies made by their founding father, A. H. A. Hogg. The appreciation of his career and the list of his published works, which open this volume, alike reveal that his concern has not been solely with hill-forts; but hill-forts have been an enduring passion of much of his archaeological life, and no apology is needed for restricting our contents to this theme. Recently, a reviewer of his *Hill-Forts of Britain* described Dr Hogg as 'the doyen of hill-fort archaeology', an accolade which few can achieve in their chosen field – but then, few have witnessed the developments and vicissitudes of 40 years' research in so dynamic a branch of archaeology and yet remained in the front line throughout.

G. G.
March 1980

Bibliography of the published archaeological works, to 1980, of A. H. A. Hogg,

C.B.E., M.A., D.Litt. (*hon. causa*), F.S.A., F.S.A.Scot.

1926 'Flint implements from Shooters Hill', *Woolwich District Ant. Soc. Annual Rep. Trans* 23:43–4.

1929 'Sweyn's Camp, Swanscombe', *Arch. Cant.* 41:13–17.

1930 'Kitchen midden, Gunwalloe', *J. Roy. Inst. Cornwall* 23.ii:325–6.

1932 'Tonge Castle', *Arch. Cant.* 44:60–6.

1934 'Dyke near Bexley, Kent', *Antiquity* 8:218–22.

1935 'Dyke on Hartford Bridge Flats', *PHFCAS* 13.i:70–4.

1937 (with O'Neil, B. H. St J.) 'A causewayed earthwork in West Kent', *Antiquity* 11:223–5.
(with Stevens, C. E.) 'The defences of Roman Dorchester', *Oxoniensia* 2:41–73.

1938 'Preliminary report on the excavation of a long barrow at West Rudham, Norfolk', *PPS* 4:334–6.

1940 'A long barrow at West Rudham, Norfolk. Final report', *Norfolk Archaeol.* 27:315–31.

1941 'Earthworks in Joyden's Wood, Bexley, Kent', *Arch. Cant.* 54:10–27.
(with O'Neil, B. H. St J. and Stevens, C. E.) 'Earthworks on Hayes and West Wickham Commons', *Arch. Cant.* 54:28–34.

1942 'Excavations in a native settlement at Ingram Hill, Northumberland', *Arch. Ael.* 20:110–33.
'The native settlement at Gunnar Peak', *Arch. Ael.* 20:155–74.

1943 'Native settlements of Northumberland', *Antiquity* 17:136–47.

1944 'Cist at Clifton Farm near Morpeth', *Procs Soc. Ant. Newcastle upon Tyne* 10:156–61.

1945 'Gwynedd and the Votadini', *Antiquity* 19:80–4.
'Roman fragments from Castle Dykes near Cockburnspath and from St Abb's Head', *PSAS* 79:172–3.

1946 'Llwyfenydd', *Antiquity* 20:210–11.
(with Frere, S. S.) 'An iron age and Roman site on Mickleham Downs', *Sy AC* 49:104–6.

1947 'A new list of the native sites of Northumberland', *Procs Soc. Ant. Newcastle upon Tyne* 11:140–79.

1948   'The date of Cunedda', *Antiquity 22*: 201–5.
       'Northumbrian forts and farms' (résumé of paper read to Prehistoric
       Society and Cumberland and Westmorland Antiquarian and Archaeo-
       logical Society in Carlisle, 1948), *Arch. Newsletter 1*: 11–12.
1949   'Earthwork at Old Yevering', *Antiquity 23*: 211–13.
1951   'The defences of Craigluscar Fort', *PSAS 85*: 165–70.
       'The Votadini', in *Aspects of Archaeology in Britain and Beyond*, ed.
       W. F. Grimes: 200–20.
1954   'Caernarvonshire field-systems' (report of conference of Prehistoric
       Society in London, April 1954), *Arch. Newsletter 5*: 13–14.
       'A 14th century house-site at Cefn-y-Fan, near Dolbenmaen, Caernar-
       vonshire', *Trans Caernarvons. Hist. Soc. 15*: 1–7.
1955   'Castell Carndochan', *J. Merioneth Hist. Rec. Soc. 2(3)*: 178–80.
1956   Secretary of Royal Commission on Ancient and Historical Monuments
       in Wales for publication of *An Inventory of the Ancient Monuments in
       Caernarvonshire*, I: *East*.
       'Caerau Brynkir' (report of meeting of Cambrian Archaeological
       Association at Nefyn, 1955), *Arch. Camb. 105*: 160.
       'Further excavations at Ingram Hill', *Arch. Ael. 34*: 150–60.
       (with Hogg, N.) 'Doddington and Horton Moors', *Arch. Ael. 34*: 142–9.
       (with Griffiths, W. E.) 'The hill-fort on Conway Mountain,
       Caernarvonshire', *Arch. Camb. 105*: 49–80.
1957   'Four Spanish hill-forts', *Antiquity 31*: 25–32.
       'A fortified round hut at Carreg y Llam, near Nevin', *Arch. Camb. 106*:
       46–55.
1958   'The secondary iron age in Britain', *Antiquity 32*: 189–90.
1959   *The Roman fort at Llystyn, Bryncir Station, Caernarvonshire. First interim
       report, 1957–8* (RCAHMW).
       'Roman fort at Pen Llystyn, Bryncir Station, Caernarvonshire', *Trans
       Caernarvons. Hist. Soc. 20*: 1–5.
1960   Secretary of Royal Commission on Ancient and Historical Monuments
       in Wales for publication of *An Inventory of the Ancient Monuments in
       Caernarvonshire*, II: *Central*.
       'Garn Boduan and Tre'r Ceiri, excavations at two Caernarvonshire
       hill-forts', *Arch. J. 117*: 1–39.
1961   'An earthwork near Sutton Hoo', *Antiquity 35*: 53–5.
       'A Roman milestone from Aber', *Trans Caernarvons. Hist. Soc. 22*: 6–8.
1962   'List of hill-forts in Cardiganshire', *Bull. Board of Celtic Studies 19*: 354–
       66.
       'Archaeology' in *Wales Survey*, supplement to *The Times*, 31 January.
       'King Olaf's Castle?', in G. J. Wainwright, 'The excavation of an earth-
       work at Castell Bryn-Gwyn, Llanidan Parish, Anglesey', *Arch. Camb.
       111*: 56–8.
1963   'Some unfortified hut-groups in Wales', *Celticum 6*: 245–56.
       (with King, D. J. C.) 'Early castles in Wales and the Marches', *Arch.
       Camb. 112*: 77–124.

(with Forde, C. D., Griffiths, W. E. and Houlder, C. H.) 'Excavations at Pen Dinas, Aberystwyth', *Arch. Camb. 112*: 125–53.

1964   Secretary of Royal Commission on Ancient and Historical Monuments in Wales for publication of *An Inventory of the Ancient Monuments in Caernarvonshire*, III: *West*.
'The survival of Romano-British place-names in southern Britain', *Antiquity 38*: 296–9.

1965   'Rheged and Brigantia', *Antiquity 39*: 53–5.
'The early iron age in Wales', in *Prehistoric and Early Wales*, ed. I. Ll. Foster and G. Daniel: 109–50.
review of W. Gardner and H. N. Savory, *Dinorben* (1964), in *Arch. J. 122*: 240–1.

1966   'Native settlement in Wales', in *Rural Settlement in Roman Britain*, ed. C. Thomas (CBA Research Report 7): 28–38.

1967   (with Jones, G. D. B.) 'The Roman marching camp at Esgairperfedd (Radnor)', *Bull. Board of Celtic Studies 22*: 274–6.
(with King, D. J. C.) 'Masonry castles in Wales and the Marches', *Arch. Camb. 116*: 71–132.
review of E. G. Bowen and C. A. Gresham, *History of Merioneth*, I (1967), in *Arch. Camb. 116*: 213–15.

1968   'Pen Llystyn: a Roman fort and other remains', *Arch. J. 125*: 101–92.
review of A. Thom, *Megalithic Sites in Britain* (1967), in *Arch. Camb. 117*: 207–10.

1969   'Cefn Graeanog: a native site of the Roman period', *Trans Caernarvons. Hist. Soc. 30*: 8–20.
'A sample of French hill-forts', *Antiquity 43*: 260–73.
review of D. L. Clarke, *Analytical Archaeology* (1968), in *Post-Medieval Archaeol. 3*: 227–8.

1970   (with King, D. J. C.) 'Castles in Wales and the Marches: additions and corrections', *Arch. Camb. 119*: 119–24.
(with Bark, D. R.) 'A hut-group near Llyn Ogwen, Caernarvonshire', *Arch. Camb. 119*: 131–2.

1971   'Some applications of surface fieldwork', in *The Iron Age and its Hill-Forts*, ed. D. Hill and M. Jesson: 105–25.
'A promontory fort at Tre-coll, Llanbadarn Odwyn', *Ceredigion 6(4)*: 436–7.
(with Davies, J. L. and Hague, D. B.) 'The hut-settlement on Gate-holm, Pembrokeshire', *Arch. Camb. 120*: 102–10.

1972   'Hill-forts in the coastal area of Wales', in *The Iron Age in the Irish Sea Province*, ed. C. Thomas (CBA Research Report 9): 11–24.
'The size-distribution of hill-forts in Wales and the Marches', in *Prehistoric Man in Wales and the West: essays in honour of Lily F. Chitty*, ed. F. Lynch and C. Burgess: 293–306.
'The Government organisation of field archaeology in Britain', in *Field Survey in British Archaeology*, ed. E. Fowler: 68–71.
'Cerdic and the Cloven Way again', *Antiquity 46*: 222–3.

1973 'Hill-forts and Herefordshire', *Trans Woolhope Nat. Field Club* 41: 14–21.
'Presidential address. Field archaeology in Wales', *Arch. Camb.* 122: 1–17.
'Excavations at Harding's Down West Fort, Gower', *Arch. Camb.* 122: 55–68.
'Gaer Fawr and Carn Ingli: two major Pembrokeshire hill-forts', *Arch. Camb.* 122: 69–84.
'A "stone gun" at Arthog, Merioneth', *Arch. Camb.* 122: 179–81.
review of D. W. Harding, *The Iron Age in the Upper Thames Basin* (1972), in *Arch. Camb.* 122: 189–91.

1974 'The Llantwit Major villa: a reconsideration of the evidence', *Britannia* 5: 225–50.
'Carn Goch, Carmarthenshire', *Arch. Camb.* 123: 43–53.

1975 *Hill-Forts of Britain.*
'Rescue excavations and research in hill-forts in Wales', *Archaeol. in Wales* 15: 11–22 (CBA Group 2).
review of *Field Archaeology in Great Britain* (O.S., 5th edn, 1973), in *Arch. Camb.* 124: 121–2.
review of S. C. Stanford, *Croft Ambrey* (1974), in *Ant. J.* 55: 143–4.

1976 Secretary of Royal Commission on Ancient and Historical Monuments in Wales for publication of *An Inventory of the Ancient Monuments in Glamorgan,* I: *Pre-Norman.*
'Castle Ditches, Llancarfan, Glamorgan', *Arch. Camb.* 125: 13–39.
(with Livens, R. G.) 'Unfortified hut-groups in Wales', *Archaeol. in Wales* 16: 8–12 (CBA Group 2).

1977 'Two cairns at Aber Camddwr, near Ponterwyd, Cardiganshire', *Arch. Camb.* 126: 24–37.
review of E. W. MacKie, *Science and Society in Prehistoric Britain* (1977), in *Times Literary Suppl.*, 4 November: 1300.
review of J. Forde-Johnston, *Hillforts of the Iron Age in England and Wales: a survey of the surface evidence* (1976), in *Ant. J.* 57: 371.

1978 'Sample excavation', *Current Archaeol.* 6: 125–7.
review of P. Barker, *Techniques of Archaeological Excavation* (1977), in *Arch. Camb.* 127: 145–7.
review of J. W. Wood, *Sun, Moon and Standing Stones* (1978), in *The Listener*, 13 July: 60–1.

1979 *British Hill-Forts: an index*, BAR 62.
'The problems in Wales', in *Invasion and Response: the case of Roman Britain*, ed. B. C. Burnham and H. B. Johnson, BAR 73: 285–98.

1980 *Surveying for Archaeologists and Other Fieldworkers.*

The editor wishes to acknowledge the help and advice of Leslie Alcock, Stephen Briggs, Penny Guilbert, Jeffrey May, Ian Ralston and Hugh Thompson in compiling this bibliography.

A. H. A. Hogg during a Hill-Fort Study Group field meeting in the Welsh Marches, April 1977 (photograph G. Guilbert).

STEPHEN BRIGGS

A. H. A. Hogg – an appreciation

Although Dr Hogg was christened Alexander Hubert Arthur, he is known to his closer friends as Bob, but to the rest, through endearment rather than familiarity or disrespect, he is just plain Hogg. And as Hogg he will be known for the purposes of this short essay.

Hogg's juvenile interest in archaeology can have been no surprise to the family. His grandfather, who worked in the City, had found considerable pleasure in acquiring or studying material derived from London's Roman levels. His father, A. F. Hogg, who was head of Woolwich Polytechnic, served as President of the Woolwich and District Antiquarian Society, though his interests were to a greater degree geological and botanical. Hogg still enjoys telling the tale of his grandfather's collection. Among the samian ware it included a fine pressure-flaked dagger. This fascinating piece was endowed with a small, brittle brown label which bore traces of a decaying copper-plate hand. Anxious to provide the artifact with a provenance and thereby restore it to a rightful place in history, Hogg carefully opened and deciphered the label, only to read 'This is a dagger typical of those found in Denmark' or some such – an ironic blow to his curiosity.

At the age of 18 his first article, on flints from Shooter's Hill, was published. With archaeology in his veins and such an early start at the business of writing, he might have appeared destined for an archaeological career. But a lad's archaeological interests would not have been easily channelled into such a profession in the 1920s, when careers in the past were practically unheard of. So, after an education at Highgate School, Hogg entered Sidney Sussex College, Cambridge, in 1927; there he took a first in Civil Engineering, with Part 1 of the Maths Tripos.

His first job was with MacAlpines, the contractors, as assistant engineer. Here, demands were few on his graduate skills, and Hogg was eventually sacked – an event about which he has never made any secret. He subsequently helped to build a dry dock in Southampton and to construct the experimental (and then controversial) St Albans by-pass, one of the first all-concrete roads. After a brief spell as scientific officer in the Road Research Laboratory at Oxford (1934 to 1936), he applied for a lectureship in Civil Engineering at

King's College, Newcastle upon Tyne. Taking advantage of a short vacation between Oxford and the Newcastle interview, Hogg determined to walk the Wall and get good value for his interview expenses. At Carrawburgh he duly cast his coin into the Well of Coventina and made a wish. Might the Newcastle job be his? It was.

Excepting three years spent with the M.O.D. at the Royal Naval Dockyard in Rosyth, Newcastle was to be his home until 1945. It was here that he met Nell, then a young lecturer in physiology; and they married in 1943. Rosyth held little interest for him, and Hogg is still sceptical of his contribution to the science of mine detection. In 1945 he returned to Cambridge as I.C.I. Fellow, where he conducted some important experiments into the elasticity of concrete. Later, in 1947, he took up a lectureship there.

Before continuing the narrative of Hogg's career, it might first be useful to explain more of his extra-mural activities since leaving school. Although he enjoyed a successful career in engineering, Hogg freely admits that he was never particularly excited at the prospect of teaching men to rivet ships together or of devising new methods to defend or destroy them. In fact, by the time he had returned to Cambridge, he could boast a fair archaeological library, one quite unrivalled in quantity by engineering books. His archaeological enthusiasm had grown, and he had lost no time in investigating the evidence for himself at first hand. Hogg's interests were wide-ranging, though they were and still are dominated by a love of upstanding monuments. No doubt many of these presented a challenge to the surveyor in him, for, if the engineering contractors had left any mark upon him, it remained in his extremely strong grasp of the theodolite and its uses. And engineering's loss was to be archaeology's gain. In the early stages hill-forts were perhaps less in his mind than were long barrows and dykes. Hill-forts (for him, always with a hyphen) came later.

C. W. Phillips was fortunate to acquire his services at Skendleby (*Archaeologia 85:* 37–106). For here, between contractor and research laboratory, we read that 'Mr. A. H. A. Hogg gave skilled and prolonged assistance', working for almost four months in 1934 'when the major operations were carried out . . . Mr. Hogg's skill and perception were invaluable, practically the whole of the surveying was his work, and the excavations could never have been so successful without his presence'.

On the subject of earthworks, our student went beyond the sights of his theodolite. The physical boundaries of Bexley having taken his fancy, he thoroughly followed up their history through the Anglo-Saxon Charters which originally described them. The discovery of a rectilinear earthwork close to Sutton Hoo attracted his attention after the well-known pre-War excavations had taken place. His considerable efforts to convince the authorities that this earthwork was a likely site for an Anglo-Saxon palace fell on deaf ears. The Ministry of Works was slow to act, and scheduling was not completed before the earthwork was bulldozed years after Hogg had first fussed about it.

By 1949 his accumulated experience made Hogg well suited for an archaeological post. Without this time visiting the Well, Hogg recalls that he turned again to Coventina shortly before a likely job was advertised, and he was interviewed for and appointed Secretary to the Royal Commission on Ancient and Historical Monuments in Wales and Monmouthshire. Replacing Ralegh Radford (resigned 1948) and his predecessor W. J. Hemp (retired 1946), it was Hogg's task to complete the Inventories of Caernarvonshire, work upon which had been proceeding since Anglesey was published in 1937. W. E. Griffiths, C. N. Johns and D. B. Hague were already in Aberystwyth when Hogg arrived, and Hemp continued as part-time Senior Investigator until 1950. During the early 1950s P. Smith, C. H. Houlder and W. G. Thomas were appointed.

In these early days the whole staff would turn out to survey a single monument. Some, like Caernarvon and Conway castles, took several weeks to complete. Excavations, though more recently abandoned as a feature of Commission policy, were at that time an integral part of the investigation programme, and this policy resulted in some signal contributions. Besides Hogg's own memorable work at Tre'r Ceiri and Garn Boduan, W. E. Griffiths' excavations of important cairn and hut groups, C. H. Houlder's examination of the Mynydd Rhiw stone axe factory, and D. B. Hague's survey of St Tudwal's early Christian site are noteworthy from this most stimulating period for Welsh archaeology.

Some interesting tales come down from those days. Hogg himself relates how he was surveying a hill-fort one Sunday when a thunderstorm blew up and he was struck to the ground by lightning – as he said, by the Almighty, for not observing the Sabbath in Welsh Wales. Another story comes from the Tre'r Ceiri dig, when the whole office staff was billeted in a pub in the Lleyn. One evening the inmates were disturbed from their well-earned rest by an anxious young journalist who burst into the lounge bar to inquire where he might find the team of gynaecologists who were digging up the mountain!

Not everyone shared Hogg's enthusiasm for the early start in temperature extremes. Few others have sported a knotted handkerchief on the pate during heatwaves or a balaclava in a blizzard with quite the élan or nonchalance of Hogg. Naturally, such zeal attracted good-humoured leg-pulling. To counteract Hogg's enthusiasm for surveying on a wintry day, one colleague of genius poured feathers from a first-floor window of the office; they swirled past Hogg's window and history has it that fieldwork was abandoned in consequence.

Personal transport has always been of importance to Hogg. Today we may be regaled with the advantages of the Citroën, its high ground clearance, and, more important, its starting handle. But in the early Caernarvonshire years a Jeep was the order of the day. Its occupants did not always enjoy captivity at high speeds (a characteristic for which Hogg is still renowned); so a primitive governor in the form of a coconut shell was fixed beneath the accelerator pedal to frustrate its driver but to bring relief to his passengers. Hogg cannily carried a stick the same width as the vehicle so that all narrow farm gates could be measured in advance – a most sensible tactic.

Upon completion of the Caernarvonshire trilogy in 1964, work in Glamorgan was begun. Here the investigators were to tackle the monuments period by period. Fresh problems meant new sites to excavate, and Hogg enjoyed digs of both iron age and Roman date. The Prehistoric, Roman and Early Christian volumes of Glamorgan were completed in 1973 and published by 1976. Having seen these to the press, Hogg retired.

Retirement has not interfered with his occasionally helping D. M. Browne and C. H. Houlder survey the hill-forts of Brecknockshire, and in 1975 virtually the whole Commission office once more turned out under his guidance to survey Builth Castle.

Later life has brought just rewards; a C.B.E. in 1973 and a D. Litt. from the University of Wales for services to scholarship in Wales in 1974. For long an enthusiastic Cambrian, he was President of the Cambrian Archaeological Association for 1972–3. He continues to write prolifically, and his *Hill-Forts of Britain*, published in 1975, was the first such volume devoted exclusively to that topic. His latest venture, *Surveying for Archaeologists and Other Fieldworkers* (1980), is dedicated to his former colleagues at the Commission.

It is a pleasure for one of a younger generation to know that Hogg is always ready to assist those with less experience than himself. His detached and dispassionate advice is valued by many and is given with deference and modesty. What is more, Dr Hogg displays that faculty to review and retract his own established opinions in the light of new evidence which is surely the mark of a true man of science. For this, as well as his descriptive and synthetic works, he will always be respected and remembered.

RICHARD BRADLEY

From ritual to romance:
ceremonial enclosures and hill-forts

'Juxtaposition is great, – but, you tell me, affinity greater': A. H. Clough (1858), *Amours de Voyage*, Canto III.

The theme of this paper was suggested by the Southampton conference on hill-forts held in 1971. In the opening lecture of that meeting Christopher Hawkes spoke of 'fort sites and sanctity: older religion' (Hawkes 1971:5–6), and Barry Cunliffe's paper included religious foci among the classes of monument from which fortified centres might develop (Cunliffe 1971: 55–7). Hawkes drew attention to a remarkable sequence of ritual sites at Maiden Castle, running, with some interruptions, from the earlier neolithic to the late Roman period, and Cunliffe described the role of plateau enclosures in hill-fort origins, adding the provocative comment that 'it is tempting to see the plateau enclosures as following in the tradition of the Neolithic causewayed camps'. Cunliffe related hill-forts more directly to causewayed enclosures in a paper published three years later (Cunliffe 1974b: 248). Paul Ashbee had already drawn attention to the proximity of certain 'ritual' enclosures and hill-forts (Ashbee 1970: 104), and more recently Hawkes' arguments have been renewed by Geoffrey Wainwright in discussing the monuments around Dorchester (Wainwright 1979a). Since Hawkes' original statement Dennis Harding has offered a careful account of the antecedents of iron age ritual sites (Harding 1974: 103) and Bernard Wailes has done the same for Ireland (Wailes 1976: 337). Still more recently Euan MacKie has conceived an elaborate thesis which unites megalithic metrology, astronomy and the Druids (MacKie 1976a). The evidence is being stretched and threatens to recoil. It is time to examine the original idea in the field.

   The starting point for many of these suggestions is the juxtaposition of hill-forts and ritual monuments. Almost all this evidence actually relates to causewayed enclosures. This may be explained by their frequent hill-top siting, in contrast to that of henges which normally occupy lower ground. At the same time it should be remembered that an essential ingredient of any case for ritual continuity is a direct functional relationship between these two classes of ceremonial site. This is still contentious.

Most of the evidence in fact comes from only part of the distribution of earlier neolithic enclosures and from a still more limited segment of the overall distribution of hill-forts (fig. 1). The siting of both types of enclosure coincides at 11 points. This figure includes Maiden Bower, where the nature of the neolithic enclosure is uncertain, and Carn Brea, which was surrounded by a wall. Another possible site is at Blewburton in Berkshire (Harding 1976b: 142). Major open sites, like Liddington Castle, Ham Hill and Poundbury, are not included in this account. Six of the sites where the two distributions coincide are in Wessex; two are in south-west England; and there are single examples from the Cotswolds, the Chilterns and the South Downs. In the latter area four causewayed enclosures have no apparent successor.

The chronology of these 'ritual' sites is fairly well established. The evidence from the structural phases of causewayed enclosures suggests that they were built and maintained between the late fourth and mid-third millennia bc (Palmer 1976). Their disappearance coincides with a decline in the building of public monuments and with environmental evidence for the regeneration of a number of clearings (Bradley 1978). Artifacts continued to be deposited on these sites into the early bronze age. Henges present more of a problem.

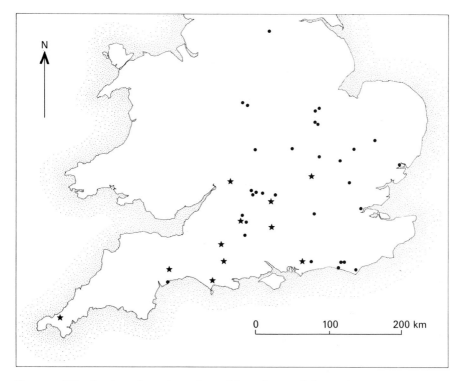

Figure 1. Distribution of certain and possible earlier neolithic enclosures in southern Britain, with those succeeded by hill-forts distinguished (stars). Sites after Palmer (1976), with the addition of Blewburton in Berkshire and Carn Brea in Cornwall.

There is no evidence that these were a single phenomenon and it now seems likely that their origins are with neolithic ring ditches rather than the larger enclosures (Kinnes 1979). There is some sequence of structural types (Catherall 1971) and the available evidence suggests a currency from the middle neolithic to the mid-second millennium. Like causewayed enclosures, they can contain later artifacts but the evidence for continuous activity effectively ceases by the middle bronze age. Among the last of these sites to be built are enclosures like Rams Hill and perhaps the Priddy Circles. Although these sites had quite complex ramparts, there is no evidence that they developed directly into 'hill-forts', even on sites like Norton Fitzwarren which were later defended (cf. Bradley and Ellison 1975: 167). Colin Burgess may well be correct when he sees a major transformation at the end of the early bronze age (Burgess 1974: 194). There are changes in the burial record, with the development of urnfields alongside barrows, and a social landscape built around ceremonial and funerary monuments eventually yielded to the needs of intensive agriculture.

The chronology of the hill-forts is much less clear-cut, and not all those on earlier sites have so far been excavated. It is necessary to enlarge the scope of the argument to cover later activity on all the ritual sites. This has the incidental advantage of showing how far the defended sites form a distinct pattern. If earlier ritual usage was an ingredient in hill-fort origins, two conditions should be met. These are propositions which can be tested against physical evidence:

1. Those defended sites which succeeded the ceremonial enclosures should be among the earliest hill-forts.
2. Since causewayed enclosures and henges were not built at the same time, the more recent sites should have a greater chance of re-use, and the later henges should be re-occupied before the others. This applies to secondary occupation of all kinds and not specifically to hill-forts.

In the discussion which follows the chronology is that of John Collis (1977b: 6).

Of the hill-forts which overlie causewayed enclosures, only one, Crickley Hill, begins life in the late bronze age, with radiocarbon dates lying at the very end of this period (Dixon 1973). There is a latest bronze age hoard from Carn Brea, but the hill-fort on the site was built late in the iron age (Mercer 1975). The Trundle, Maiden Bower and Blewburton seem to have been built at a much earlier stage in the iron age (Curwen 1954; Matthews 1976; Harding 1976b: 139), but Maiden Castle may be a little later (Wheeler 1943). Maiden Castle did produce a middle bronze age spear-head, but no other material of this period. Hembury was not re-used as a hill-fort until the later part of the iron age, although the date of its palisaded phase is not clear (Liddell 1936). There is no real evidence from the remaining sites.

Other causewayed enclosures contain pottery of early iron age date. The earliest of these sites may be at Orsett (Barrett 1978), but there are other sherds from Offham, and possibly Combe Hill (Drewett 1977; Musson 1950: fig.3).

Windmill Hill produced two early iron age sherds and several small finds of this period (Smith I. F. 1965: 170), whilst Briar Hill contains pits of the 'pre Belgic' iron age (Bamford 1976). Three of the sites were also used late in the iron age. The enclosure at Briar Hill is skirted by a pit alignment, and a new enclosure was constructed alongside the neolithic earthwork at Knap Hill (Cunnington 1911). Some of the pottery on the latter site is probably of late iron age date. Contemporary pottery also came from the outer ditch at Whitehawk (Curwen 1934). Seven of the sites have produced Roman pottery and at Windmill Hill, Knap Hill and Staines there may have been a phase of sustained settlement of Roman age (for Staines see Robertson-Mackay 1962). Finally, at Langford and at Cardington causewayed enclosures are obscured by crop marks of unknown date (Palmer 1976).

There is less evidence from published henge monuments. Only the site at Barford shows any activity in the late bronze age. Here a supposedly iron age pit contained a distinctive bronze chisel (Oswald 1967: fig. 16). Most records of iron age material are vague or incomplete, but at Durrington Walls there is early iron age pottery from high in the ditch (Wainwright and Longworth 1971: 21). This site also included a middle iron age palisade and some pits. Early and middle iron age pottery came from the ditch at Arminghall (Clark J. G. D. 1936: 16), but the one henge re-used as a hill-fort was the anomalous site of Castell Bryn-Gwyn, which is not closely dated (Wainwright G. J. 1962). Mount Pleasant also saw renewed activity, and at least one late iron age house was constructed on the site of the neolithic timber circle (Wainwright G. J. 1979a). Iron age pottery of unspecified phase is known from Dorchester-on-Thames and the Devil's Quoits (Atkinson et al. 1951), and a pit circle henge at Maxey was cut by an iron age enclosure (Simpson W. G. 1967). In the third century BC, Hanborough site IV was levelled for agricultural purposes (Case et al. 1965: 55). Sherds were deposited at Stonehenge at about the same time (Atkinson 1956), and more pottery was deposited there in the late iron age, as also at Arminghall. It may have been at this stage that one henge at Llandegai was converted for use as a settlement (Houlder 1968). There is Roman iron age pottery from the Stones of Stenness (Ritchie J. N. G. 1976: 22). Only Cairnpapple was certainly re-used for ritual, and iron age graves were there dug into a henge monument which contained nothing later than collared urns (Piggott S. 1948). The bank around Maes Howe was also enlarged in the iron age (Renfrew et al. 1976: 198). The Irish evidence is not considered in this paper.

Three observations arise from this detail. First, it is clear that more causewayed enclosures than henges include iron age material, even though the latter are more frequent and more widely distributed. Second, there are suggestions that a higher proportion of causewayed enclosures show activity *early* in the iron age: such material is known from at least seven causewayed sites, but from only two henges, although some site reports do not provide enough detail. Finally, there is a hint that some of the earlier henges were re-used before the later ones. It is interesting that Arminghall and Barford are among the earliest of all these sites. Although Llandegai may not conform to this pattern, it is clear that renewed activity on the later sites at Hanborough, Stonehenge and Mount Pleasant was itself at a developed phase of the iron age. None of these observations are consistent with the two propositions from which this discussion arose. In fact there appears to have been a considerable hiatus on every site and the date at which they came back into use seems to be directly related to the duration of this interval. It seems as if ritual use of these locations 'sterilized' them for a period, after which they were again available for settlement. The break usually runs throughout the later bronze age.

To see this change in more detail it is worth returning to Rams Hill, for it is still the one excavated site which was only briefly deserted. Between the early bronze age and the middle to late bronze age transition it appears to have been a hilltop enclosure, dominating an area rich in burials, and confined by a considerable earthwork. Throughout this period there was little evidence for domestic activity on the site and it can be argued that this enclosure was in an already archaic tradition (Bradley and Ellison 1975). But after a short interval of disuse, perhaps in the eleventh century bc, the surrounding area was cleared and the earlier enclosure was replaced by an important settlement. This contained a number of houses and an arrangement of four-post structures. Although these structures are normally interpreted as granaries, there was no direct evidence of arable farming from the site and it was originally suggested that the economy was based mainly on livestock. This perhaps needs modification. The surrounding area contains several large field systems, very probably of bronze age date (Bradley and Richards 1978), and the evidence from Rams Hill would be equally consistent with its interpretation as a food store, much as Cunliffe has suggested for other early hill-forts (Cunliffe 1976b: 347). If this were the case, there would be no need to find a novel function for the four-posters on the site, and the absence of carbonized cereals would be explained if grain had been introduced after processing. It may be significant that Rams Hill did in fact develop into a hill-fort. The nearby field systems belonged to a very different landscape from that of the earthworks of the first phase. Hill-forts proper grew out of this period of economic change.

The changes at Rams Hill came some time after the desertion of other enclosures. It remains to be asked how the abandoned enclosures were treated and whether these changes were general, or were confined to these rather special sites. Because of their greater numbers, it is worth extending the discussion to bronze age barrows.

The break in the use of large enclosures extends over a wide range of ritual structures. On a number of these sites, including ring ditches in the Thames valley and henge monuments on the chalk, there is evidence that open features were soon being filled with wind-blown silt, perhaps from arable land or over-grazed pasture (Cornwall 1953; Evans in Wainwright G.J. 1979a: 210ff.). At least two of the deserted henges were fenced off from productive farmland. This may be the function of a Deverel-Rimbury land boundary close to the Stonehenge Avenue (RCAHME 1979: 25) and of another middle bronze age ditch cutting off the enclosure at Durrington Walls (Wainwright and Longworth 1971: 310). Domestic settlements are known close to both of these monuments, one at Winterbourne Stoke crossroads, close to Stonehenge (MPBW 1967: 11–12), and the other the Durrington Egg, south of Woodhenge (Cunnington 1929). Round barrows may show a similar pattern. Some gravel sites show evidence of clearance around their mounds (Green 1974; Bradley and Richards, forthcoming), and on the chalk of Wessex, where the sites of neolithic enclosures and hill-forts often coincide, it is very common for groups of round barrows to have been preserved in areas of pasture. Indeed it is to this feature that they owe their survival to the present day. A number of these barrow cemeteries were enclosed by ditches in the later bronze age. A good example is on Snail Down in Wiltshire (Bowen 1975: 106-7). A similar pattern is seen near Oakley Down in Dorset and provides more chronological detail. Here a long barrow and two bronze age mounds were cut off from arable fields by a shallow ditch. The fields carefully respected this division, which probably separated arable from pasture, and even continued to do so when one of these plots was taken out of use and adapted as a middle bronze age settlement (Toms 1925; RCAHME 1975: 70). Such attention to barrows is a very widespread phenomenon, and other boundary ditches, first established in this period, were aligned on earlier mounds. Virtually the same patterns are seen in areas of arable, both on the chalk and the gravels. Barrows normally lie at the edge of field systems or were incorporated in the boundaries of individual plots. It is not likely that many of the mounds were actually disturbed. There are few items of later bronze age date from barrow ditches in southern England, apart from obvious secondary burials. The following figures are taken from reliably published sites in three environments:

Finds from barrow ditches	Downland of Wiltshire and Dorset	Upper Thames valley	Heathlands of central southern England	
Later bronze age	3	3	0	sites
Iron age	7	18	1	sites
Roman	21	19	5	sites
Size of sample	46	40	37	sites

As this table suggests, pressures really built up in the iron age, except on the degraded heathland soils. Unfortunately it is seldom possible to date such material more precisely. The table also indicates an increasing contrast between the chalk and the river gravels during the iron age. On the downland it would seem that a higher proportion of barrows were preserved intact, whilst on the gravels more sites were eventually destroyed (cf. RCAHME 1976: lv). It is not certain whether burial monuments in the two areas had been built on an equivalent scale (Case 1963), but it is clear that more ring ditches on the gravels were in areas which saw later settlement. The evidence of crop marks seems to show that the Upper Thames gravels were now at a premium. Isolated mounds could be preserved but few barrow ceme-teries can be found without other crop marks, usually of iron age or Roman date. The following table illustrates this pattern:

	In isolation	With other crop marks
Single ring ditches	32	24 sites
Multiple ring ditches	21	48 sites

Sources: Benson and Miles 1974, Gates 1975 and RCAHME 1976.

On the chalk there is less evidence for drastic change, but in some instances all respect for ritual sites had been lost. The Dorset cursus was overlain by a settlement (RCAHME 1975: 24), and the number of earlier prehistoric burials from the sites of hill-forts suggest that older cemeteries were being forgotten or ignored. For example, at Overton Down a flat cemetery was damaged by an iron age settlement and its fields (Fowler 1967); the rampart at Old Win-chester Hill impinged on a group of barrows; and the Long Mound at Maiden Castle was cut in half by the first iron age defences (Wheeler 1943).

On the gravels the treatment of these sites was far more drastic. It is some-times possible to recognize successive stages in this process. At Stanton Har-court in the Thames valley wind-blown silts in the filling of ring ditches indicate some form of agriculture in the area not long after they were built; and by the middle of the iron age a nearby henge and several barrows were being levelled to allow cultivation (Cornwall 1953; Case et al. 1965: 55). At Abingdon, further downstream, two ring ditches which had been respected throughout the later bronze age were removed by an iron age settlement (Par-rington 1978). It is interesting to notice how this settlement first developed alongside these monuments and only gradually expanded across them. The whole process took about 200 years. The evidence from the Great Ouse valley is very similar. It is known that the areas around a number of ring ditches were later cleared for pastoral land use (Green 1974). A few secondary burials also belong to this phase, which usually occurred in the middle bronze age. A similar pattern is present in the Thames and Kennet valleys (Bradley and Richards, forthcoming). At Roxton in Bedfordshire there is evidence for middle bronze age domestic activity in a small cemetery of earlier date (Peter Woodward, pers. comm.). This particular site is especially informative since excavation has also shown a second phase of land use in the iron age, this time associated with ditches which ran up to the mounds and incorporated them in the new field boundaries. At this stage the areas between the barrows were ploughed and their ditches filled. By the Roman period it was possible to plough across the mounds. A heavier plough was now available and this change could account for the high proportion of Roman finds on such sites. There is evidence for iron age ploughing close to other ring ditches in the Ouse valley (Green 1974).

In short, the pattern shown by the neolithic enclosures is repeated by the burial sites, and by the beginning of the iron age a wide variety of the sites of ritual monuments were being re-used. There is no reason to believe that the new use was connected with ritual and on some sites there is clear evidence of agriculture. The interval of desertion ends at various stages in the first millennium, but it is clear that the sites most recently used for ritual were among the last to be disturbed. Similarly the earliest of the ritual sites were often the soonest forgotten. There is no one explanation for the presence of later artifacts. A few enclosures were re-used as settlements, but many of these finds may be manure-deposited refuse associated with the expansion of agriculture. The destruction of antiquities has a very long history and it would seem that later use of these sites is not related to their earlier function. It is not a sign of continuing respect: it actually shows that any inhibitions had been lost.

Seen in this light, the re-use of these sites is only part of the expansion of settlement which is the hallmark of the first millennium, and in particular of the iron age. It is the counterpart of colonization in other areas. To some extent this is related to the new range of agricultural tools, including iron axes, mattocks and ard tips, and of the careful provision for grain storage characteristic of defended and unenclosed settlements. It would appear that ritual use of a site merely 'neutralized' it for later settlers until a lengthy interval had elapsed.

These broad generalizations also conceal a geographical pattern, for it was mainly in a limited area that old causewayed enclosures were adapted as hillforts, however widespread the evidence for iron age activity of other kinds. This is essentially a Wessex phenomenon and contrasts with the evidence from Sussex, where only one site out of six became a hill-fort. It is possible that the Wessex chalk was far more extensively enclosed than other areas; in the later bronze age it was this area that was divided up by an elaborate network of ditches, and it was this area again which contained an unusual proportion of iron age enclosures, as opposed to open settlements (cf. Perry 1969: 39). These two processes could well be related: the careful allotment of land in the later bronze age may already reveal greater competition than in other areas. But, whatever the merits of this view, Wessex was unusually densely settled. If causewayed enclosures were occupying usable soils – and especially if they formed gaps in a crowded landscape – it would be surprising if some of their earthworks had not been renewed. If their earlier role supplies an ingredient of ritual, this new use of hilltops for defence and display provides the rest of my title.

Such a cycle of events was to be repeated. It has been seen in the location of Saxon settlements on Roman and earlier religious sites (Miles 1974: 40); and it appears again in the modern pressures on urban graveyards. In the end it is not the coincidence of location that really matters, but the conflicts within society between the requirements of ritual and those of subsistence. This is a question which has exercised anthropologists, who have access to the rituals and myths which elude the prehistorian. It is a theme of particular significance and should concern iron age scholars as well.

MICHAEL AVERY

Furrowed bowls and carinated Hawkes A pottery

The chronology of hill-forts and of other settlement sites of the first millennium BC in southern Britain depends on the stratified Hawkes A potsherds which offer *termini post quem*. The calendar dating of the multifarious forms of Hawkes A pottery has always been hung round two key styles: the furrowed bowls which are most notably known from All Cannings Cross; and the carinated pottery which has conventionally been ascribed to the fifth century BC. I shall here suggest a revised dating for both of these styles. Consequently I shall suggest a revised date-range for all Hawkes A pottery and for the sites dated by that pottery.

Although a limited number of radiocarbon determinations now provide a useful skeleton of calendar dates for the first millennium BC, these remain an adjunct to the pottery, not a substitute. The best chronologically-ordered division of the pottery is still the Hawkes ABC system (Kendrick and Hawkes 1932: 153–208; Hawkes 1961; Harding 1972; 1974); essentially the same system has been used by Hodson, albeit under a different nomenclature (Hodson 1964: fig. 1), and forms the basis of the ideas outlined by Cunliffe (1974a). The calendar dating, however, has long been obscured by the persistent interpretation of all this pottery as 'iron age'. The terms 'Hawkes A', 'Hawkes B' and 'Hawkes C' are used here to eliminate this cultural gloss from a fundamentally ordinal system of pottery classification and dating. I shall argue that much more Hawkes A pottery belongs to the bronze age than has usually been allowed; and firmly back in the bronze age, not in a 'proto-iron age' limbo of the eighth century BC. Swan has shown that, at the other end of the time-scale, some Hawkes C pottery should be dated later than the Roman Conquest (1975). No nomenclature which titles this pottery 'iron age' or 'pre-Roman iron age' can now eliminate misleading overtones. It is perhaps appropriate to stress that use of the ABC terminology does not imply the view that A, B and C pottery styles mark three successive cultures,[1] much less that they first appeared in Britain through invasion. It has been clear since at least the mid-1970s that something was radically wrong with the dating of much that was conventionally ascribed to the iron age. Champion (1975) has very cogently argued that much of this 'iron age' material could be ascribed to the late bronze age, if Continental parallels were allowed to date the British material without interference from preconceptions.[2] I have myself suggested removing 'iron age' from the title of the pottery (1976: 38, n.93), to clear away one preconception. It remains to give more substance to the possibilities, by trying to establish firm specific dates in the bronze age for specific items of the erstwhile iron age.

Hill-forts where Hawkes A pottery is vitally important for dating include Budbury,[3] Hollingbury,[4] Bindon,[5] and the cross-rampart of the small fort of period 1 at Torberry.[6] The hill-fort most crucially affected by a re-dating, however, is Maiden Castle, Dorset. Here carinated pottery was found within the make-up of the rampart of period 1, the small fort.[7] Period 1 ended with a long interval of abandonment and ditch silting, which was then succeeded by the enlarged fort of periods 2, 3 and 4. This carinated pottery has always been the crucial evidence which required a date after the fifth century BC for Maiden Castle 1 and similar timbered structures,[8] and imposed a date hardly before 100 BC on the developed dump ramparts found at Maiden Castle in period 4 and elsewhere. The re-dating propounded below allows Maiden Castle potentially an extra half-millennium of life. This permits the evidence of long-lived development to be given its full weight, at Maiden Castle and at other hill-forts.

It is now some 20 years since Margaret Smith dramatically altered the later British bronze age. In 1959, she transferred much of what had until then been thought of as late bronze age metalwork back into the second millennium BC, as her Ornament Horizon. The impact of this, however, spread wider than metalwork. With the Ornament Horizon bronzes, Deverel-Rimbury pottery and settlement sites were also emptied out of the late bronze age into the middle bronze age (Smith M. A. 1959: 155–9). This left a void in the British late bronze age, between Deverel-Rimbury and All Cannings Cross. The void has not proven easy to fill. For the past 50 years or so, most of the known pottery and sites later than Deverel-Rimbury have been dated to the iron age, that is, later than the seventh century BC. There have been two reasons for this dating. Firstly, a number of bits of evidence, individually slight but cumulatively impressive, combine to suggest that the earliest pottery recovered from settlement sites later than Deverel-Rimbury consists of the furrowed bowls of the type found at All Cannings Cross by Cunnington (1923). These furrowed bowls have been dated later than the seventh century BC because of a bronze example in the hoard found at Welby, Leicestershire, which has been dated to about 650 BC.[9] Secondly, much of the pottery has been dated later than the fifth century BC, because of the conclusion that in that century there was a period of use of carinated pottery; carinated pottery has been dated by comparing it with fifth-century BC pottery in the Marne region of north-eastern France.[10]

Consequently, over the past 20 years a paradoxical situation has developed: the period from the eleventh to the seventh centuries BC has been well-peopled with sophisticated bronze-using societies, but devoid of settlement sites.[11] The settlement sites have all appeared to come in with a bang in the seventh or sixth century BC, as the metalwork disappeared.

The paradox can be resolved by reconsidering the Continental parallels for furrowed bowls. Continental parallels for British pottery are never as exact as one would ideally like, but in the case of furrowed bowls they seem sufficiently close to call for a revision of conventional datings. Some parallels can be found in France, particularly in the region of the Upper Rhine. Much better parallels, however, occur in the region of the Middle Rhine, in South-western Germany; these German parallels can be quite precisely dated to Hallstatt A2, conventionally taken as the eleventh century BC. Moving nearer to Britain, the Lower Rhine has produced only limited evidence of pottery and metalwork comparable to that of South-western Germany at this date. In the region east and south-east of Paris, however, including the Marne, there is evidence of pottery and metalwork comparable to that of Hallstatt A on the Middle Rhine; it is likely that this region will eventually prove to have brought furrowed bowls nearer to southern Britain in Hallstatt A times. There is supporting evidence from Britain for such a date and, even allowing for 'time-lag', there is no reason to suppose that furrowed bowls should be dated later than about 1000 BC.

The British evidence, as always, depends heavily on settlement sites, usually a palimpsest of successive re-occupations. The re-occupation problem vitiates all attempts to argue that items are of the same date simply because found on the same site. If, however, we reject such arguments, the purely insular evidence for dating dwindles dramatically. Radiocarbon dates are few, their contexts commonly reported with a singular lack of precision; when their error terms are increased by calibration into real years, they often allow any date within half a millennium. The Continental evidence is based much more firmly on reliable associations in graves, and on far closer contacts with the much better-dated Mediterranean. Where detailed study has taken place, a much more finely-divided chronology is possible. The main problem with Continental parallels is that the pottery styles of British settlement sites are never exactly the same as those found in south German graves. Should the differences be explained as the result of a difference in date, the traditional 'time-lag', or as the result of a spatial difference, perhaps correlating with a poorer economy in peripheral Britain?

Pottery typologists have strongly favoured the 'time-lag' viewpoint, usually in an extreme form. Bronze typologists, in contrast, have increasingly abandoned it.[12] This difference in approach is a crucial factor underlying the paradox of a late bronze age with bronzes but no pottery. The intellectual underpinning of the 'time-lag' viewpoint was always the theory that the spread of ideas from Central Europe was a very slow process of gradual folk movement of 'Urnfield people(s)', to be traced most significantly by the gradual spread westwards of cremation cemeteries,[13] until a final wave lapped onto British shores from Belgium in the first century BC. Reliable independent evidence of stratigraphy, association and dating has been slight, and theories such as this have been relied on to fill the gap. The view that this change in burial rite shows a change in ethnic group, rather than a change in religious belief or social observance, has never (as far as I am aware) been given detailed documentation. If the theory is questioned, there is no warrant for invoking a time-lag of more than a few decades before the appearance in Britain of ideas which have Continental parallels in Central Europe.

The demise of the 'ethnic' approach to later prehistory, with its emphasis on 'diffusion', has coincided with the growth of an 'isolationist' approach of 'independent innovation'. For the study of late bronze age pottery in Britain, this has been an unfortunate coincidence. The late datings justified by the 'ethnic' interpretation of change had dissociated furrowed bowls sharply from their Continental parallels. Independent, isolated development has gained credence as the only possible interpretation, given the appearance in Britain of styles for which no Continental parallels exist contemporary with the conventional date of the British material. It has been impossible to suppose that eleventh-century Hallstatt A2 bowl forms on the Continent had anything to do with the eighth- or seventh-century British bowls, contemporary with Hallstatt B3 or Hallstatt C. The British bowls cannot have been developed from Continental forms which had been superseded and abandoned centuries before. Whatever the similarities, the British examples must have been independently innovated.

Isolationism carried to such lengths seems implausible. Britain in the middle and later bronze age had a flourishing economy, keen to adopt from Europe and develop the most significant new advance of the period, the sword. If one is to suppose that pottery manufacture should be treated as isolationist, whereas bronze manufacture was internationalist, it seems necessary to suppose that pottery manufacture was purely a traditional craft, hidebound by village tabus which forbade adoption of ideas from 'outside'. In the case of furrowed bowls, the supposition is particularly difficult to reconcile with the evidence of a distribution of this distinctive style throughout southern Britain, presented in Appendix A.

In general terms, then, it seems implausible to accept the currently conventional 'isolationist' approach to British late bronze age pottery, divorcing its development from contemporary Hallstatt A and B developments. In the case of furrowed bowls, neither the material itself nor the intellectual climate of the time call for this. Isolationism is more plausibly seen as a modern historical accident, born out of the late datings which are the child of the 'ethnic' approach. The detailed evidence presented below, gathered from the Continent and from Britain, suggests that furrowed bowls should be viewed as evidence of a roughly parallel development in British and in Continental Hallstatt pottery. That differences exist is hardly surprising, in view of the spatial distance between southern Britain and southern Germany; they are better viewed as the result of spatial distance than as the result of temporal distance.

Parallelism between Continental and British pottery in this period has implications also for the date of carinated pottery in Britain. Between the end of Hallstatt B1 at about 900 BC and Hallstatt D2 just before 500 BC, Hallstatt pottery is characteristically round-shouldered, not carinated. Recognition of this has been symbolized since the 1930s by ascription of carinated Hawkes A pottery to a fifth-century BC, 'Marnian' date. Associated groups and distinctive styles of pottery do exist in southern Britain which must be dated to around the fifth century BC, and an attempt will be made below to isolate and define some of these and their associations more closely. The most distinctive styles are carinated. In recent years, however, it has become increasingly clear that not all carinated Hawkes A pottery can be dated as late as the fifth century BC. Various attempts have been made to push some examples a century or so earlier. These attempts, however, place that pottery at dates when carinated Continental parallels are rare or non-existent. Such attempts require an 'isolationist' approach which sits oddly with the evidence of clear general parallels in development between British and Continental Hallstatt C and D, and close parallels in the distinctive pottery styles of the fifth century BC. It seems more plausible to maintain parallelism, and to date such carinated pottery to the Hallstatt A/B1 'carinated horizon' around 1000 BC; an earlier dating of furrowed bowls (also of course carinated) readily permits this. The detailed evidence for placing at this early date all carinated pottery which is not of the fifth century BC is not as well documented as is the case for dating furrowed bowls to a Hallstatt A2 date. There is, however, evidence for dating some British carinated pottery as early as this. The marked absence of carinated pottery from Continental Hallstatt B2/3 and Hallstatt C contexts, during centuries when the British metal industries were clearly in contact with the Continent, places the onus of proof on those who would seek to date British carinated pottery between 900 and 500 BC.

Furrowed bowls

In form, furrowed bowls are carinated, open bowls. They usually have a flaring or slightly everted short lip or longer neck, demarcated from a clear and sloping shoulder (upon which the furrowing occurs); a carinated or sharp-shouldered division between the shoulder and the lower body; and an omphalos base. The bowls are found in two main types (fig. 2): round-bottomed, U-section 'wave' furrows, probably done with a finger, are usually found with the short lip; flat-bottomed 'groove' furrows, apparently done with a stick or other tool, are usually found with the longer neck. Both types occur with a red, haematite coating in Wessex (Wiltshire, Hampshire and Dorset), though the type with wave furrows and short lip is apparently rarer (fig. 4 and Appendix A).[14]

It has long been traditional to derive them from the little half-scale model cast in bronze which was found in a hoard at Welby, Leicestershire (fig. 2. 4); and to suggest that the pottery bowls must be later than this metal example.[15] Except that it is cast in bronze and at half-scale, the Welby example is a normal furrowed bowl with wave furrows and short, everted lip. The Welby bowl and comparable wave-furrowed bowls in pottery should be of very much the same date. It seems, however, more likely that the Welby bowl is a copy of

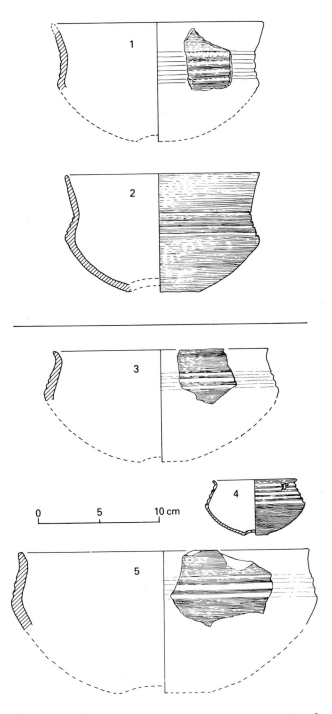

Figure 2. Furrowed bowls. Nos. 1 and 2 with groove furrows and neck; 3, 4 and 5 with wave furrows and lip.
No.1 from Winklebury, Hants. (after Piggott C. M. 1943: no.7); no.2 from Boscombe Down West, Wilts. (after Richardson 1951: fig.7, no.15); no.3 from Langton Matravers, Dorset (or Gallows Gore?) (drawn by the present author in Christchurch Museum); no.4 (in bronze) from Welby, Leics. (after Smith M. A. 1957: G. B. 24.2(2), no.6); no.5 from Hillbrow, Pokesdown, Bournemouth, Hants. (drawn by the present author in Christchurch Museum). All ⅓ life size. (See Appendix A for details.)

pottery examples than *vice-versa*. Its size suggests this; and so also does the fact that the technique of producing wave furrows is better adapted to producing pottery than to producing the quite complex clay mould in which the Welby bowl must have been cast.

It has been usual to think of the Welby hoard as deposited after 650 BC, but there is no reason for a date this late.[16] There is no very good reason to suppose that it was even a single deposit.[17] Assuming that it was, its *terminus post quem* need be no later than about 900 BC.[18] The furrowed bowl, however, need not be that late. In the hoard were found also two cross-handles from a 'cross-handled bowl'. This is a type found most frequently in Hungary, but found also in more westerly European deposits which have a consistent Hallstatt B1 date, that is, of the tenth century BC.[19] To accommodate the conventional dating of the Ewart Park sword, the cross-handle scraps must apparently have been a century old when finally buried. Consequently, other items in the 'hoard' need not have been made as late as the Ewart Park sword either. If we reject a date for furrowed bowls based on the Welby Ewart Park sword, the way is open to reconsider dating for the Welby and other furrowed bowls based directly on dated Continental comparanda.[20]

The furrowed bowl, as is well known, finds generalized parallels in some of the French Urnfield 'rilled' and 'furrowed' wares. Furrowed wares of various sorts are almost the universal common denominator of French Urnfield pottery. A few distinctions must, however, be drawn before it is possible to look for specific parallels. I shall take 'furrowing' to be horizontal lines of various sorts around the vessel, set in various positions (from the interior edge of the lip to the exterior edge of the base). This should be distinguished from 'rilling', that is, from lines which are not horizontal. Rilling is found as vertical or diagonal rilling, usually on the lower part of the body; as curved rilling round some of the 'knobs' or 'nipples' which appear on some vessels ('Buckelurnen'); and as criss-cross or 'basket-weave' rilling, which is occasionally used to form patterns. There are relatively few rilled vessels which are not also furrowed; but there are many furrowed vessels which are not rilled. The techniques of both furrowing and rilling are various.[21] Continental furrowing, like British furrowing, may consist of close-set, fairly deep, U-section 'wave'-furrowing; or of wide-set, fairly deep, flat-bottom-section 'groove'-furrowing. Vertical and diagonal rilling nearly always has wide-set, U-section lines, very shallowly impressed indeed; curved rilling round 'nipples' and 'basket-weave' rilling may instead be close-set.[22] There are apparently few rilled sherds known from Britain.[23] What is of concern for parallels with Britain is furrowing. Furrowing is a general characteristic of French Urnfield pottery, and may still have been in use in Hallstatt C times,[24] but it is usually on vessels of shapes quite different from furrowed bowls. Consequently, it is not simply furrowing alone which must concern us, but furrowing on low, wide-mouthed, carinated, omphalos-based bowls. In France, these form a more restricted selection.[25] Almost all of the Continental examples have the short, sharply-everted lip of Welby, rather than the longer, vertical or slightly out-turned neck which is more common on British pottery.

In France, a number of unassociated or undated examples are known to me,[26] but there are also better-dated examples. Some occur in the regions of eastern France which border on the Upper Rhine. The example from the Combe Bernard (Côte d'Or) is probably of Bronze Moyen 3, though the association is a little uncertain;[27] the rather poorly-dated example from Veux-haulles (Côte d'Or) is presumably of Bronze Final I or II;[28] the example from Champlay (Yonne) is apparently of Bronze Moyen or Bronze Final II.[29] The example from Rouffach (Haut-Rhin) is rather better dated, to Bronze Final IIa.[30] This furrowed bowl is merely one variant of a range of low, open bowls with omphalos base and sharply-everted lip which are found in the Haut-Rhin. They come in a variety of forms with shoulders more or less carinated and sometimes with vertical rilling;[31] and they seem to be of Bronze Final IIa, or at least apparently not later.[32] In adjacent areas of France, bordering on Switzerland, some of these carinated bowls are ascribed to the slightly earlier date of Bronze Final I.[33] In the rest of France, later examples of furrowed bowls might be claimed, but the associations used to support this claim are doubtful.[34]

Thus in the Centre-East of France there are parallels to the Welby furrowed bowl which have quite well-dated associations; and these associations range from Bronze Moyen 3 to Bronze Final IIb. These French examples appear to be one variant of a general style of low bowl, often carinated, which was particularly common in or about Bronze Final IIa and which it is difficult to find firmly dated at a later date.

Nearer to Britain, in the Middle Rhine, more compelling parallels emerge. In that area are a whole range of close parallels for the Welby bowl, and also of less close parallels. These appear to have had a limited life, and the best parallels can be quite firmly tied down to Hallstatt A2.

The most notable and key example is the wave-furrowed bowl, only slightly different from the Welby example, which was found, made in black ware, in the Hallstatt A2 grave at Erbenheim with the eponymous sword itself (fig. 3).[35] But this does not stand alone. From Hessen in particular have been published a range of Hallstatt A2 furrowed bowl variants. Close parallels to Welby have been found in graves with Hallstatt A2 metalwork,[36] as also have less close parallels.[37] Some of the close parallels to the Welby bowl have been found alone, or merely with pottery, not with easily datable metal objects;[38] but these are apparently even so of Hallstatt A2, not later.[39] There are hints that the type of furrowing associated with Hallstatt A1 bronzes was a little different from that of the Welby bowl.[40] Consequently, a Hallstatt A2 date seems the nearest fit. Similar bowls are found throughout south-western Germany during Hallstatt A,[41] and again it seems that the closest parallels for the Welby bowl are associated with Hallstatt A2 metalwork.[42]

It is not easy to correlate in detail between the French Bronze Final I/II/III systems, based in the end on that of Hatt (1955a; 1955b; 1956; 1959; 1961), and the German Bronzezeit D/Hallstatt A/Hallstatt B systems, based in the end on that of Müller-Karpe (1959). For the areas discussed above, there is a broad

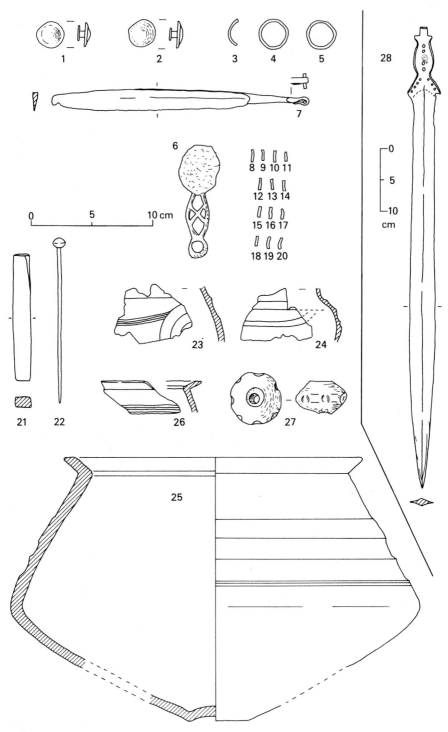

Figure 3. The Erbenheim grave-goods (Grave 1 of Merten's Brickworks, Wiesbaden-Erbenheim) (after Herrmann 1966: Taf.99.C). All ⅓ life size, except no.28 which is ⅙ life size.

correlation between Hallstatt A1 and Bronze Final IIa, and between Hallstatt A2 and Bronze Final IIb; and the calendar dates of Bronze Final II and Hallstatt A occupy roughly the period between 1200 and 1000 BC.[43] There is therefore some suggestion that parallels for the Welby bowl are found earlier in the Upper Rhine region (say, in the twelfth century BC) than in the Middle Rhine region (say, in the eleventh century BC).

From the Upper and Middle Rhine, there are two routes along which one might search for traces of furrowed bowls: northwards down the Rhine, and westwards across France. Neither seems yet to produce datable traces, but the French route seems more promising. Moving towards Britain northwards, down the Rhine, the Urnfield period in the Neuwied Basin still seems obscure,[44] but provides some clear parallels with Hallstatt A and B pottery further up the Rhine.[45] Good examples of Hallstatt A2 metalwork and pottery have been found but not, as far as I am aware, any furrowed bowls.[46] Furrowed bowls of a sort appear there in what is probably a late stage of the Laufeld group, lasting as late as early Hallstatt D.[47] But what these lack is carination; they have apparently been modified by the more rounded forms of Hallstatt B and Hallstatt C, and if anything they emphasize the earlier connections of the carinated, British, furrowed bowls. Near the mouth of the Rhine, good Hallstatt A pottery is somewhat lacking, and no close parallels for furrowed bowls exist. The nearest parallels appear to be small 'beakers', of a rather different shape, used as accessory vessels in some graves in Flanders; dating is difficult, parallels being found in both Hallstatt A2 and Hallstatt B3 contexts.[48]

Moving towards Britain by the French route, it is notoriously difficult to establish parallels near the Channel coast. The datable items come from hoards or as stray finds, and cemeteries with pottery are rare.[49] A little further from the Channel coast, however, three cemeteries found to the east and southeast of Paris show that the material culture of mid-France was very similar to that of the Upper and Middle Rhine. These are the cemeteries of Pougues-les-Eaux (Nièvre), Aulnay-aux-Planches (Marne) and Gours-aux-Lions (Seine-et-Marne). Pougues-les-Eaux seems to have started in Bronze Final I (roughly equivalent to the German Bronzezeit D), but probably continued later.[50] Aulnay-aux-Planches had at least three good Hallstatt A graves,[51] though this cemetery also continued later. No exact parallel for the Welby bowl was found at either of these sites. Pougues-les-Eaux had a couple of open bowls, probably of Bronze Final I, which appear generally similar but not identical.[52] Aulnay had a number of bowls which are very like those of the Middle Rhine Hallstatt A1 and Hallstatt A2,[53] though again none is a satisfactory parallel for the Welby bowl. At Gours-aux-Lions (Marolles-sur-Seine), Nécropole I had bronzes of Bronze Final I and more especially of Bronze Final IIa; the pottery included many urns and bowls which were furrowed but also usually had rilling. Partly because of the rilling, there were no exact parallels for British furrowed bowls,[54] and the impression is given that Bronze Final IIa (which equates with Hallstatt A1) is perhaps a little early for good parallels. In view of the unassociated or undated examples known in France, it would not be surprising if the idea of the furrowed bowl reached Britain through France; but good Hallstatt A or Bronze Final II associations are still scarce in central and northern France, and the trail is still obscure.

At Welby there were thus two items for which Central European parallels date to about 1000 BC: the furrowed bowl around the eleventh century, and the cross-handled bowl around the tenth century. If the hoard was a unitary deposit, these must have been old when buried with the eighth-century BC Ewart Park sword. The cross-handled bowl certainly was: only its handles survived, even the rivets being lost. The furrowed bowl was in a much better condition but, being cast as one single casting, it may have lasted better. It is clear that the cross-handled bowl was imported; perhaps the furrowed bowl was also. Although the furrowed bowl is unique, and it is therefore surprising to suppose that such a thing was cast in Central Europe or eastern France at this date, it would be equally surprising to suppose that it was cast in Britain at any date.

Turning from the Welby bronze bowl to other wave-furrowed bowls in pottery, a date about 1000 BC for the latter is supported by some evidence from Britain. A date in the eleventh century BC would make sense of some radiocarbon dates. It lies at the early end of the range for the radiocarbon determinations from the round-houses of Longbridge Deverill Cow Down, where were apparently found, as yet unpublished, furrowed bowls.[55] The houses need not all have been in use simultaneously, and the radiocarbon determinations allow a long range. At the 95 per cent probable level, there could have been a house at the site at any time between the twelfth and the fourth centuries BC; at the 99 per cent probable level, between the fourteenth and the third centuries.[56] A date in the eleventh century BC lies at the later end of the ranges for the Deverel-Rimbury sites of Shearplace Hill and Itford Hill. At Shearplace, the 95 per cent probable range is from the twentieth to the tenth century BC, and the 99 per cent probable range is from the twenty-first to the ninth century BC;[57] at Itford, the ranges are from the sixteenth to the tenth century BC and from the seventeenth to the ninth respectively.[58] Deverel-Rimbury pottery does include some furrowing, partly on settlement site pottery and partly on globular urns.[59] At Barmston, a thin birch stake produced a radiocarbon determination with a 95 per cent probable range from the sixteenth to the ninth century BC; the stake had apparently lined a pit cut down from the surface of a layer of peat upon which lay a furrowed bowl.[60]

A crucial point, however, is that one of the vessels from Shearplace was a carinated, wave-furrowed vessel. It was not drawn as such, and was interpreted as a globular urn, but a carination was noted at a late stage of the publication.[61] This furrowed vessel was reasonably well associated by stratification with the radiocarbon samples, and there is no good reason to suppose that it was a much later relic.[62] Association of furrowed bowls with large round-houses as at Shearplace is demonstrated both by the Longbridge Deverill evidence and also by the discovery of furrowed bowls in post-holes of both the round-houses at Little Woodbury.[63]

Thus furrowed bowls could have been in use in Britain in the eleventh century BC. There are other hints in the same direction. At Rainsborough, for example, was found a decorated fine-ware bowl, with flaring rim and rounded shoulder, for which a Hallstatt B2/B3 date should now certainly be suggested (that is, the ninth or eighth century BC). With it, however, and scattered over the site, were extremely abraded tiny scraps of furrowed bowls, clearly older, surviving rubbish.[64] Indeed, when All Cannings Cross was first published, back in the 1920s, the similarity between Deverel-Rimbury pottery and All Cannings Cross pottery was noted.[65] An early date for furrowed bowls perhaps allows one to make more sense of globular urns. These come in wave-furrowed and groove-furrowed forms, like furrowed bowls;[66] and some examples of globular urns show very shallow furrowing, more in the style of rilled ware than is usual on furrowed bowls.[67]

This theory would put furrowed bowls back to the Penard phase of the British middle bronze age, immediately after the Taunton phase or Ornament Horizon. It is not surprising to find strong parallels with Central Europe in this early Urnfield phase. At this time were introduced also a range of Hallstatt A2 metal types, which influenced the later bronze industries in Britain very greatly, such as Erbenheim and Hemigkofen swords, the first true swords in Britain.[68] This does not imply that one should think of an invasive Continental group: far too much of the Continental pottery, and more particularly the Continental metalwork, is missing from Britain. What one can suppose, however, is that the pottery industry in Britain managed its own rather provincial imitations of the bowl styles of the Rhineland, at the same time as the bronze industry was also aware of the products and techniques of Central Europe.

Groove-furrowed bowls are conventionally dated later than wave-furrowed bowls, though no evidence for this order has been published.[69] Groove-furrowed bowls were found in pit 1 at Darmsden, Suffolk, with carinated pottery lacking furrows.[70] In the same pit were also found sherds of larger, furrowed urns, with flaring neck and round shoulder. These could be simplified provincial variants of Hallstatt B2/B3 pottery,[71] but they could equally well be simplified provincial variants of Bronze D/Bronze Final I-IIa urns; the latter are very similar to Hallstatt B2/B3 pottery in the general outline which is all that is reproduced at Darmsden.[72] It is probably not fortuitous that this pit also produced one of the few possible British attempts at the knob, wart, Buckel or nipple characteristic of Bronze D/Bronze Final I pottery.[73] Unfortunately, however, pit 1 at Darmsden does not carry complete conviction as a reliable sealed association of homogeneous date. Published records of its internal stratification are poor, revealing only that it was of large size. Amongst its contents were reportedly two pedestal bases, for which it is very difficult to find dated parallels before Hallstatt D (see below, p. 44). There must therefore be a real possibility that this pit had accumulated debris from a palimpsest of successive occupations.

Both groove- and wave-furrowed bowls occur with a reddish, haematite coating in Wessex (Wiltshire, Hampshire and Dorset), and this is usually taken to be the full extent of the phenomenon.[74] But furrowed bowls are not restricted to that region. Red-coated examples occurred at Rainsborough, Northamptonshire, and Linford, Essex, in addition to the bronze example from Welby, Leicestershire (Appendix A). The red coating is not apparently true haematiting, but the form of the vessel is the same as in Wessex. True haematiting is a regional trait of the Wessex area, extending to peripheral regions like Surrey and the Upper Thames, but not usually much further afield.[75] In Wessex, not only does it occur on furrowed bowls, it also occurs on Hawkes B bead-rims.[76] An even wider distribution of furrowed bowls appears if black or grey bowls of groove-furrowed design are also accepted as furrowed bowls (fig. 4 and Appendix A). Black and brown furrowed bowls occurred at All Cannings Cross and elsewhere, together with haematite-coated examples, and there is no reason to reject examples which merely lack haematite coating. Hawkes B bead-rims, of course, are common in versions without haematiting, and there is no reason to distinguish in date between those with haematite coating and those without; the same is true of furrowed bowls. This extension, however, provides a distribution of furrowed bowls throughout England, from Cornwall to Yorkshire, from Shropshire across to Suffolk, and down to Surrey (fig. 4). In this, I return to the view which was originally held of many of these bowls in the 1940s.[77] The view has been eclipsed by the more recent interpretation of some of these furrowed bowls as of the fifth century BC. I shall return to this later (p. 42).

Carinated pottery

A revised dating for furrowed bowls implies also, as its most important by-product, that the dating of carinated pottery must be re-assessed. Carinated pottery appears to fall into two separate phases: an earlier phase around 1000 BC; and a later phase around the fifth century BC. With furrowed bowls moved to the eleventh century BC, it is no longer necessary to force carinated pottery into the period between the ninth and the fifth centuries BC when, on the Continent, rounded shapes were much more in vogue. On closer examination, the pottery which can be reliably ascribed to the fifth century BC appears to be of a distinctive type of carinated shape. It is necessary to be more cautious about ascribing carinated pottery to the fifth century than has sometimes been the case in the past, and to restrict this ascription to those vessels for which precise Continental parallels can be found. It is not perhaps surprising that there has been confusion in Britain between pottery of Hallstatt A date and pottery of Hallstatt D or La Tène I date; the same confusion over carination has occurred even in the Marne region of France.[78] It is not possible here to provide a corpus of British carinated pottery, but some of the styles discussed below are illustrated in fig. 5.

For the past 50 years, it has been normal to ascribe all (or at least some) of the carinated Hawkes A pottery to the late fifth or fourth century BC. The reason has been that carinated pottery is found in fifth- and fourth-century graves in the Marne region of France. It has been usual to interpret this pottery in terms of a 'Marnian invasion'.[79] There have been two main strands to the Marnian invasion theory. One strand has held that carinated pottery is evidence of an invasive 'Marnian culture'; the other has held that various relics and hill-forts in Sussex are evidence of a Marnian invasion. We are concerned here with the carinated Marnians, not with the hill-fort Marnians.[80]

Definitions of British Marnian carinated pottery have varied over the years. Recently, it has been 'triconic' or 'tripartite angular' pottery which has been most firmly ascribed to the Marnians and to the fifth century BC. As defined,

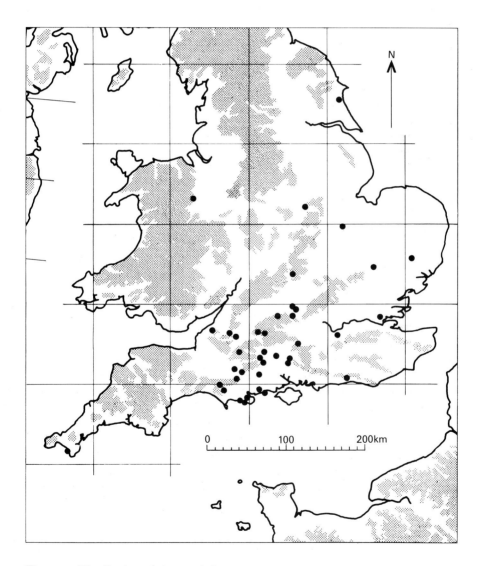

Figure 4. Distribution of sites with furrowed bowls (see Appendix A for list). Land over 250m stippled.

this comprises low bowls and also taller, larger jars. The classic profile has a flaring or out-turned neck; this is demarcated from, and sharply joined to, a shoulder; and this shoulder is itself sharply joined to the lower body at a carination.[81] There is in Britain also 'biconic' carinated pottery, with beaded rim in place of the flaring neck.[82] In Britain, the biconic style has not been as firmly ascribed to the fifth century, though it is certainly ascribed to a La Tène I date in the Marne region, together with the triconic style.[83] The classification of triconic pottery is unfortunately not as clear-cut as the definition of the classic profile might seem to suggest. There is a range of profiles, extending from those with a clear and sharp demarcation between a flaring neck and a shoulder to those where an upright neck and a shoulder form one concave curve.[84] The whole spectrum of the range can in fact be found on one and the same site, as at Long Wittenham, Berkshire, Allen's Pit, Dorchester, Oxfordshire, and Chinnor, Oxfordshire.[85]

The re-dating of furrowed bowls propounded above forces a reconsideration of carinated pottery. In eastern England, furrowed bowls appear to be associated with examples of triconic pottery which have been picked out specifically as of the fifth century BC: both jars, at Linford, Essex, and perhaps also bowls, at Darmsden, Suffolk.[86] This triconic pottery should be much earlier than the fifth century BC. Indeed, other evidence supports an early date. In phase IIc at Eldon's Seat, Encombe, Dorset, were found carinated plain bowls (not triconic, but with curving concave necks),[87] and a few scraps of furrowed bowl and of pottery with the white-filled decoration found also at All Cannings Cross.[88] At the Breiddin, Montgomeryshire, carinated scraps were found stratified earlier than a rampart which is very unlikely to have been built as late as 600 BC, and could be distinctly earlier.[89] At Minnis Bay, Birchington, Kent, carinated bowls were apparently deposited earlier than a late bronze age hoard (Appendix B). The conclusion that some carinated pottery must be earlier than the fifth century BC is not new. Several authors have suggested dating individual vessels and sites earlier than that century.[90] The dates offered, however, have been restricted to the sixth, seventh and, occasionally, eighth century BC. They are clearly dictated by the view that this pottery cannot be divorced from the conventional iron age, starting with Hallstatt C in the seventh century BC (or, as some would maintain, in the eighth century).[91] The Continental evidence provides no support for such datings, nor for the view that there was a significant break in pottery styles around the eighth or seventh centuries BC.[92] Hallstatt B2/3 and Hallstatt C pottery apparently forms a continuum of rounded shapes within which no clear break is identifiable.[93] With the re-dating of furrowed bowls, an earlier dating, around 1000 BC, may be suggested for the carinated pottery which is not of the fifth century BC, divorcing this pottery quite clearly from the iron age. Hawkes A pottery, far from being restricted to the iron age, should be viewed as following Deverel-Rimbury after, at most, a short gap.

By implication, carinated pottery should be divided into two clearly distinct horizons. There is good evidence of a resurgence of triconic pottery in the iron age: at least one distinctive style of about the fifth century BC can be

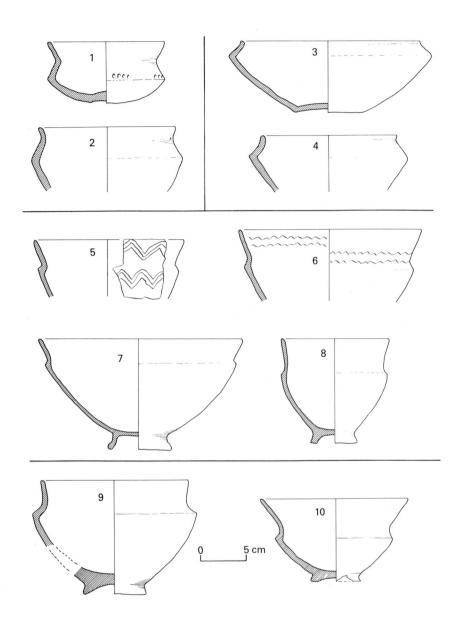

Figure 5. Carinated pottery. Nos. 1 and 2 triconic; 3 and 4 biconic; 5, 6 and 7 'Puddle-hill style'; 8 les Jogasses; 9 and 10 British comparanda for the 'Puddlehill style'.

Nos. 1 and 2 from Long Wittenham, Berks. (after Harding 1972: pl. 50, A and J); nos. 3 and 4 from West Harling, Norfolk (after Clark and Fell 1953: fig. 15, nos. 69 and 72); nos. 5 and 6 from Puddlehill, Beds. (after Matthews 1976: fig. 30, no. 5, and fig. 41, no. 4); no. 7 from Wandlebury, Cambs. (after Hartley 1957: fig. 7, no. 16); no. 8 from les Jogasses (Chouilly, Marne) tombe 69 (after Hatt and Roualet 1976: pl. 20, no. 926); no. 9 from Orsett, Essex (after Barrett 1978: fig. 41, no. 74); no. 10 from Wisley, Surrey (after Bishop 1971: fig. 6, no. 42). All ¼ life size.

quite precisely defined. The key pottery may be termed the 'Puddlehill style'. At Puddlehill, Bedfordshire, were found some ten quite distinctive bowls, decorated with multiple zig-zag lines with white infill; these had a markedly and distinctively narrow shoulder, barely more than a 'kick'. This is a regional style, not a feature of Puddlehill alone, and its centre seems to lie on the chalk of the Chilterns. Decorated examples have been found at Chinnor and at Ravensburgh, plain examples with the same profile at Wandlebury, Cambridgeshire, and Linford, Essex, and comparable shapes in the same area.[94] At Chinnor, Ravensburgh and Wandlebury, the vessels had pedestal bases. No bases were found attached to the examples at Puddlehill, where bases of all sorts were notably rare in the pit groups from which these vessels came. Combining these, it is possible to isolate a Puddlehill style with distinctive triconic profile, often with distinctive decoration, and a pedestal base (fig. 5.5–7).

The Puddlehill site itself provided key dating evidence. Large pieces of the fine triconic bowls were found in three pits with coarse pottery (both plain and finger-tip decorated) which is very similar to the coarse pottery found at Chinnor. Although the coarse pottery is crude, the shapes are notably repeated in several pit-groups, and the similarities in the coarse pottery reinforce the similarities in the fine bowls. Two of the Puddlehill pits produced pieces of iron with the bowls. A pit which lacked fine bowls but had the coarser pottery produced a simple ring-headed pin; this reinforces the discovery of these pins at Chinnor.[95] Puddlehill and Chinnor may be taken as of very much the same date, a regional group definitely not earlier than the introduction of iron in the seventh century BC.

If the Puddlehill style is later than 700 BC, however, it immediately becomes necessary to consider parallels with Hallstatt D2 and La Tène I pottery in the Marne region of France. These seem quite compelling. There are good general parallels in that region both for the triconic vessels of the Puddlehill style and also for the other triconic vessels found associated with that style at Chinnor; these parallels are found in the Hallstatt part of the cemetery at les Jogasses, and also in the La Tène I part of that cemetery and in La Tène I cemeteries elsewhere. There are also parallels for other, less common pottery shapes found with Puddlehill-style vessels at Chinnor[96] and at Puddlehill itself.[97] Etruscan *stamnoi* probably provided the model for the curious handle skeuomorphs found at Chinnor.[98]

The best parallels for the rather simple profiles of the Puddlehill style are those from the Hallstatt D2 part of the cemetery at Jogasses. A few of the pedestalled vessels from Jogasses provide remarkably exact parallels;[99] others are a little less close.[100] Although there is controversy about the exact calendar date of the cemetery,[101] and about the sequence within the cemetery,[102] the whole of the Hallstatt D2 part clearly lies somewhere between 550 and 450 BC, and probably earlier within that bracket rather than later. Triconic pottery from graves of the succeeding La Tène I periods in the Marne region is less simple, more sophisticated, often with comparatively exaggerated necks and pedestals.[103] The Puddlehill style and its associata may be closely contemporary with the Hallstatt D2, Jogassian examples which they most nearly resemble; or may be simplified versions of the later La Tène I grave styles, appropriate to provincial settlement sites. In either case, the Puddlehill style is no earlier than the late sixth century BC. One may note the prevalence of pedestal bases at Mont Lassois, presumably of the same date, to judge from the preponderance of Hallstatt D2 fibulae there.[104]

Pottery of the preceding period in the Marne apparently differed from triconic carinated pottery. At any rate, in the seventh century BC there is evidence that distinctive, round-bodied, vertical-necked bowls were in use at Saint Vincent in the Ardennes and 6okm further south at Haulzy in Champagne.[105] Some of the pottery from Jogasses has rounded shoulders,[106] and it is reasonable to suppose that a change-over took place in the sixth century. The best parallels for the Puddlehill style are thus unlikely to be earlier than the late sixth century BC.

Despite the similarities between the Puddlehill style (with its associata) and pottery from the Marne, there are many differences in detail; and the La Tène I pottery from the Marne normally includes shapes which are found either only rarely or not at all in Britain.[107] It is true that there are dumpy 'pear-shaped' foot-ring bowls of 'South-Eastern B' type in Britain, which do have Marnian parallels; one parallel was even found in a Hallstatt D four-wheel cart burial at Jogasses itself.[108] Significantly, however, these occur in Britain on sites other than those which produce Puddlehill-style pottery, and seem to occupy a different area.[109] In addition, the British sites lack the metalwork of Marnian Hallstatt D2 and La Tène I sites.[110] It is true that six Hallstatt D daggers have been found in the lower Thames, but these have a distribution rather different from that of Puddlehill-style bowls, which is based on the Chilterns.[111] It is significant that there are no Hallstatt D2 fibulae from this part of Britain at all, such as are commonplace at Jogasses and Mont Lassois.[112] It is more significant still that the Puddlehill style of pottery is found with the distinctively British ring-headed pin as a dress-fastener, in lieu of fibulae of Hallstatt D2 or La Tène I.

It is, then, reasonable to suggest a date around the fifth century BC for the Puddlehill style and its associata. The evidence hardly supports an invasion from the Continent, for too much is missing. The Puddlehill style is based on the chalk area, from Cambridgeshire southwards down the Chilterns, which later became the centre of considerable prosperity and of the tribe of the Catuvellauni.[113] The fifth-century distribution is hardly suitable for one to base tribal boundaries upon it. It would not be surprising, however, if a relatively rich farming area on the periphery of Europe knew of, and reflected in a pale, provincial version, the distinctive styles of pottery current in the wealthy areas of eastern France.

Carinated pottery can thus be divided into two groups. An earlier group is found with omphalos-based, furrowed bowls, and should be dated around 1000 BC. A later group is found with the narrow-shouldered, pedestalled, triconic vessels of the Puddlehill style, and these should be dated around the fifth century BC. A number of sites with triconic pottery show neither of these distinctive features, and are more difficult to apportion. It seems reasonable to suggest that Long Wittenham may be of the earlier phase,[114] as may Allen's Pit, Dorchester (because of the furrowed bowl from that site);[115] while Woodeaton is perhaps more likely to belong to the later phase, because of its ring-headed pins, although the bases were 'mostly flat'.[116]

Between the two periods of angular pottery, one would expect most pottery styles to be rounded in shape. Continental pottery styles seem to be basically rounded rather than angular between the end of Hallstatt B1 (around 900 BC) and the start of Hallstatt D2 (at, say, 550 BC).[117] There are thus still problems in dating British sites which have produced angular pottery and also bronzes that should be dated within that 400-year range. The most notable examples, perhaps, are Staple Howe, which had Hallstatt C bronzes that ought to be of the seventh century BC, and Ivinghoe Beacon, which had bronzes that ought to be of the eighth and seventh centuries BC. These two sites have always posed problems of interpretation, for the bronzes should be distinctly earlier than the fifth-century date which the carinated pottery has been taken to suggest. The easiest way to resolve the problem is to emphasize the evidence that these sites had structures of more than one period. The angular pottery may then be thought of as later than the bronzes (as has been the practice hitherto) or earlier (as now seems possible).[118]

Conclusion

The work of Margaret Smith 20 years ago opened up a void in the British late bronze age, between Deverel-Rimbury and All Cannings Cross. There is, however, evidence both on the Continent and in Britain that the void should be filled by closing up the gap: the Hawkes A furrowed bowls of All Cannings Cross should follow directly on from Deverel-Rimbury, after little if any gap, at a date in the eleventh century BC.

The consequences for the succeeding 600 years are considerable. Firstly, this conclusion opens up the question of Continental bronze age and Urn-field parallels for all types of Hawkes A pottery. The tendency hitherto has been to seek parallels only in iron age contexts, and to neglect the possibilities in earlier periods. This has cramped a bewildering multiplicity of styles into much too short a period. Hawkes A pottery has always been rightly thought of as paralleled by Hallstatt pottery. The mistake has been to construe 'Hallstatt' as 'Hallstatt iron age', limiting it to Hallstatt C and D, and neglecting the justified insistence of German scholars that the Hallstatt period is more properly seen as one unit, comprising the whole of Hallstatt A to D.[119] The view that the iron age is radically different from the late bronze age has lived on in the British Isles, in a 'time-lag' perpetuated by the terminology used, despite lip-service to an imprecisely defined concept of 'continuity'.[120] Accepting that Continental parallels are legitimate opens up a range of possibilities for dating 'iron age A' pottery distinctly earlier than the iron age, and for dating 'later bronze age' pottery earlier still.[121]

Secondly, the re-dating of furrowed bowls strongly suggests a re-dating of some of the carinated or triconic pottery which has commonly passed as fifth century BC material. It appears that there were two phases of carinated or 'metallic' pottery in Britain: one which parallels the 'metallic' shapes of Continental Hallstatt A and B1, around 1000 BC; and another which parallels the 'metallic' shapes of Hallstatt D2 and La Tène I, around the fifth century BC. In both periods, southern British potters managed simplified provincial versions of Continental styles, probably acquired through Eastern France. In between these dates, Continental parallels suggest that pottery forms, including bowls, were almost certainly rounded in shoulder profile. The Hallstatt A bowls mark apparently an introduction to Britain of bowl forms capable of standing firm upon a surface such as a table. They should presumably be interpreted as 'porridge bowls', wide and open for eating. If so, they mark an introduction, at some levels of society, of new table manners and customs; and perhaps of new grain foods, bruised or rolled by saddle querns, and ante-dating the ground foods symbolized by the introduction of rotary querns at the time of Hawkes B pottery. The large multi-ring round-houses conventionally ascribed to the iron age, such as at Longbridge Deverill and Little Woodbury, can be dated back with furrowed bowls before 1000 BC, nearer to the date of the Shearplace Hill round-houses. The prosperous farmers which these presumably imply provide a social context for the new table manners.

Thirdly, the carinated and other Hawkes A pottery which is stratified beneath the defences of the earlier hill-forts of southern Britain may now be taken to offer a general *terminus post quem* of around 1000 BC. For some time, there has been a conflict between the late bronze age dates which our limited supply of radiocarbon determinations suggests for the start of early hill-forts and the later date suggested by the stratified Hawkes A pottery. The earlier dating of Hawkes A pottery makes it possible to give full weight to the evidence of long-lived development of hill-fort defences, and to permit some of these defences to be of the latest bronze age.

Notes

1. This is the view which Hawkes originally propounded (1931: 64), but tacitly abandoned some years ago (1973b).

2. While himself cautiously interpreting individual cases as perhaps only possibilities (Champion 1975: 136–8), Champion suggested that furrowed bowls might be of the tenth century, on the grounds that the metalwork of the Welby hoard could be of that date. Otherwise, he limited himself to parallels with the Low Countries. For chronological purposes, however, the key to dating both the Low Countries and also Britain must lie in Central Europe.

3. Pottery found in Area III, layer 7, which apparently did not extend outside the limits of the inner rampart (Wainwright 1970: 123 and fig. 5, layer 7). The classes of pottery found in this layer are detailed on Wainwright's table II.

4. Sherd 'with finger-printing on the lip' from ditch preceding rampart (Curwen 1932: 12).

5. Wheeler 1953: fig. 3, nos. 1–8, 10–15, 18–20 and 22–9.

6. One or two pots (Cunliffe 1976a: 15, pot no. 1 and possibly pot no. 2) plus possibly also a bronze ring (*ibid.*: 14, S.F.4).

7. The rampart of the original 6.5ha fort of period 1 was apparently of two successive stages. These show in the section taken between the portals of the eastern entrance (Wheeler 1943: pl. XI): period 1a appears as 'Rampart 1', period 1c as 'Ramp. 2'. Period 1c clearly followed rapidly on period 1a, before the upright timbers had had time to decay. Unpublished manuscripts in Dorchester Museum record that carinated Hawkes A pottery was found below 'Ramp. 2'. I am grateful to Mr R. Peers of Dorchester Museum, and to Mr R. Alcock, for permission to see the documents and for generous assistance in examining them.

8. Wheeler, accepting the date of about 400 BC for carinated pottery (1943: 187), necessarily concluded that Maiden Castle 1 started 'at a date which is not likely to have been far removed from 300 BC' (*ibid.*: 32).

9. See, for example, Hodson (1964: 108), Cunliffe (1974a: 31–3) and Harding (1974: 149), all following Hawkes (1961: 11). Hawkes obtained this dating from Hawkes and Smith (1957: 154–5) and M. A. Smith (1957: G.B. 24), and with it supported the dating which he had suggested long before for All Cannings Cross (Hawkes *et al.* 1930: 156).

10. See, for example, Cunliffe (1968; 1974a: 36–7) and Harding (1974: 157–76), following Hawkes (1940; 1962), Savory (1937) and Wheeler (1943: 185–90).

11. Burgess 1974: 205–11 and 214–21.

12. See, for example, Burgess 1979: 271.

13. See, for example, Bosch-Gimpera (1939) and Kimmig (1951: 65–72; 1954b: 41–2 and 95–8; 1970: 39–40). The theory has now been abandoned by Kimmig (1979: 202).

14. See also Harding 1972: 144, with list of sites, and pl. 3, with map; 1974: 148–53, with repeat of map and drawings of examples from All Cannings Cross.

15. See, for example, Hawkes (1961: 11, n.23), Harding (1974: 148–51) and Cunliffe (1974a: 31–3). For the Welby hoard, see Powell (1948) and M. A. Smith (1957: G.B. 24). A few of the pottery examples are as small as the Welby example (Cunnington 1923: 144), but most are distinctly larger.

16. The dating 'after 650 BC' derives from M. A. Smith (1957: G.B. 24) and Hawkes and Smith (1957: 154–5). Powell offered an even later date (1948: 39–40). The arguments given by Hawkes and Smith do not, however, establish the *terminus post quem* which they have been taken to offer. They note that the cross-handled bowl fragments found at Welby were hesitantly ascribed by von Merhart (1952: 14) to his class C, of Hallstatt C date; if that attribution is correct, then a Hallstatt C date (i.e. after 700 BC) is correct. But Hawkes and Smith questioned that attribution, observing correctly that the handles from Welby are much more like those of von Merhart's class B1. This would permit a date before 700 BC.

17. The record of its discovery is not encouraging (Powell 1948: 40).

18. See M. A. Smith (1957: G.B. 24) for the sword; and see Burgess (1968: 17–26; 1974: 209–11; 1979: 271) for the date of Ewart Park swords, which, most recently and very plausibly, he suggests started at around 900 BC.

19. Champion (1975: 136) was right to point out that this allows an early date. Indeed, the Continental evidence more than allows an early date; it seems to require one. Of the very few examples of class B1 cross-handles found west of Hungary (von Merhart 1952: 63 and Karte 1), Müller-Karpe has put into his Hallstatt B1 phase not only that from Unterglauheim (1959: 167, Abb. 41 and Taf. 169) but also those from Linz (*ibid.*: 127–8, Abb. 40 and Taf. 137–9), Seifenau (*ibid.*: 139) and (if there was a cross-handle there) that from Ehingen (*ibid.*: 167 and Taf. 168).

20. M. A. Smith drew attention to the earlier parallels for the furrowed bowl (1957: G.B. 24, card 2(2), section 6 (Comparisons), no. 6), noting the bowl from Mannheim-Seckenheim published by Kimmig (1940: Taf. 11.C.4). She rejected the Hallstatt A date, however, on the grounds that furrowed bowls 'may be expected also to survive into Hallstatt (C) times' at the Camp de Montmorot (Jura), as noted by Sandars (1957: fig. 54, nos. 3–4). There are, however, no good associations at Montmorot, and Sandars' dating of its pottery appears to be based on her iron age dating of All Cannings Cross (*ibid.*: 139 and 225). Since All Cannings Cross is itself dated by reference to Welby, the circular argument is not compelling.

21. The lines may be done with a U-section or with a flat-bottomed section. Secondly, the lines may be close-set, leaving no space between adjacent lines, or they may be wide-set, leaving an undisturbed band of the original vessel surface between adjacent lines. Thirdly, the lines may be deeply or else shallowly impressed.

22. In most general discussions of the date of furrowed and rilled pottery, these distinctions do not appear to be drawn, and consequently one cannot be sure exactly what phenomenon is being discussed. Thus Sandars distinguished between rilling and fluting; in the terminology which I have adopted, these are, respectively, wide-set and close-set lines; but she did not distinguish between horizontal lines and vertical or diagonal or curved lines (1957: 130). She then applied the term 'rilled ware' not only to vessels which are 'rilled' in her definition (*ibid.*: figs. 31–4), but also to various sherds which appear to be, in her terminology, 'fluted' (*ibid.*: figs. 29 and 30). In discussing the bowls from Combe Bernard, Veuxhaulles and Champlay (*ibid.*: 89–91, 96–8), she appears to wish to connect these with rilled ware, despite the fact that they do not have vertical rilling, only horizontal furrowing, and despite the fact that at least the example from Champlay (*ibid.*: fig. 25, no. 7) and probably also that from Veuxhaulles (*ibid.*: fig. 21, no. 5) apparently have fluting, not rilling in her terms. Consequently, it is not entirely clear what is plotted on her maps and lists (*ibid.*: 361 and 365). The same sort of uncertainty about terminology affects also, for example, the discussion of 'céramique cannelée' by Millotte (1963: 128–30), the discussion of 'poterie godronnée' by Niederlender *et al.* (1966: 94–7 and 171–3), the discussion of 'céramique à cannelures et godrons' by Daugas and Pétrequin (1970) and the comments by Boudou *et al.* (1961). All these authors draw useful distinctions, but they have not been applied in any comprehensive study.

23. A slightly dubious example from Brecknockshire has been illustrated by Savory (1971b: fig. 1, no. 4). Some globular urns have the shallow lines (Calkin 1962: 24–6). A possible example was found at Little Woodbury (Brailsford and Jackson 1948: fig. 4, no. 2d).

24. Wamser accepts the existence of furrowed Hallstatt C pottery in Burgundy and the Jura (1975: Taf. 17 and Taf. 2), but a check through the lists of published references suggests that the associations between this sort of pottery and Hallstatt C metalwork are often rather dubious. Brisson and Hatt (1967: figs. 23–5) have also accepted the existence of furrowing of Hallstatt C and even of Hallstatt D date, but the evidence for this is not clear to me; their groups of pottery are far from being single simultaneous deposits. One of the problems, of course, is to know whether one should accept that iron may be present in Hallstatt B contexts (as does Chertier 1976: 158) or define iron as

diagnostic of Hallstatt C (as apparently do Brisson and Hatt 1953: 212, à propos of Aulnay tombe B12). This problem has not yet been fully resolved.

25. It is possible that their infrequency reflects merely the greater range of shapes on which furrowing is found. Carinated furrowed bowls do not stand out as a distinctive type in quite the way they do in Britain. It may be that examples of furrowing on other vessel shapes have been chosen for illustration instead of carinated bowls. Relatively little close attention has been paid to the varying shapes of vessel upon which furrowing is found. The discussion by Daugas and Pétrequin (1970) marks a welcome new development. It is likely that a thorough literature and museum search would reveal more furrowed bowls.

26. From the Camp de Chassey (Kimmig 1954a: fig. 10); from Liverdun (Kimmig 1952: fig. 29, F.2); perhaps from Ecury-le-Repos, Chemin de Connantray (Brisson and Hatt 1966: fig. 9, no. 14), but this has fine-line furrowing; perhaps from Ecury-le-Repos, le Popelin (*ibid.*: fig. 16, no. 9); perhaps from le Fort Harrouard (Philippe 1937: fig. 69, no. 18; Sandars 1957: fig. 78, no. 10).

27. Sandars 1957: 88–90 and fig. 21, no. 1. There is some uncertainty about the association. Françoise Henry apparently illustrated this vessel as one of the grave-goods from her 'sépulture centrale', or 'sépulture A' (Henry 1933: 28 and 148 and fig. 2); but the only furrowed bowl which she lists is from a second grave, 'sépulture B', which also contained iron (*ibid.*: 148). If the association in sépulture A is valid, the spiral-ended anklet (*ibid.*: fig. 2, bottom left) is of Bronze Moyen I type (Hatt 1955a: fig. 2; Ziegert 1963: Taf. 6, Ztgr. 4); the rilled-headed pin (Sandars 1957: fig. 21, no. 2) appears however to be of Bronze Moyen III (Hatt 1955a: fig. C; Ziegert 1963: Taf. 6, Ztgr. 5; Zumstein 1976: pl. II, no. 6; Bonnamour *et al.* 1976: fig. 2, no. 10; Bocquet 1976: fig. 2, no. 13).

28. Sandars 1957: 89–90 and fig. 21, no. 5. This is of rather uncertain date because the character of the sword is not clear.

29. Sandars 1957: 96 and fig. 25, no. 7: 'second recorded grave'. This was found with a bronze pin and a bracelet: the bracelet was apparently 'a version of the Geispolisheim bracelet'. For Sandars' Geispolisheim bracelets, see her pp. 80–2 and fig. 25, no. 5 and pl. IV, nos. 3 and 4. Unfortunately bracelets generally similar to these are found throughout Bronze Moyen (Hatt 1955a: figs. A, B and C; Ziegert 1963: Taf. 6; Zumstein 1976: pl. I, no. 5 and pl. II, no. 2), and also in Bronze Final IIa (Zumstein 1976: pl. III, no. 123; 1964: fig. 7, no. 123 and fig. 27, no. 123; Hatt 1961: fig. 2). Thus the published information is not really adequate for a precise dating.

30. The furrowed bowl is no. 409 of Sépulture I at Rouffach-Gallbühl (Zumstein 1965: 46 and fig. 61). Zumstein dated this grave to his Bronze Final IIa (1964: 48–9), and the argument seems convincing, although it is complex because based on pottery not on metalwork. The large cordoned urn from this same grave at Rouffach (Zumstein 1965: fig. 61, no. 404) has good parallels with two similar large cordoned urns, each of which was associated with metalwork which suggests a Bronze Final IIa date; the Rouffach urn has slight differences from a third urn which appears to be of Bronze Final I. The first urn was found in Tombe I of the Casernes de Cavalrie site at Colmar, with a Bronze Final IIa pin and knife (Zumstein 1964: 48; 1965: 176–8 and fig. 21, nos. 61–3). The second urn was one of the urns from Algolsheim-Brunnenzug (*ibid.*: 162–4 and fig. 12, no. 2). This urn was found with a pin, and though the precise pin is not known, the range of pins from this site consists of Bronze Final IIa and IIb pins (*ibid.*: fig. 13, nos. 14–21). The third urn was found at Wittelsheim (Zumstein 1965: 53–4 and fig. 64, no. 443), with a Rixheim sword (*ibid.*: no. 442). The Rixheim sword in this area Zumstein attributed to his Bronze Final IIa (1964: 45–7), but Schauer (1971: 71–3) has shown quite convincingly that Zumstein's arguments were weak, and that the Rixheim sword should really be dated earlier than Zumstein's other Bronze Final IIa metalwork. Thus the Bronze Final I date which Zumstein inconsistently gave to the Wittelsheim urn should stand (1964: 45–7). The Wittelsheim urn is slightly different from the Rouffach urn, and this can be taken to mark a difference in date, allowing the Rouf-

fach urn and furrowed bowl to be of Bronze Final IIa.

31. The group of four vessels from a grave at Bolwiller-Grassweg (Zumstein 1965: 174 and fig. 18) offers very close parallels to the groups from Rouffach-Gallbühl (see n. 30 above). This implies some consistency in the shapes manufactured by potters in the region.

32. Contrast the examples from Rouffach-Gallbühl and Bolwiller-Grassweg (nn. 30 and 31) with the Bronze Final IIb and Bronze Final III pottery shown by Zumstein (1964: figs. 8–10; 1976: pl. III) and by Hatt (1961: figs. 3–5).

33. Zumstein 1976: pl. IV, top left, from tumulus I of Haguenau-Kirchlach; Bocquet 1976: fig. 3; Unz 1973.

34. For example, Reculée de Ney, Courchapon and Baume-les-Messieurs (Sandars 1957: 213–17). In addition, in the Arcachon region, in the far south-west of France, are found tumuli and urnfields with a number of furrowed bowls as accessory vessels, sometimes furrowed but usually with the presumably later, rounded shoulders of Hallstatt B (Mohen and Coffyn 1970: pls. XVII and XVIII; Kimmig 1954b). Many of the cremation urns have good general parallels with Central European Hallstatt A and B pottery, though most have the everted neck found in Central Europe in Hallstatt B2 contexts (Müller-Karpe 1959: Abb. 52–3) or, more usually, in Hallstatt B3 contexts (*ibid.*: Abb. 61–2), rather than the vertical cylindrical necks of Hallstatt A or B1 (*ibid.*: Abb. 29–31, 35–9, 42). Kimmig argued (1954b: 90–1) that all were of Hallstatt C or D date, but this seems to conflate potentially earlier pottery together with distinctive, later, Hallstatt D 'urnes à mamelons' (Mohen and Coffyn 1970: type I urns; see p. 105 and pl. IV; pl. IV, no. 4 is the same as that published by Kimmig (1954b: Abb. 17B) as from Trouc-du-Bourdiou grave 19; the group is published by Mohen and Coffyn as their nos. 120–6 from Trouc-du-Bourdiou grave 18). Urn covers of the type found in Arcachon have been seen as of Hallstatt C/D date (Kimmig 1954b: 90; Mohen and Coffyn 1970: 108–9), but similar covers are also a general Hallstatt A/B feature (Herrmann 1966: *passim*). Most of the carinated furrowed bowls from the Arcachon region are strictly speaking unassociated, but two have a very doubtful association with an iron spear-head at Tumulus K of le Gaillard (Mohen and Coffyn 1970: 22–3). Mohen and Coffyn conflated together all the furrowed bowls, sharp and round-shouldered, and emphasized a limited number of them in drawing comparisons with Haulzy type III (1970: 109, type X); see n. 105 below for Haulzy type III bowls, which are not good parallels for most of these bowls from the Arcachon. Thus the conclusion that furrowed bowl parallels from the Arcachon are of iron age date is based on doubtful evidence.

35. For the Erbenheim grave (Grave 1 of Merten's Brickworks) see no. 255 of Herrmann (1966: 101 and Taf. 99.C.25) and also see Cowen (1955: Abb. 4). The Hallstatt A2 dating depends on the knife, razor and pin rather than the sword: see Herrmann (1966: 30–5 and Abb. 5) and Müller-Karpe (1959: 176, 197 and Abb. 38 and 39). Cowen, who named the sword type, dated it a little early (1951: 198–200 and 209–10; 1955: 73–6 and 108–9).

36. Friedenau, Frankfurt-Sindlingen, cremation grave vessels (Herrmann 1966: 62 and Taf. 74.A.1 and 2) with a Hallstatt A2 knife and razor (*ibid.*: Taf. 74.A.7 and 8; cf. *ibid.*: Abb. 5, nos. 9 and 12).

Eschborn, stone cist grave 2 (*ibid.*: 73–4 and Taf. 83.C.3), with a Hemigkofen sword (*ibid.*: Taf. 84, no. 1), a Hallstatt A2 pin (*ibid.*: Taf. 84, no. 6; cf. Abb. 5, no. 15), a Hallstatt A2 bracelet (*ibid.*: Taf. 84, no. 5; cf. Abb. 5, no. 11) and just a hint of something later in the form of a Hallstatt B1 knife (*ibid.*: Taf. 84, no. 2; cf. Müller-Karpe 1959: Abb. 42).

Hochheim, Falkenberg, produced two furrowed bowls (Herrmann 1966: 32 and 75, and Taf. 85.B.1 and 6, and Abb. 6, nos. 5 and 9), from two graves of which the contents were mixed together, but which both contained Hallstatt A2 knives (*ibid.*: Taf. 85.B.3 and 4; cf. Abb. 5, no. 9 and Müller-Karpe 1959: Abb. 39, nos. 8 and 9).

At Södel, with a cremation found in a modern sand-pit, was a furrowed bowl (Herrmann 1966: 131–2 and Taf. 122.B.8), found with a Hallstatt A2 razor handle (*ibid.*: Taf.

122.B.4; cf. Abb. 5, no. 12) and the clay core of a Hallstatt A bronze pin (ibid.: Taf. 122.B.4; cf. Abb. 5, nos. 2, 3 and 27–30).

At Darmstadt, in the primary grave (beneath a later grave) in a barrow, was found a furrowed bowl (Herrmann 1966: 154–5 and Taf. 146.A.1 and 2), with a Hallstatt A2 knife (ibid.: Taf. 146.A.8) and a Hallstatt A2 bronze ring (ibid.: Taf. 146.A.9; cf. Abb. 5, no. 11).

At Niedernberg, with an urn burial, was found a furrowed bowl (Müller-Karpe 1959: Taf. 206.B.3), with a Hallstatt A2 knife (ibid.: Taf. 206.B.1; cf. Abb. 39, no. 8) and a Hallstatt A or A2 pin (ibid.: Taf. 206.B.2; cf. ibid.: Abb. 39, no. 2 and Herrmann 1966: Abb. 5, no. 27).

37. From Dietzenbach, stone cist grave 1, came a bowl (Herrmann 1966: 185 and Taf. 171, nos. 12 and 14) with a Hallstatt A2 razor (ibid.: Taf. 171, no. 6; cf. Abb. 5, no. 12), Hallstatt A and A1 pins (ibid.: Taf. 171, no. 2; cf. ibid.: Abb. 5, no. 17 and Müller-Karpe 1959: Abb. 31, no. 7).

From Horlach, Russelsheim, grave 3, came a bowl (Herrmann 1966: 182 and Taf. 168.A.3), with a Hallstatt A1 pin (ibid.: Taf. 168.A.6; cf. Abb. 5, no. 5) and a Hallstatt A2 bronze ring (ibid.: Taf. 168.A.9; cf. Abb. 5, no. 11).

From Pfungstadt, Pabsts' Vineyard, grave 1, came bowls (Herrmann 1966: 161 and Taf. 153.B.1 and 5), with bronze pins (ibid.: Taf. 153.B.10 and 11) of Hallstatt A2 (Müller-Karpe 1959: Abb. 39, no. 3) or Hallstatt A (Herrmann 1966: Abb. 5, no. 28).

38. At Osthafen, grave 10 (Herrmann 1966: 64 and Taf. 67.C.4); at Frankfurt-Niederursel, Falkenhan Brickyard, grave 7 (ibid.: 58 and Taf. 72.D.3); at Butzbach, Bouchenröder's Field, stray find (ibid.: 112 and Taf. 105.B); at Darmstadt-Arheiligen, Kranichsteiner Park, grave 2 (ibid.: 155 and Taf. 145.D.1 and 2); at Rüsselsheim-Königstädten, with a cremation (ibid.: 184 and Taf. 169.A.2); at Hanau, Beethoven-Platz, grave 2 (Müller-Karpe 1948: 65 and Taf. 10.C.7); at Hanau, Lehrhofen Heide, grave 11 (ibid.: 68 and Taf. 16.C.4); one of the graves at Grosskrotzenburg (ibid.: 71 and Taf. 22.C.3); a grave at Langendiebach (ibid.: 75 and Taf. 29.C.2); at Borsdorf, barrow 15 (ibid.: 78 and Taf. 38.A.3); and in grave 1 at Wisselsheim (ibid.: 79 and Taf. 39.B.6).

39. Note the association with 'Adelskeramik' at Osthafen, grave 10 (Herrmann 1966: Taf. 67.C.1) and Frankfurt-Niederursel, grave 7 (ibid.: Taf. 72.D.1). 'Adelskeramik' is taken by Herrmann (1966: 32–5) as distinctive of his Hallstatt A2 phase, and was found at Eschborn, stone cist grave 2 (ibid.: 73–4 and Taf. 83.C and 84) with a rather less close parallel for the Welby bowl and with Hallstatt A metalwork (see n. 36 above). No bowl variants at all comparable with that from Welby are present in the graves which Herrmann lists for his Hallstatt B1 and B3 phases (1966: 34–5). Müller-Karpe suggested that one furrowed bowl variant should be attributed to Hallstatt B1, that from Grossauheim, grave 4 (1959: 319 and Abb. 42, no. 20; 1948: 70 and Taf. 20.B.2).

40. Oberwalluf, stone cist grave B had a bowl (Herrmann 1966: 84–5 and Taf. 89.B.22 and 23), with a Hallstatt A1 knife (ibid.: Taf. 89.B.1; cf. ibid.: Abb. 5, no. 17 and Müller-Karpe 1959: Abb. 31, no. 7) and a Hallstatt A1 pin (Herrmann 1966: Taf. 89.B.8; cf. Abb. 5, no. 6).

The Gambach, 'Altstadter Rossfeld' cremation had a bowl (Herrmann 1966: 118 and Taf. 110.A.6 and 8), with a Hallstatt A1 pin (ibid.: Taf. 110.A.3; cf. Abb. 5, no. 7) and a possible Hallstatt A2 pin (ibid.: Taf. 110.A.1; cf. Müller-Karpe 1959: Abb. 39, no. 3).

The cremation found in 1939 at Lampertheim, Falkenflug, had a bowl (Herrmann 1966: 149–50 and Taf. 140, no. 16), with a Hallstatt A1 razor (ibid.: Taf. 140, no. 9; cf. Abb. 5, no. 1) and a Hallstatt A pin (ibid.: Taf. 140, no. 8; cf. Abb. 5, no. 3 ?).

Cremation grave 3 from Pfungstadt, Pabsts' Vineyard, had a bowl (Herrmann 1966: 162 and Taf. 154.B.3) with a Hallstatt A1 knife (ibid.: Taf. 154.B.1; cf. ibid.: Abb. 5, no. 18 and Müller-Karpe 1959: Abb. 31, no. 7) and a Hallstatt A1 pin (Herrmann 1966: Taf. 154.B.2; cf. Abb. 5, no. 4).

41. Müller-Karpe 1959: Abb. 29, no. 23; Abb. 30, no. 2; Abb. 37, no. 28; Abb. 38, no. 7.

42. For example, that found with a cremation at Oftersheim (Kimmig 1940: Taf. 9.G.8), with a Hallstatt A2 knife (ibid.: G.10). Though the bowls from Baden (Kimmig

1940) are of very much the same shapes as the bowls from Hessen (Herrmann 1966), the metalwork published from Baden does not seem as commonly associated with the bowls as in Hessen.

43. The similarities are fairly evident between Hallstatt A1 of Müller-Karpe (1959: Abb. 29 and 30) and Bronze Final IIa of Zumstein (1964: 40 and fig. 7). Zumstein ascribed the Rixheim sword to his IIa, but Schauer (1971: 71–3) has shown that it should go back to Bronze D, where Müller-Karpe put it (1959: Abb. 25). With this modification, Zumstein's IIa parallels Hallstatt A1 quite closely.

44. Joachim (1968: 30) relies on an unpublished thesis of 1940 by Löffler.

45. Desittere 1968: 11–15 and figs. 1–18.

46. See, for example, the grave from Heimbach, Kr. Neuwied (Desittere 1968: fig. 9).

47. These are basically the Schüsseln of Joachim (1968: 23), and the crucial dating associations are those of graves 20, 22 and 23 of Bassenheim 3 (*ibid.*: 31 and 88, and Taf. 11.C, D and E).

48. For the area near the mouth of the Rhine, see Desittere (1968). The nearest approach to furrowed bowls seems to be some of the little furrowed beakers found as accessory vessels, especially at Temse-Veldmolenwijk (De Laet 1958: nos. 80, 111, 120, 147). But these characteristically have a pointed or narrow, flat base and high, vertical or flaring neck. With the few of these which are furrowed apparently go a number of similarly shaped vessels which are very much less like furrowed bowls (*ibid.*: nos. 91, 106, 148, 150, 151, 170 and 180). Desittere illustrates no nearer parallels to furrowed bowls than these (1968: figs. 95–6 and *passim*). Some of these beakers can be paralleled in the grave with Hallstatt A2 metalwork at Heimbach, Kr. Neuwied (*ibid.*: fig. 9, no. 5). Desittere ascribes the great majority of them to Hallstatt B (1968: 34–6 and fig. IV), and this is probably true of the example from Voerde, grave 20, no. 10 of Desittere (1968: 113 and fig. 37); the flaring neck of the associated urn (*ibid.*: no. 8) is a Hallstatt B feature, not Hallstatt A. Kimmig (1970: 45) has argued that the other vessel in that grave, no. 9 of Desittere (1968: fig. 37), could not be earlier than Hallstatt C–D in south-west Germany. This view, however, seems to place excessive reliance on the absence of a sharply everted lip on that vessel; with this exception, the general shape of no. 9 is well paralleled in Hallstatt B3 contexts, and found with vessels comparable to the little beaker, no. 10. One may note, for example, Fundgruppe 4 from barrow C at Ihringen (Kimmig 1940: 140–1 and Taf. 25) or the Hallstatt B3 metalwork and pottery which comprised the lower group from Gündlingen barrow A (*ibid.*: 137–40 and Abb. 3 and Taf. 28.B).

49. For some of the evidence, see Verron (1976) and Mohen (1972).

50. See Kimmig (1952: 140 and figs. 19–22) and Sandars (1957: 146–7 and figs. 33–5). Early-looking pottery is the rilled ware on Kimmig's figs. 19 and 20. For this rilled ware, see Sandars (1957: 130–54); she rightly emphasized the early connections of the bronzes, but allowed some of them (such as crook-headed pins) to last on later than now really seems likely. For rilled ware ('leicht gerillte Keramik'), see also Holste (1953: 95–7), Ziegert (1963: 26, 38–9 and Taf. 15) and Müller-Karpe (1959: 183 and Abb. 22 and 23); they emphasize its Bronze D date and distinctness from Hallstatt A pottery. Although Kimmig (1952: 140) and Cordier (1972: 88) suggest a Bronze Final II (= Hallstatt A) date for the start of the rilled ware at Pougues-les-Eaux, it is not easy to see why the starting date should be depressed so late. The bronzes also seem to have a Bronze D/ Bronze Final I air: cf. Hatt (1961: fig. 1) and Müller-Karpe (1959: Abb. 25). The pottery from the site does, however, seem to include later forms, of Hallstatt A and perhaps even of Hallstatt B (Kimmig 1952: fig. 21, B to D; Sandars 1957: 146, n. 1 and figs. 33–5).

51. Brisson and Hatt 1953: tombe Z.2 (figs. 42 and 53), tombe Z.9 (fig. 42) and tombe Z.1 (fig. 43). See also the drawings of Chertier (1976).

52. See Kimmig (1952: fig. 20, nos. B.2 and C); these were illustrated also by Sandars (1957: fig. 33, nos. 16 and 17 respectively).

53. Compare the pottery of Aulnay tombe Z.2 (Brisson and Hatt 1953: fig. 42, nos. 3

and 4) with the Hallstatt A1 bowls from Oberwalluf, Gambach, Lampertheim and Pfungstadt cited in n. 40 above. Brisson and Hatt ascribed tombe Z.2 to Hallstatt A1 (1953: fig. 40); although Müller-Karpe (1959: 175, n. 1) objected that the knife from tombe Z.2 should not be older than his Hallstatt A2, Herrmann was prepared to accept such knives as also found in Hallstatt A1 (1966: Abb. 5). Compare the bowl from Aulnay tombe Z.9 with the Hallstatt A2 bowls from Friedenau and Darmstadt cited in n. 36 above.

54. A number of bowls illustrated by C. and D. Mordant (1970) are to be distinguished from furrowed bowls both by rilling and also by differences in the rim or lip profile and by more rounded shoulders (e.g., *ibid.*: fig. 8, no. 11; fig. 10, no. 2).

55. See Chadwick (1961) for the site. The relevant C14 determinations are three. NPL-104 was from a sample which came from a post-hole of an unspecified house, and is cited as 2480 bp (5568) ± 90 (Callow *et al.* 1966: 340). NPL-105 was from a sample which came from a post-hole of House 1, and is cited as 2580 bp ± 155 (Callow and Hassall 1968: 115). NPL-106 was from a sample which came from a post-hole of House 2, and is cited as 2450 bp ± 90 (*ibid.*: 115).

56. The range of NPL-104 calibrates at the 95% probable level to 900–420 BC (Clark R. M. 1975) or 990–390 BC (Wendland and Donley 1971); at the 99% probable level to 970–410 BC (Clark 1975) or 1090–300 BC (Wendland and Donley 1971). The range of NPL-105 calibrates at the 95% probable level to 1100–480 BC (Clark 1975) or 1190–440 BC (Wendland and Donley 1971); at the 99% probable level to 1320–210 BC (Clark 1975) or 1310–320 BC (Wendland and Donley 1971). The range of NPL-106 calibrates at the 95% probable level to 880–400 BC or 950–350 BC respectively; at the 99% probable level to 940–240 BC or 1050–260 BC respectively.

57. The Shearplace Hill estimate is NPL-19, cited as 3130 bp ± 180 (Rahtz and ApSimon 1962: 289–90; Callow *et al.* 1963: 36). The phasing of the scattered charcoal which produced the sample was interpreted by Avery and Close-Brooks (1969: 347, n.1). The 95% probable range is from 1900–980 BC (Clark 1975) or 1960–1050 BC (Wendland and Donley 1971); the 99% probable range is 2050–870 BC or 2100–920 BC respectively.

58. The pottery from the Itford Hill cemetery, published by Ellison (1972), is admittedly more like that from Shearplace than is the pottery from the Itford settlement site, recorded by Burstow and Holleyman (1957); but parts of what appear to be the same vessel were recorded at both Itford locations. The C14 determination from the Itford settlement (Holden 1972: 89) was presumably obtained from barley from pit 26 of Hut E (Burstow and Holleyman 1957: 177–8). The determination is GrN-6167, cited as 2950 bp (5568) ± 35 (Holden 1972: 89). This gives a 95% probable range of 1520–950 BC (Clark 1975) or 1590–960 BC (Wendland and Donley 1971); and 99% probable ranges of 1580–890 BC and 1690–870 BC respectively.

59. See the pottery from the Ash Hole cave, Brixham (ApSimon 1968); and for globular urns, see Calkin (1962: 24–9).

60. This is the wood stake from which was taken sample BM-123, cited as 2890 bp ± 150 (Barker and Mackey 1963: 105; Varley 1968: 14, stake from site A at 30ft). This was apparently one of the birch stakes (each about 8cm across) which surrounded a 'cooking'-pit cut down from the surface of the peat (Varley 1968: 14, 22 (section A, component (i)) and fig. 8, Pit at 30ft). The furrowed bowl lay on the surface of that peat underneath a layer of clay (*ibid.*: 24 (I.A.P.3) and 16), some 30m away from the pit (*ibid.*: figs. 5 and 9). BM-123 is an old British Museum determination, cited with an error term arbitrarily increased to ± 150 (Barker and Mackey 1963: 104): the 'counting statistics' error is apparently ± 78. The determination calibrates at the 95% probable level to 1450–900 BC (Clark 1975) or 1570–840 BC (Wendland and Donley 1971). Another stake produced determination BM-122, cited as 2960 bp ± 150 (Varley 1968: 14; Barker and Mackey 1963: 105) but the exact stratified location of this is variously reported and it may have lain beneath the peat (Varley 1968: fig. 8).

61. For the vessel, see Rahtz and ApSimon (1962: 311–13, no. 18). Calkin's obser-

vation that some of the Shearplace pottery was iron age (1962: 28) reflects the close similarity between the Shearplace material and some of the pottery conventionally ascribed to the iron age.

62. Sherds of the furrowed vessel, no. 18, were found in post-hole 46 (Rahtz and ApSimon 1962: 313) in 'lower dark soil'. This post-hole is one of those of House A.2 (*ibid.*: fig. 5; Avery and Close-Brooks 1969: 347, n.3); that is, the post-hole was of period 2 (*ibid.*: 345), and the C14 determination was obtained from charcoal of periods 1 and 2 (*ibid.*: 347, n.1).

63. From the south-western hole of the four central post-holes of House 1 at Little Woodbury came a furrowed bowl, type 2a.1 of Brailsford and Jackson (1948: 10), and two furrowed bowls also came from post-holes of House 2. The other published sherds from the round-houses came solely from post-holes of House 1: from other central post-holes came types 3b, 14f and 16e, plus sherds with finger-tip decoration; from post-holes of the entrance came sherds with finger-tip decoration. From the 'drain' of House 1 (if this feature was connected with House 1) came type 19a, a sherd possibly with rilling (see n.23 above).

64. The Hallstatt B2/B3 bowl is no. 75 of Avery *et al.* (1967); the furrowed bowls are no. 78 and nos. 33 and 34.

65. See Cunnington (1923: 21–2) and Hawkes *et al.* (1930: 143 and 155–7). Amongst the multifarious items found poorly associated at the site was a vessel of very fine, polished black ware with nipples and furrowing (Cunnington 1923: pl. 29, no. 2). Although this has been ascribed to the eighth to seventh century BC by Cunliffe (1974a: fig. A.2, no. 10), there really are no Continental parallels for nipples and furrowing later than the Buckelurnen of Bronze D/Bronze Final 1. It is particularly noticeable that the sharply-everted lip of the All Cannings Cross vessel is also of this early Urnfield character.

66. Types IIa and IIb of Calkin (1962: 25–6).

67. Type I of Calkin (1962: 24–5).

68. Burgess 1974: 205 and 217–18.

69. It should be noted that grooved furrows appear in eastern France in the same general Urnfield contexts as wave furrowing: see Chertier (1976: figs. 22–7) and Brisson and Hatt (1953: *passim*; 1966: *passim*; 1967: fig. 27).

70. Cunliffe 1968.

71. Compare nos. 24–6 of Cunliffe (1968) with Hallstatt B3 examples illustrated by Müller-Karpe (1959: Abb. 61–2).

72. Compare, for example, Müller-Karpe (1959: Abb. 23, nos. 35 and 38), Hatt (1961: fig. 1), Kimmig (1952: fig. 22, no. 3) and C. and D. Mordant (1970: fig. 5, no. 1; fig. 9, no. 1; fig. 10, no. 5).

73. Cunliffe 1968: fig. 3, no. 27.

74. Harding 1972: 145 and pl. 3; 1974: 148–53.

75. Wheeler 1943: 192–4 and map at fig. 55; Burchell and Frere 1947: 45–6.

76. Wheeler 1943: 203 and 223 and no. 134B.

77. By Burchell and Frere (1947: 43–5), Hawkes and Fell (1943: 205, discussing no. J.1) and Fell (1952: 38).

78. See Chertier 1973: 567–9. Hallstatt A comparanda for these vessels can be seen published by Herrmann (1966).

79. See, for example, R. A. Smith (1925: 89), Hawkes *et al.* (1930: 89), Favret (1936: 104–5), Savory (1937: 6–11; 1939: 253–4), Hawkes (1940; 1961: 11; 1962: 85–7), Wheeler (1943: 187–90), Kenyon (1952: 50 and 55–7), Cunliffe (1974a: 36) and Harding (1974: 157–76).

80. I have outlined elsewhere the history of the Sussex hill-fort Marnian theory (Avery 1976: 31–4). It will be sufficient to add here that the Sussex Marnian and the carinated Marnian theories appeared initially almost as rival constructions, but co-existed happily for some 20 years, not always being clearly distinguished one from another. The Sussex Marnians had their impact more directly on hill-fort dating, es-

tablishing a doctrine that hill-forts did not start until 250 BC; the carinated Marnians had their impact rather on pottery. The effect of the carinated Marnians on hill-forts, however, was to reinforce the late datings. Carinated pottery was taken to be the earliest iron age pottery (Savory 1939: 252–3; Wheeler 1943: 187–90); indeed, on one view, carinated furrowed bowls were held to be of the fifth century BC (Favret 1936: 104–5). This was taken to show that all hill-forts with early iron age pottery, Hawkes A pottery, were later than the fifth century BC. As we shall see below, the view that carinated pottery was amongst the earliest Hawkes A pottery was correct, but the calendar dates were about 500 years too late. The more recent history of the carinated Marnians has been complex. The two Marnian theories were still recognizably distinct in the late 1950s (Hawkes 1961: 11 – Long Wittenham as final First A; *ibid.*: 13 – Southern First B), but successful criticism of the Sussex hill-fort Marnians by Hodson (1962) led Hawkes to hold temporarily that there was a single, 'big-bang' carinated Marnian invasion about 400 BC (1962; and lectures in Oxford, 1963/64). Arguments and evidence which Hawkes adduced in 1963/64 for the 'big-bang' theory were faithfully reproduced by Harding (1974: 157–76), but the significance of the Marnians had been radically reduced in the interim by Hawkes himself, emphasizing the greater importance for British development of repeated, small impulses from the Continent (1973a: 622).

81. Harding has presented the most recent version of the view (1972: 86–96, 145 and pl. 5; 1974: 157–76 and fig. 53). He gives a list of sites, though unfortunately he does not specify which individual vessels he accepts from these sites.

82. See, for example, Clark and Fell (1953: nos. 65, 66, 69, 72, 97, 98) and Brewster (1963: fig. 35, no. 4 and fig. 40, no. 7).

83. See, for example, Rowlett *et al.* (1969: 125 and fig. 30, nos. 27 and 45, 'biconic plates') and Bretz-Mahler (1971: pls. 109, 114, 121; 1961: pls. X-XII and XXIV-XXV).

84. See, for example, Cunliffe and Phillipson (1968: fig. 16).

85. For Long Wittenham, see Savory (1937: fig. 2) and Harding (1972: pl. 50). For Allen's Pit, see Harding (1972: 89–90 and pl. 54, A-F), Bradford (1942b) and Leeds (1935). For Chinnor, see Richardson and Young (1951: figs. 7 and 8).

86. For Linford, pit G.15, see Hawkes (1962: fig. I, nos. 1–5); for Darmsden, pit 1, see Cunliffe (1968: figs. 2 and 3).

87. Cunliffe and Phillipson 1968: nos. 110–17, 119–22, 124, 125.

88. *Ibid.*: nos. 140–3 and 148.

89. Musson 1976.

90. See Harding (1974: 138–45) and Challis and Harding (1975: i, 37). See also the sites of Kirtlington (Harding 1966; 1972: 80–1 and pl. 49), New Wintle's Farm (Harding 1972: 80) and Bampton (*ibid.*: 81 and pl. 46.A.). Cunliffe (1968: 176) wished to transfer the carinated pottery of West Harling to the sixth century BC: he drew comparison with carinated pottery from Staple Howe, where he apparently felt that the Hallstatt C bronzes should be transferred from the seventh to the sixth century BC in order to accommodate a radiocarbon date. The argument seems unconvincing, in view of the inherent imprecision of the radiocarbon date and the multi-period character of Staple Howe. Cunliffe later ascribed carinated vessels to various of his groups, spanning the eighth to third centuries BC (1974a: figs. A.1 to A.12). Except at Eldon's Seat (for which, see above, p. 42), evidence of association and stratigraphy seems too slight to establish the date suggested. Even for Eldon's Seat I ('Ultimate Deverel-Rimbury'), Cunliffe originally suggested a date as late as 750 BC (1974a: 29–30) or seventh–sixth centuries (Cunliffe and Phillipson 1968: 231). Barrett (1978: 278) has suggested eighth- to sixth-century dates for vessels with carination, and has also (1976: 294–5) coined the term 'post Deverel-Rimbury' to include such material as Eldon's Seat I, which he views as earlier than furrowed bowls (ascribed by him to the eighth–fifth centuries).

91. The conventional date for the start of Hallstatt C is around 700 BC, based on the conclusion that the earliest date is late in the eighth century (Dehn and Frey 1962: 199–200; Kossack 1957: 220–3). Sandars has proposed starting Hallstatt C firmly in the

eighth century (1971: 25 and 28, n.34), basing herself on the discussion by Joanna Close-Brooks (1968). It is not clear to me that the case for the earlier dating of Hallstatt C is yet made.

92. The gap between the end of Deverel-Rimbury and this 'iron age' pottery has recently been termed 'post Deverel-Rimbury', implying still that a significant break in pottery styles should be identifiable around the eighth or seventh century (Barrett, cited in n.90 above). For a comment on the date of such 'post Deverel-Rimbury' pottery, see n.121 below.

93. As illustrated by Müller-Karpe (1959: Abb. 52–3 and 61–2) and Kossack (1959: Taf. 15–17). See also Kimmig (1940), Herrmann (1966) and Müller-Karpe (1948).

94. At Puddlehill, these bowls appear in Group 3 of Matthews (1976: 143, fig.97, nos. 29–34). There are four of which a quantity was found (ibid.: fig. 30, nos. 5 and 6; fig. 37, no. 10; fig. 41, no. 4) and about six were found only as scraps (ibid.: fig. 37, nos. 11 and 12; fig. 54, no. 7; fig. 66, nos. 12 and 13; and perhaps fig. 39, no. 7). For Wandlebury, see Hartley (1957: fig. 7, no. 16). For Chinnor, see Richardson and Young (1951: fig. 7, nos. 37, 40 and 43; fig. 8, nos. 46, 47, 50, 51, 65 and 78); most of those from Chinnor are variants with decoration different from that at Puddlehill, but there were two examples with decoration very closely paralleled at Puddlehill (ibid.: fig. 8, nos. 50 and 65). A plain example came from Linford (Hawkes 1962: fig. III, no. 11). For Ravensburgh, see Dyer (1976: 157 and fig. 3). The Ravensburgh example was reportedly 'associated with' a La Tène Ib fibula illustrated on the same figure. Mr Dyer tells me, however, that the fibula was found in the centre of an entrance passage and the vessel at the edge of the passage, and he is not absolutely convinced that they must have been in use simultaneously. Comparable shapes in plain ware have been found at Wilbury, Herts. (Applebaum 1949: fig. 8, no. 10a); Holwell, Herts. (Applebaum 1934: fig. 3, no. 5); War Ditches, Cherry Hinton, Cambs. (Fox C. 1923: pl. XVI, no. 6); Ivinghoe Beacon, Bucks. (Cotton and Frere 1968: nos. 24 and 110); and Bledlow, Bucks. (Saunders 1971: fig. 3, nos. 12 and 13). This seems fairly clear evidence that the narrow shoulder is a regional style, but the dates of the plain ware examples have to be treated with a little more caution than the dates of the decorated examples. Pedestalled plain ware of clearly similar profile has been recorded from sites in Surrey (Bishop 1971: fig. 6, nos. 42–6, classed as his 'Form 8', with valuable discussion at p. 17) and from Orsett, Essex (Barrett 1978: fig. 41, no. 74). The whole range of such vessels would repay full listing and closer examination.

95. At Puddlehill, the three pits which produced fine ware bowls were pit 4 (Matthews 1976: fig. 30), pit 13 (ibid.: fig. 37) and pit 18 (ibid.: fig. 41); pits 13 and 18 also contained iron. Three pits produced only scraps of the fine ware bowls: pit 21 (ibid.: fig. 54), pit 17 (ibid.: fig 29) and pit 27 (ibid.: fig. 66). In these three, of course, the bowl scraps could be surviving rubbish, and the pits therefore basically later than pits 4, 13 and 18. The Puddlehill ring-headed pin was found in pit 3 (ibid.: fig. 28). For the Chinnor pottery, see Richardson and Young (1951: figs. 5 and 6); for the ring-headed pins, see Richardson and Young (1951: fig. 10) and Harding (1972: 170 and pl. 73, nos. D–F).

96. Compare no. 35 of Richardson and Young (1951: fig. 6) with three French examples found associated with triconic or bead-rim carinated vessels:

(1) a similarly-shaped vessel was found in grave 39 at Grandes-Loges (Bretz-Mahler 1961: 32 and pl. XXIII, no. 2), with two triconic vessels (ibid.: 12 and pl. III, no. 2; ibid.: 16 and unillustrated vessel no. 31.1.619);

(2) a similarly-shaped vessel was found in grave 51 of the La Tène cemetery at Jogasses (ibid.: 27 and pl. XXIII, no. 8), with a triconic vessel (ibid.: 11 and pl. II, no. 7) and two other vessels (ibid.: 14 and pl. IV, no. 2; ibid.: 20 and pl. XIV, no. 10);

(3) a similarly-shaped vessel was found in grave 105 of the La Tène cemetery at Jogasses (ibid.: 27 and pl. XXIII, no. 10) with a bead-rimmed carinated vessel (ibid.: 18 and pl. VIII, no. 8).

The furrowed shoulder of no. 48 of Richardson and Young (1951: fig. 8), found without a base at Chinnor, may be compared with the furrowed shoulder of the vessel found unassociated in grave 102 at Jogasses (Hatt and Roualet 1976); the latter has a highly significant pedestal.

97. Compare a vessel from pit 4 of Matthews (1976: fig. 30, no. 4) and a vessel from pit 39 (*ibid*.: fig. 39, no. 1) with various vessels of the same curvilinear profile, usually having pedestals, which the Puddlehill examples lack (Bretz-Mahler 1961: pls. XVII and XVIII), but sometimes lacking pedestals (*ibid*.: pls. XIX and XX, esp. no. 7). Hawkes (1940) drew attention to similar parallels for a base from Worth; despite the very fragmentary condition of that base, these parallels may be valid.

98. Champion 1977.

99. Hatt and Roualet 1976: graves 37 and 69.

100. *Ibid*.: graves 19, 82, 156 and 187.

101. Hatt and Roualet 1977: 7–10; Mansfeld 1973: 87–91; Dehn and Frey 1962.

102. Hatt and Roualet 1977: 10; Babes 1974: 25–47.

103. Chertier (1973); Bretz-Mahler (1971; 1961: pls. I-III and VIII); Hatt and Roualet (1977: pls. IV and VI).

104. Pedestal bases: Joffroy (1960: pls. 49–51). Fibulae: *ibid*.: pls. 19–27.

105. The vessels from Saint Vincent are fairly homogeneous in their profiles (Mariën 1964: 142–3, section 3 with list of many from Saint Vincent). They appear to compare closely with type III of the Haulzy cemetery (Goury 1911: fig. 19; Mariën 1964: 142–3). At Haulzy, one example was found in tumulus 30 with an iron Hallstatt C sword (Goury 1911: 40; Mariën 1964: 142 and 159); another was found in tumulus 3 with a bronze Hallstatt C razor (Goury 1911: 33 and pl. I, no. 2; Mariën 1964: 142 and 159; compare the example from Langenthal, Kr. Bern, illustrated by Jockenhövel 1971: no. 579); another was found with an iron spear-head in grave 15 (Goury 1911: 37–8 and fig. 14; Mariën 1964: 159).

106. Hatt and Roualet 1976: graves 33, 47, 72, 87 (no. 980), 168 and 179.

107. As Harding (1974: 159–61) and more especially Hodson (1975) have emphasized with regard to 'vases piriformes'. For Marnian La Tène I styles which differ from triconic pottery, see Bretz-Mahler (1971: pls. 106–7, 112–13, 115–20), Chertier (1973) and Hatt and Roualet (1977: pls. IV, VI and VIII). Curvilinear-profile vessels were distinctly more common in association with triconic pottery in the Marne than they appear to have been in Britain, judging from the two poor, provincial parallels noted above from Puddlehill (n. 97): see Bretz-Mahler (1961).

108. See Hatt and Roualet (1976: grave 16) and Joffroy (1958: 130–3). For 'South-Eastern B', see Ward Perkins (1938:154–5).

109. Hawkes, of course, recognized this difference in associations by distinguishing the carinated Marnian connection of Long Wittenham (1961: 11) from the pedestalled Marnian connection at Worth (*ibid*.: 13, n.35).

110. Thénot (1976); Hatt and Roualet (1976; 1977).

111. See Jope (1961: fig. 10) for distribution map of Hallstatt D daggers, his nos. 1–6.

112. Hodson (1971) has already emphasized the absence of such fibulae from Britain, and the lists of Mansfeld (1973) make the same point.

113. For the tribal area, as shown by coins, see Allen (1961: 219–35) and Rivet (1962: coin maps 4 and 5). For cremation cemeteries, see Radford (1954: 22–3) and Birchall (1965); for richer burials, see I. M. Stead (1967: 44–8).

114. Harding (1972: 89–90 and pl. 50); Savory (1937).

115. Bradford (1942b); Leeds (1935); Harding (1972: 89–90 and pl. 54).

116. Harding (1972: 89).

117. Müller-Karpe (1959: Abb. 52–3 and 61–2); Kossack (1959: Taf. 15–17).

118. For the Staple Howe Hallstatt C bronzes, see Brewster (1963: 111–17); for the suggestion that the sharp-shouldered pottery should be dated about 500 BC, a century or more later than the bronzes, see Brewster (1963: 108–9) and Hawkes (foreword to Brewster 1963). There is, as far as I may see, no published stratigraphical evidence for the chronological order of the three palisade trenches at Staple Howe, despite the

excavator's assertion that they were built in a specific order. For the Ivinghoe eighth/seventh-century bronzes, see Britton (1968). Cotton and Frere suggested that the pottery should be dated in the sixth century (1968: 200–3). They discounted the possibility that the habitation and pottery at Ivinghoe could be of more than one period (*ibid.*: 200), but the excavation of the interior suggested very strongly that more than one period of structure was present: it is very unlikely that the rectangular structure II was in use simultaneously with the round structure III, for they are too close (*ibid.*: fig. 7).

119. For the attempt to limit the term 'Hallstatt' to Hallstatt C and D, naming Hallstatt A and B 'bronze age E and F', see Hawkes (1948: esp. 213–14) and Childe (1948), followed by Powell (1963). The re-naming was rejected by Vogt (1950), and the rejection was accepted by Hawkes and Smith (1957: 137, n.4).

120. See, for example, Hodson (1964), Renfrew (1974) and Barrett (1978). Champion (1975) has notably dissented.

121. For example, the best parallels for 'vertical rippling' on 'post Deverel-Rimbury' pottery presumably lie in the 'rilling' of Bronze D or Bronze Final I, well before the eleventh- to ninth-century BC date suggested by Barrett (1979). The earlier dating would presumably be supported by the radiocarbon dates cited for 'post Deverel-Rimbury' pottery by Barrett (1976: fig. 17.1), if these were calibrated into real years. This leaves a convenient gap for Hawkes A pottery in the succeeding Hallstatt A to D period.

Appendix A: a preliminary list of furrowed bowls in Britain

Where information is available, I have noted the colour of the vessel(s) and whether wave or groove furrows were present. If the rim and upper region were preserved, I have also noted whether they show a (short) lip or a (longer) neck (see fig. 2).

I enter the caveat that many of the sherds I have not examined myself. Some styles of early Anglo-Saxon pottery are at first sight surprisingly similar to furrowed bowls (Biddle 1972: 101 and fig. 3, nos. 1–4, citing parallels from the Feddersen Wierde; Myres 1969: 87–8 and figs. 35–7, and especially fig. 14, no. 2102; Myres 1977: figs. 88, 89, 95, 99, 228 and 326).

A separate list of questionable, unconfirmed and rejected examples is given in Appendix B.

All Cannings Cross, Wilts. (SU–41–080634): some 170 furrowed bowls in total (Cunnington 1923: 144). Published examples include wave and groove furrows, necked and lipped profiles and haematited, brown and black fabrics (*ibid.*: 34 and pl. 28, nos. 1 6, 11, 16 and 20; pl. 37, no. 6; pl. 39, no. 1; pl. 40, no. 1; pl. 43, nos. 3, 4 and ?5; pl. 45, nos. 2, 3, 5 and 6; pl. 47a, no. 8; Harding 1974: fig. 41, A-F).

Allen's Pit, Dorchester, Oxon. (SU–41–575962): two or three examples, all grooved and in black ware, and probably all necked (Harding 1972: pl. 54, A, B and ?E; Leeds 1935: 39–41 and fig. 2, no. b – perhaps Harding's B; Savory 1939: pl. XIc, being Harding's A).

Barmston, Yorks. (TA–54–172586): one necked, grooved example in ware grey-black to orange-buff (Varley 1968: 24 and fig. 11, no. I.A.P. (3); Challis and Harding 1975: ii, 12 and fig. 21, no. 3).

Bathampton Down, Som. (ST–31–766647): one example found near but outside the hill-fort. It was buff-black in colour, with groove furrows and perhaps a long neck (Wainwright G. J. 1967: fig. 5, no. 10; Cunliffe 1974a: fig. A.7, no. 15).

Blewburton, Berks. (SU–41–547862): the shoulder only of one grooved example of unspecified colour (Bradford 1942a: no. 30) and possibly one necked example (*ibid.*: no. 42).

Boscombe Down West, Wilts. (SU–41–189399): two examples, both haematited, grooved and necked (Richardson 1951: 140 and fig. 7, nos. 14 and 15 – i.e. fig. 2.2 herein).

Budbury, Wilts. (ST–31–821611): 83 haematited examples. The 18 which have been illustrated by G. J. Wainwright (1970: 133–6, class VIII, nos. 74–91) include ten lipped examples with wave furrows (*ibid.*: nos. 74, 75, 77, 78, 80, 83, 84, 86, 87, 91) and five grooved scraps (*ibid.*: nos. 76, 79, 82, 85, 89), of which one was lipped (*ibid.*: no. 89) and one necked (*ibid.*: no. 76).

Cold Kitchen Hill, Wilts. (ST–31–833387): one haematited example (Cunnington and Goddard 1934: 115, unillustrated; Barrett 1979: 230, no. 11). Apparently wave-furrowed with lip.

Darmsden, Suff. (TM–62–097527): 11 examples with brown, grey and black surfaces (Cunliffe 1968: nos. 1–9, 60 and 61), all apparently grooved (except perhaps no. 9) and all with necks, but relatively short necks.

Eldon's Seat, Encombe, Dorset (SY–30–939776): four haematited examples, all probably grooved and apparently necked (Cunliffe and Phillipson 1968: nos. 140–3).

Fengate, Peterborough, Northants. (TL–52–206988): one grooved example (shoulder only) in black ware (Hawkes and Fell 1943: 205 and fig. 5, no. J.1).

Gallows Gore, Worth Matravers, Dorset (SY–30–978790): at least two haematited examples apparently showing (1) grooved furrows with a long neck and (2) wave furrows with a lip (Calkin 1948: 46 and pl. IIA, nos. 1ª and 1ᵈ; no. 1ª is probably that drawn by Calkin and Piggott 1939: fig. 4, no. 27). These came from the western of the two areas at Gallows Gore. The two areas were distinguished by Calkin (1948: 40–1; 1953: 48 and 52, and appendix I, nos. 16a and 16b); the eastern area was reported on by Calkin (1953: 48–52), but apparently produced no furrowed bowls. A further haematited example with wave furrows and lip was in the Red House Museum, Christchurch, in 1964 (fig. 2.3 herein), reportedly a surface find from Langton Matravers. This may have come from Gallows Gore, which was originally said to be in Langton Matravers parish (Calkin and Piggott 1939), but lies in fact in Worth Matravers parish (Calkin 1947: 42). I am most grateful to Mr J. H. Lavender for assistance with the pottery in the Red House Museum.

Hengistbury Head, Hants. (SZ–40–170908): three examples (Bushe-Fox 1915: 30 and pl. XVI, nos. 1–3 and pl. X, no. 9 (= pl. XVI, no. 1)). Two were haematited and one had a patchy surface, partly haematited, partly brown. Two were necked (pl. XVI, nos. 1 and 2), one of them perhaps having wave furrows (pl. XVI, no. 1 = pl. X, no. 9); one was lipped (pl. XVI, no. 3). In the Red House Museum, Christchurch, in 1964, were noted two haematited wave-furrowed examples: one was a rimless sherd (cf. Bushe-Fox's pl. XVI, no. 2); a second, unmarked but in the 'reserve collection from Hengistbury Head', was haematited with black patches on the lip and was perhaps Bushe-Fox's pl. XVI, no. 3 (in which case his pl. XVI, no. 3 was slightly mis-drawn).

Highfield, Fisherton, Salisbury, Wilts. (SU–41–133308): two examples, one haematited, one in black ware (Hawkes 1934: 599, nos. 18 and 21, not illustrated).

Hillbrow, Pokesdown, Bournemouth, Hants. (SZ–40–12.92.): two examples. One was given a slightly misleading illustration by Calkin (1951: fig. 13). This was in the Red House Museum, Christchurch, in 1964, labelled 'HBP.3' (fig. 2.5 herein); haematited, with wave furrows and lip. Another, unpublished example (HBP.2 in the Red House Museum in 1964) was yellow-brown, with wave furrows and probably a longer neck (but broken).

Kimmeridge (Gaulter Cliffs), Dorset (SY–30–907792): 'many small bowls in haematite ware . . . occasionally the neck . . . decorated with furrows' (Calkin 1948: 39). One example had a relatively short neck and perhaps wave furrows (Cunliffe 1974a: fig. A.3, no. 3; perhaps Calkin 1948: 46 and pl. 1B, no. 1). Davies mentions haematite ware but no furrowed bowls (1936: 215).

Kingston Buci, Sussex (TQ–51–233059): one wave-furrowed example with short lip, said to be in 'grey sandy ware' (Curwen and Hawkes 1931: 195 and fig. 15; Cunliffe 1966: 115 and fig. 3, no. 16; Cunliffe 1974a: fig. A.3, no. 11).

Kynance, the Lizard, Cornwall (SW–10–687139): 'a good deal of A.1 furrowed ware' (Thomas I. 1960: 12 and fig. 4, no. i). The six examples which I have examined were dark brown, dark grey and black in colour, had groove and wave furrows, but were merely shoulder scraps without rim or base.

Lidbury, Wilts. (SU–41–166142): 'a number of . . . very small' fragments of 'red-coated' (haematited) furrowed bowls (Cunnington 1917: 19 and 30–1 (not illustrated); cf. her pl. VI, nos. 1 and 2, both being bowls from All Cannings Cross, not Lidbury).

Linford, Essex (TQ–51–669800): one red, grooved example with neck (Hawkes 1962: fig. 1, no. 5).

Linton, Cambs. (TL–52–556464): three or four grooved examples, with fairly short neck, of unspecified colour (Fell 1952: fig. 4, nos. 22–4 and perhaps 17).

Little Woodbury, Wilts. (SU–41–150279): at least 12 fragments, including wave furrows and necks, and coloured black and grey as well as haematited (Brailsford and Jackson 1948: 10 and fig. 3, pot form 2ai).

Longbridge Deverill Cow Down, Wilts. (ST–31–887145): numerous unpublished examples of various types (Chadwick 1961; Harding 1972: 144; 1974: 153).

Marnhull, Dorset (ST–31–795198): two haematited examples, both probably lipped and both perhaps with wave furrows (Williams A. 1950: fig. 9, nos. 39 and 49).

Martinsell, Wilts. (SU–41–170633): a haematited example, perhaps with wave furrows but no rim, found outside and west of the hill-fort (Meyrick 1947: 256 and fig. III, no. 1).

Meon Hill, Hants. (SU–41–344352): 19 haematited examples (Liddell 1935: 27). The nine or ten published examples include wave and groove furrows (Liddell 1933: 149 and fig. XI, nos. P.70, P.74, P.23 and P.69; 1935: 27 and pl. 23, nos. P.150, P.150a, P.305, P.327, P.359 and ?P.331). Though most lack rims, they include a lipped example (Liddell 1933: fig. XI, P.69) and two apparently necked examples (Liddell 1935: pl. 23, nos. P.327 and P.359).

Old Oswestry, Salop (SJ–33–269310): apparently four examples, one black, the rest 'ferruginous' buff to pink; one illustrated fragment of carination had wave furrows (Varley 1964: fig. 38, no. 2; Savory 1976a: 76, nos. 126.3–6, and fig. 40, no. 7).

Orsett, Essex (TQ–51–653806): one fragment with groove furrows and neck, coloured orange to brown (Barrett 1978: 284 and fig. 42, no. 110).

Pagan's Hill, Chew Stoke, Som. (ST–31–557626): four haematited examples with groove furrows and neck (ApSimon *et al.* 1958: fig. 23, nos. 1, 2, 4 and 5).

Pimperne, Dorset (ST–31–891097): unspecified furrowed bowls, as yet unpublished (Harding 1972: 144; Harding and Blake 1963).

Poundbury, Dorset (SY–30–682911): the carination of one example in brown ware with wave furrows (Richardson 1940: fig. 5, no. 1).

Rainsborough, Northants. (SP–42–526348): two or three examples in red-brown ware, probably wth wave furrows (Avery *et al.* 1967: nos. 33, 34 and ?78).

Rams Hill, Berks. (SU–41–314863): one haematited, wave-furrowed example with relatively short neck (Piggott S. and C. M. 1940: fig. 5, no. 2; Bradley and Ellison 1975: 109–11 and fig. 3.6, no. 60).

Sandown Park, Esher, Surrey (TQ–51–128650): four examples, black and grey with groove furrows (Burchell and Frere 1947: fig. 16, nos. 15 and 16; fig. 18, nos. 32 and 33).

Shearplace Hill, Dorset (SY–30–640985): one wave-furrowed example in reddish to black ware, with neck and anomalous rim tip (Rahtz and ApSimon 1962: 311 and fig. 17, no. 18).

Twyford Down, Hants. (SU–41–483269): one sherd of the shoulder of a furrowed haematited bowl, comparable to All Cannings Cross (Stuart and Birkbeck 1937: 197, unillustrated).

Welby, Leics. (SK–43–723214): one bronze example in a hoard of bronzes. It was wave-furrowed and with lip (Powell 1948: pl. VI; Smith M.A. 1957: G.B. 24.2(2), no. 6; Harding 1974: fig. 42; Cunliffe 1974a: fig. 3.3, no. 2; and fig. 2.4 herein).

Winchester, Hants. (SU–41–48.29.): numerous sherds of haematited furrowed bowls. Two illustrated examples show neck and lip, and both perhaps had grooved furrows (Cunliffe 1964: 1, 2, 21, 33, 55 and fig. 12, nos. 1 and 2; see his fig. 1 for location).

Winklebury, Hants. (SU–41–613529): 'a few' furrowed bowls (Smith K. 1977: 86), of which eight or nine have been illustrated. One was a necked vessel with groove furrows, said to be haematited (Piggott C. M. 1943: no. 7 – i.e. fig. 2.1 herein; for location, see Williams-Freeman 1940: 270). Two shoulder scraps were both grooved, being dark grey-brown and burnished dark red in colour (Robertson-Mackay 1977: 150, nos. 15 and 17, the same as his fig. 8, nos. 19 and 21). Five more shoulder scraps were probably all wave-furrowed (Smith K. 1977: 98–9 and fig. 31, nos. 27–31) and one necked rim possibly had furrows (*ibid.*: no. 26); all were flint-gritted (*ibid.*: 89, group 1); none were haematited (*ibid.*: 86), but colours are not specified.

Wittenham Clumps, Berks. (SU–41–565925): furrowed bowl(s) reported by Harding (1972: 144), though denied by Rhodes (1948: 24).

Appendix B: questionable, unconfirmed and rejected examples of furrowed bowls in Britain

Hayes Wood, Freshford, Som. (ST–31–772608): three body scraps of unknown colour, perhaps from grooved furrowed bowls but questionable (Stone 1935: 142 and fig. 2, nos. 8, 12 and 13).

Hinderclay, Suffolk (TM–62–020755): two possible examples in black ware, possibly parts of the same vessel (Cunliffe 1968: fig. 5, nos. 64 and 65).

Hockwold cum Wilton, Norfolk, Area 7088 (TL–52–70.88.): one possible example, dark grey with groove furrows and neck (Salway 1967: 60 and fig. 12, no. B.9).

Hollingbury, Sussex (TQ–51–322078): one possible scrap in black ware (Cunliffe 1966: 114 and fig. 2, no. 58).

Liddington Castle, Wilts. (SU–41–209797): one scrap with grooved decoration, apparently a Hawkes B decorated sherd (Passmore 1914: pl. 1, no. 7). G.J. Wainwright interpreted the sherd as a furrowed bowl (1970: 136), but this appears to be an error.

Minnis Bay, Birchington, Kent (TR–61–284697): a furrowed sherd of unspecified fabric, but clearly not carinated (Worsfold 1943: fig. 8, no. 4), and several carinated bowls without furrowing (*ibid.*: fig. 6). The pottery was probably deposited before a gravel bank was laid (*ibid.*: 29 and fig. 3) and into the gravel bank had been inserted a late bronze age hoard of bronzes (*ibid.*: 33–5 and pls. XI and XII).

New Wintle's Farm, Hanborough, Oxon. (SP–42–432108): one grooved carinated bowl in brown-black ware, with an anomalous long neck and everted lip, and with a flat base instead of an omphalos (Harding 1972: 155 and pl. 49, E). This was interpreted as a pre-Roman furrowed bowl by Harding (1972: 144). However, the shape has better parallels in early Anglo-Saxon pottery where the furrowing is also found (Myres 1969: figs. 35–7 and especially fig. 14, no. 2102). The site produced other early Anglo-Saxon remains (Hawkes and Gray 1969).

Old Sarum, Wilts. (SU–41–137327): one grey carinated necked vessel, no furrows being visible (Rahtz and Musty 1960: 368, unillustrated).

The Trundle, Sussex (SU–41–877110): example(s) were reported by Harding (1972: 144), but are not identifiable in the publications by Curwen (1929; 1931).

Upavon, Wilts. (near SU–41–13.55.): furrowed bowl(s) reported by Harding (1972: 144) have not been located in any other publication.

Yarnton, Oxon. (near SP–42–47.12.): one possible example (Bradford 1942b: 56 and fig. 12, no. 57), but this was not confirmed by Harding (1972: 144).

Cunliffe has listed nine unpublished sites in eastern England with examples of his 'Darmsden type 1' class (1968: 179–80). This class includes both furrowed and unfurrowed examples of carinated bowls, and consequently it is not clear how many of these sites had furrowed bowls.

JOHN COLLIS

A theoretical study of hill-forts

With the collapse of the ABC system for the British iron age and the rejection, at least by some of us, of the historical paradigm which lay behind it, there has been a tendency for iron age studies to disintegrate into regional studies. Given our state of knowledge this is both inevitable and necessary, and on the whole there is considerable agreement about the way in which research should be conducted, with, for example, large-scale surveys to reconstruct settlement patterns and landscapes, followed up by large-scale excavation of key sites. There is much implicit theory behind this recent work, though this is generally within a regional context, and as yet there is little explicit model-building of a general or inter-regional kind. In this paper I hope to demonstrate the need for such theoretical work if we are to avoid misinterpretations of our data, and also to suggest a way in which we might start model-building to explain the nature of one class of field monument, the hill-fort.

In many ways the study of hill-forts exemplifies the development of British iron age studies. Under the historical paradigm the major question to be answered was 'When?' – the dating of hill-fort horizons as indicators of tribal and political unrest. The excavation methods of Wheeler and Hawkes in the 1930s were almost entirely orientated to this problem, with great emphasis on the trenching of ramparts and the clearance of entrances, but little work on interiors. The 'Why?' of hill-forts was answered either in terms of their being the bases of successful conquerors, on the model of Roman forts or Norman castles, or as centres of native resistance, like the Saxon *burhs*. The question 'How?', the function of the hill-fort in its social and economic environment, was hardly voiced.

Hodson's paper of 1964 on the 'Woodbury Culture' cleared the way for hill-forts to be studied as an indigenous development, but it was not until 1971, due to considerable conservatism in theoretical conjecture by iron age scholars, that the first two papers discussing why hill-forts should appear were published (Cunliffe 1971; Bradley 1971). Both start from a regional base, Bradley from the downlands of Sussex, Cunliffe from the chalk areas of Wessex. Both deal with the emergence of hill-forts in the late bronze age and early iron age as part of a social and economic evolution, brought about mainly by internal processes. But both are inductive models, arguing from the authors' interpretations of field data, rather than deductive ones, involving the setting up of theoretical situations to be tested against the data.

Bradley's complex model derives essentially from Boserup (1965), who suggests that change will only occur within systems, especially agricultural, when forced by factors such as population pressure. Cunliffe's less explicit model is rather Malthusian, with population rising to new thresholds as each technological innovation allows greater productivity, eventually leading to conflict which is accelerated as trading contact with the Continent increases. He has developed his model further to explain the appearance of urban settlements in Britain (Cunliffe 1974a; 1976c; 1978).

These models present problems, both in the limitations of using them as a basis for more general theory and application, and also because some of the assumptions implicit in them are questionable. As the authors themselves are no longer happy with the models, it is not worth while going into detailed criticisms, though a few points should perhaps be made. Both are obviously regional in their application, specifically to southern England. Present data in the form of C14 dates suggest that hill-forts were already in existence in other areas such as the southern Pennines under very different economic and environmental conditions long before those of Sussex and Wessex. Also these models are arguing backwards from the data – we have hill-forts, therefore there was conflict, and conflict is most likely to come from population pressure. This does not explain why areas such as the chalk wolds of Yorkshire and Lincolnshire, where the same processes and pressures might be expected, have virtually no hill-forts, and even those are early and short-lived.

At certain periods in some areas there are hints of an elite class: for instance, the large houses at Little Woodbury and Pimperne, or the luxury imports at Owslebury; but it is interesting to note that these hints come from 'minor' settlements, suggesting that if there was an elite it did not reside in the hill-forts. A similar pattern is suggested in the Hunsrück-Eifel where there are burials of a rich, elite class. The burial evidence from south-east England in the first century BC, the inscribed dynastic coinage, the speed of the collapse of the centralized Catuvellaunian state at the time of the Roman Conquest, all imply that a highly centralized, hierarchical organization had emerged in that area by the time of the Roman Conquest; but it is one of the areas without hill-forts. By contrast, in the hill-fort area of Dorset, we find no evidence for inscribed coinage, little for foreign trade or rich burials, a limited range for the size of huts within hill-forts, and no evidence that the Durotriges were capable of acting under a centralized leadership; rather, Vespasian had to reduce each hill-fort individually. The picture here is of a decentralized, relatively egalitarian society, as opposed to the hierarchical one assumed by Cunliffe.

Both models are also gradualist, talking of the evolution of hill-forts and hill-fort functions. Cunliffe, particularly in his more developed model, sees the gradual emergence of individual hill-forts to dominance over larger and larger territories. At the end of this process the 'developed' hill-fort has, according to Cunliffe, acquired a number of 'central place' functions, and this leads him to suggest that these sites can be termed 'proto-urban'. I would agree with much of his interpretation (though I am sceptical about the redistributive function of hill-forts), but 'proto-urban' seems to me an unfortunate term as I consider these sites to be below the urban threshold, representing a 'dead-end' rather than a stage in the process towards urbanization (Collis, forthcoming).

Hill-fort systems and change

In an earlier article (Collis 1977b) I attempted to define a group of hill-forts in central Hampshire in terms of their surface morphology, and by using Thiessen polygons went on to suggest that a group of smaller hill-forts also belonged with these larger sites because of spatial relationship. However, there was a number of hill-forts which did not belong to this system, notably a group of much larger sites in the north-west of the area, of which one, Balksbury, has been excavated and demonstrated to have been built and deserted early within the hill-fort sequence of this region. In other words, Balksbury may belong to a different system which overlaps the other one only partially in chronological and geographical terms.

I would suggest that this way of looking at hill-fort systems might help us unravel some of the complexities of our field data. A system of hill-forts can be localized or widespread, and may be adjacent to areas where there are no hill-forts. Also we should assume different types of hill-fort system: hierarchical, non-hierarchical, nucleated (i.e. large and few) or non-nucleated (small and many), each reflecting a different social and economic function. In table 1 I have hypothesized three different areas with different developments and phases of hill-fort construction. This is shown in geographical terms in fig. 6. We can assume that some of these sites were suitable for re-occupation at various phases, others were not. A further complexity assumed, though not shown, on the diagram is the increase or decrease in size of some sites. The final result as the archaeologist might see it is shown at the bottom of fig. 6, which I would suggest represents the kind of complexity we see in the archaeological record.

I have still to state why I prefer to see these successive systems as representing *breaks* rather than as a continuous process. Firstly, from a methodological point of view it is better for an archaeologist to understand how one system works (a 'static' model), before he can suggest how it changes into another system (a 'dynamic' model). It is a criticism of both the Bradley and Cunliffe models that they are dealing with the change of one unknown system to another. I would not, however, suggest that we should not speculate in this way. Such speculation can throw light on the static situations, and in any case we are never likely to be able to reconstruct completely two succeeding systems; but the limitations of the approach should be recognized.

Secondly, and more important, the archaeological record itself is more suggestive of breaks, rather than continuity. The very construction of a fort is the

	Area A	Area B	Area C
Period 1	Large, widely-spaced hill-forts, non-hierarchical	No hill-forts	Dense pattern of small hill-forts, non-hierarchical
Period 2	No hill-forts	Hierarchical system of large and small hill-forts	No hill-forts
Period 3	No hill-forts	As Period 2	Area B system spreads to area C

Table 1. Hypothetical systems of hill-forts in three adjacent regions.

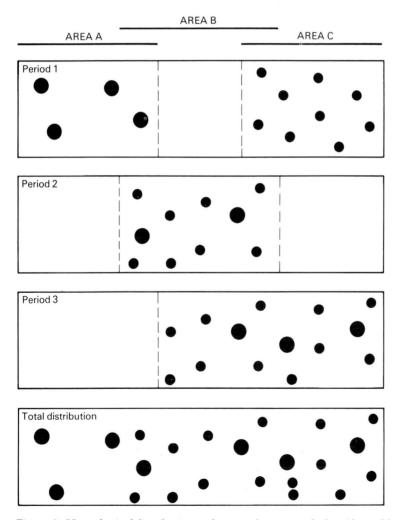

Figure 6. Hypothetical distributions of sites in three periods, based on table 1, and the final pattern as seen by the field archaeologist. Large circles indicate major sites, small circles indicate minor sites.

act of a moment of time, forced by political and social pressures; likewise the reconstruction and refurbishing of a fort. The evidence from Moel y Gaer implies successive disjointed re-use of the fort (Guilbert 1975a). The Danebury evidence is at present difficult to interpret. The layout seems to have remained fairly static: an early phase with circular houses surrounding small square structures, replaced by a more regular layout of square four- and six-post structures. Later again, at least some of the square buildings were abandoned, though the ring of circular houses continued in use. Whether this represents gradual change within the system or a thorough refurbishing at one moment in time, as could have happened with the defences, remains to be seen. I do not wish to imply that a system necessarily remained static – the very process of building an enclosure around a population can allow greater central control, for instance; but we should distinguish between the change which appears from the archaeological record to have been slow and the sudden change to a completely new system.

With these points in mind, we can return to the area of Wessex under consideration here. The dating evidence for certain hill-forts in this region was illustrated by Cunliffe (1976c: fig. 1) who sees in it an early period with large numbers of hill-forts which gradually became fewer as one site became dominant and took on more central place functions. An alternative interpretation is summarized in fig. 7 and may be described as follows, though it should be stressed that the dates are no better than notional since I do not have a complete list of C14 dates for the area.

1. c.700–600 BC. Large hill-forts with mainly circular houses (e.g. Balksbury), and possibly palisaded enclosures with round-houses and small square structures to the south (e.g. Danebury).
2. c.600–400 BC. Univallate hill-forts of c.4–10ha with a planned layout of rectangular houses and some circular buildings; non-hierarchical? (e.g. Danebury).
3. c.400–100 BC. Univallate hill-forts as before, but possibly hierarchical, with large sites of 20–30ha (e.g. Maiden Castle, Hod Hill and, later, Winchester), medium-sized hill-forts of c.8–10ha (e.g. St Catharine's Hill and Danebury), and small hill-forts of c.2–3ha (e.g. Tidbury); other small sites, such as Oliver's Battery, Alresford, may have been complementary rather than subsidiary.
4. c.100 BC–AD 40. No hill-forts east of the Test, except perhaps the rectangular forts at Ashley and Egsbury; and for some of this time there may have been none in western Hampshire either.
5. c.AD 40–50. Hill-forts west of the Test, possibly with re-occupation of Danebury and Bury Hill; many multivallate. No hill-forts east of the Test.

Though this represents a simplification (omitting, for example, the forts off the chalk), I believe that it offers a better interpretation than that suggested by Cunliffe. It also pin-points gaps in our knowledge: what is the date of the rectangular forts, what is going on inside the small hill-forts?

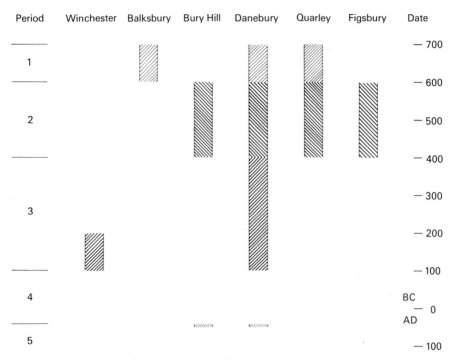

Figure 7. Occupation phases of certain hill-forts in western Hampshire and eastern Wiltshire.

Although the historical paradigm may be under suspicion, I would follow Hogg (1978: 126) in making a plea that the need for dating is ever-present and that sample excavation can fulfil this need. Single trenches through ramparts can still be very informative in telling us to which system a fort belongs, as long as the trenches are big enough to identify the forms and phases of construction (Guilbert 1975b).

Inhabitants

As already mentioned, behind most previous interpretations of hill-forts there have been assumptions about the nature of the inhabitants (e.g. a stratified society with an aristocracy, or invaders, or the total population), or about the function of the fort (that it should be a central place with administrative and redistributive functions). These are, however, assumptions, and I would like now to attempt to clear the ground for a more objective view of the problem. Essentially we are dealing with two variables: the length of time a fort is occupied, and the segment of the population resident. Function, I assume, is largely dictated by the nature of the population resident.

Firstly there are the variables for period of occupation:

a. Permanent residence
b. Seasonal residence
c. Sporadic visits during the year (e.g. for exchange, social gatherings, etc.)
d. Residence in time of need
e. Never resident

Some of the population groups we might postulate are:

1. Total population
2. People whose land lies nearest
3. People whose normal residence lies nearest
4. Social elite (e.g. chieftain, landed gentry)
5. Non-agricultural population (e.g. artisans, craftsmen, traders)
6. Age-set (e.g. young men receiving military training)
7. Ethnic group (e.g. conquerors)

This allows us to set up a matrix of variables which we might like to test, and this is also useful to show which categories and combinations we cannot demonstrate. Though there may be simple combinations – e.g. Moel y Gaer might be category d(1), total population resident in times of need – in the case of the 'pre-industrial city' we might expect a(4,5,6) c(3), i.e. a resident social elite with artisans and servants to supply their needs, probably foreign merchants, and yet visited by the majority of the population at some time. In the case of some of the forts in the Welsh Marches with their planned layouts of little square houses, one wonders whether it might be a(6), a permanent residence for young men of fighting age, a sort of iron age Catterick Camp (cf. Hogg 1975: 77). Some such selection of the population seems implied by these strange structures; they seem too small to hold full nuclear families, and as Stanford (1974a: 231) has suggested, this would produce an unexpectedly high population figure.

Patterns of residence

We should distinguish between three phases of a hill-fort's development – what we might term the pre-crisis, crisis, and post-crisis situations. Clearly the size, siting, inhabitants and layout of the fort will be dictated by the social structure and settlement pattern in the period immediately before it is established, and by the nature of the crisis. We can set up a series of models, assuming for instance a hierarchical social structure, and suggest ways in which each might react to a given crisis, and what might happen after the crisis has disappeared. We must remember that hill-forts show an enormous range in nature, from defences built around single farms to fully urban sites. In the Netherlands one group of sites has been identified where the only buildings within the forts seem to be for storage, the farmers themselves continuing to live on the surrounding farmsteads (Waterbolk 1977). In the case

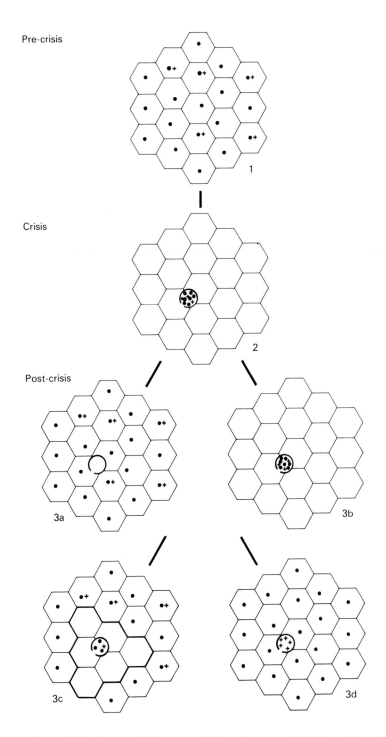

Figure 8.   A model for the establishment and abandonment of hill-forts. Dots indicate farmers, crosses indicate craftsmen.

of the 'oppida', nucleation produced an urban complex, implying that some sort of state organization had come into existence by the time of crisis.

The variations are obviously numerous but, to demonstrate how theoretical models can be derived which are capable of testing, I will take one situation and follow through what might happen. In fig. 8.1 I have postulated a dispersed non-hierarchical settlement pattern of small farming settlements. Industry is carried out on a part-time basis, or by specialists scattered throughout the area. Fig. 8.2 represents the crisis. The population builds a hill-fort, perhaps selecting one or two individuals to organize defence, just as Cassivellaunus was chosen to lead resistance against Caesar. Everyone then moves into the fort. When the crisis ends, a number of possibilities is available, influenced by the length of time for which centralization was necessary (e.g. how much time was expended on building new houses), the suitability of the new sites for permanent residence (accessibility, exposure, etc.) and the nature of the social structure. Even within a single system the reaction may vary from one site to another depending on local factors. Some of the post-crisis variables are shown in fig. 8.3:

a. A return to the pre-crisis situation.
b. The whole population remains in the hill-fort. In terms of access to land, this will lead to the gradual impoverishment of the population, especially for those whose land lies furthest from the fort. As there are no dependent settlements, the hill-fort cannot be classed as a 'central place'.
c. Farmers whose land lies furthest from the fort return home, while those who live nearest may be tempted to stay, giving a zone of land which is exploited from the fort, signified in fig. 8.3c by the thickened line. It is important to notice in this situation that the fort has no central place functions other than defence. The long-term effects of this pattern could have two results: either greater co-operation may occur between the inhabitants of the fort, leading to specialization; or, those who remain in the fort will only be exploiting their farms in a 'satisfising' way, i.e. they will be getting satisfactory return for their labour, but not the maximum because of the amount of time expended in travelling to and from their farms (Chisholm 1962). Those on the periphery who have returned to their farms, however, will be in an 'optimising' situation, and they may finally end up the richest members of the society.
d. Those engaged primarily in agricultural activity return to their farms, but those with no specific reason for returning (e.g. craftsmen) may stay in the fort, in which case the fort may start to acquire central place functions in addition to that of defence.

This general model may explain apparent distributions of wealth in the first century BC in southern England; why, for instance, inhabitants of small farming settlements such as Owslebury seem to have been able to acquire wine, whereas amphorae are rare on hill-forts, and also why silver coins seem to be more common outside hill-forts than from the forts in the Dorset area (Collis 1971).

Further comments

One or two other points seem to be worth making. Firstly, we have assumed that defences are constructed primarily for defence. This may not always be so, and in some cases we can suggest that prestige was more important. A number of sites show an impressive entrance façade, but minimal defences 'round the back'. The innermost defence at Burley Wood, Bridestowe, Devon, is one case (Fox A. 1961), and it is also found at minor settlements such as Owslebury, and most markedly at Gussage All Saints (Wainwright G.J. 1979b). This may also account for 'hill-forts' in non-defensive situations, such as the hill-slope forts of western England (Fox A. 1961).

A second matter is whether we can distinguish between hill-fort systems which are due to external stimulus, in contrast to those which are due to internal stress. One clue may be offered by the similarity or otherwise of the hill-fort structures themselves. Presumably each site was designed by an 'expert' known for his knowledge in such matters – 'specialist' or 'architect' may be too strong a term. Where there was co-operation and sharing of ideas a marked regional style might emerge, as Jope (1963) has suggested for aspects of medieval culture. The detailed similarities of 'guard-chambers' in the Welsh Marches, or in areas of Wessex might be quoted. But also general methods of rampart construction could spread between mutually antagonistic groups, as with the *murus gallicus* in first-century BC Gaul. This also raises the interesting question of how ideas were transmitted from one generation to another.

We should not forget that there were also long periods and large areas in the first millennium BC which did not have hill-forts. I have never liked the equation 'hill-forts = conflict'. If we were to make a simple numerical count of surviving weapons in Britain, the iron age would come out as a peaceful period, especially in comparison with the late bronze age. The hill-fort may have been a successful solution to keeping the peace. Another solution is the centralization of power, and this is what may have been happening in the areas without hill-forts. Cunliffe's map of gold torcs (which may indicate a social elite) shows them to be largely exclusive of the hill-fort areas (Cunliffe 1974a: 285), and, as mentioned before, the development of centralized states and of urbanism appears to have nothing to do with hill-forts.

Conclusions

What I have presented here represents, I believe, a different way of looking at hill-forts, and one which may start to give us more explicit models for testing. It can transcend the more regional approaches of Cunliffe and Bradley. Indeed, it has potential for any area where hill-forts and defended sites appear in simple societies. I have emphasized the aspect of sudden shift or break in the system as against the more gradualist models, since the establishment of a hill-fort is an act of discontinuity, and I think we may find terms such as 'origin' and 'development' are not particularly useful concepts.

Acknowledgments

My thanks to Barry Cunliffe for commenting on and correcting an earlier version of this paper, and to those students and colleagues who have discussed hill-forts with me in recent years.

IAN RALSTON

The use of timber in hill-fort defences in France

Amongst the most impressive physical remains to survive from the later pre-historic periods in Europe, from the Iberian peninsula to northern Scotland and to the central heartland of the Continent, are the varieties of fortified enclosure to which the generic term 'hill-fort' may be applied. Of course this epithet obscures the range of locations that such sites occupy: hill-slope positions and others of more negligible defensive properties, as illustrated in England and Wales by Forde-Johnston (1976), may be contrasted with others on summits, naturally difficult of access, and on sea-girt promontories. In defining such sites, an essential characteristic is the presence of at least a partial circuit of man-made defences (Hogg 1979: 1).

These defences are often the most indestructible element of a site, so that all that may be apparent today is the layout of a set of banks, walls and ditches, still present as surface features and delimiting an area that is, superficially, archaeologically featureless. The organization of hill-fort interiors and the nature and extent of inter-site relationships have been attracting greater attention in recent Anglo-American treatments of, in particular, the late pre-Roman iron age in France, especially since the emergence of urbanization as a theme in the archaeology of the later La Tène periods (Crumley 1974; Collis 1975; Cunliffe and Rowley 1976; Nash 1978). This paper, which I write with pleasure for Dr A. H. A. Hogg, whose *Antiquity* article of 1969 set me off in quest of French *enceintes*, will concentrate on some aspects of the defences of sites on the other side of the English Channel.

Primarily for the reason stated above, evidence of defensive architecture, albeit of very varying quality, is more plentiful than that relating to internal structures and layout for many French hill-forts. Although recent French work is, rightfully, more concerned with the settlement aspects of these sites, much of the evidence derives from a major spate of activity, partially stimulated by the interest of Napoleon III, and lasting from the mid-nineteenth century until the First World War, during which a principal concern was to establish the constructional (and destructional) sequence of the defences and to elaborate cultural parallels on the basis of architectural similarity.

There was a considerable range of constructional variation present in defensive architecture in Europe north of the Alps during the last millennium BC. The increasing application of isotopic dating techniques, especially radiocarbon, to these later prehistoric structures has been a major contribution to our comprehension of the wide chronological span over which forts were constructed, though precise chronologies must probably still elude us in view, *inter alia*, of dated samples coming from mature constructional timbers (Coles and Jones 1975) and the evidence provided by the close-dating of the gateway timbers from Cullykhan, Banffshire (Campbell *et al*. 1978). Although there is as yet little reason to envisage a continuous tradition of fort-construction for many areas of Europe, there is equally little evidence to suggest that each perceived chronological episode of hill-fort building will allow of a generalized explanation, and local factors will need to be sought. Population displacements, such as that of the Cimbri and Teutones, remain one factor inescapably to be taken into account, but are unlikely to provide a satisfactory rationale for hill-fort construction in many instances. In France, as elsewhere, there is now plentiful evidence to suggest that many of these forts had been abandoned considerably before the appearance of the Roman military over much of central and western Europe, and hence before the best-documented conflicts in which such forts were to be involved. To anticipate the next section, there can be little doubt that the appearance of Roman armies in France north of the Mediterranean coastal strip in 58 BC must have given a considerable fillip to the defensive aspect of hill-forts, though, like many 'events' in protohistory, this is in many instances notoriously difficult to substantiate unequivocally from the available archaeological evidence. It may be suggested that the critical difference between the Romans and their Celtic adversaries did not lie in military technology, even though artillery, such as catapults, and siege-towers were surely novel threats to the security of Celtic fortresses. Although Celts and Romans had been in conflict for several centuries, and Celts had served as mercenaries in the armies of the Mediterranean world, the critical difference between Roman and native in the military sphere was rather in terms of organization, of the ability to sustain military activity. Prior to the appearance of the Roman armies, hill-forts fulfilled a function in societies where warfare may be presumed to have been of a markedly different character. Whilst warfare amongst High Barbarian groupings such as the Celts will have been a more elaborate undertaking than amongst less complex societies, we are far removed from the era of total war (Harris 1975). Records of inter-barbarian warfare are few, since this lay beyond the interests of classical authors, but Irish literary sources, amongst others of a slightly later date, point to the often desultory character of military campaigning amongst the protohistoric Celts. The character of warfare they portray is often essentially 'heroic', with larger-scale engagements limited to raids, ambushes and, by later standards, short-lived battles. The role of fortified strongpoints in warfare of this type is liable to be over-estimated, particularly when there is no reason to suspect that late bronze age and iron age societies observed a frequent convention of medieval military etiquette, which demanded of an attacking force that it should not confine its activities to plundering an enemy's territory, and that it was honour-bound to besiege any stronghold the defenders had chosen to protect.

In the absence of explosives, the range of fire from a fort is greatly diminished, so much so that they are essentially passively defensive in character. It is thus difficult to support a view of hill-forts dominating a surrounding tract of country in any direct military sense. The only exception to this is the use of chariots by Celtic societies, though by the time Caesar was writing in the first century BC the military use of these vehicles seems to have been in decline on the Continent. Harding (1974) has pointed out that the chariot could have been used to convey a mobile force from a hill-fort to confront an approaching enemy on lower ground: cavalry, for which the Gauls were later to become famous in the Roman Empire, would represent another means of extending the aggressive potential of a hill-fort beyond its very immediate environs. In general, though, such military considerations as underpinned the forms of Temperate European iron age defensive architecture may be suggested to have been restricted to the likelihood of raids and attacks of limited duration. Only in the final stages of their use were they sometimes pressed into service against the Roman military machine.

Two principal competing strands can be noted in the military technologies of the last centuries BC in France. One of these is rooted in native craftsmanship, the other is influenced by contacts with the Mediterranean world. Taking France as an entity, the evidence of status artifacts, wine containers of various kinds and other material, suggests that Mediterranean influence was not all-pervasive, chronologically, socially or spatially, during the course of the local iron age. Whilst certain types of iron age fortified site in France show very clear Mediterranean influence – the masonry bastions and layout of Entremont (Benoit 1975) are a clear example – other aspects of French protohistoric fortifications are perhaps less readily assimilated to Mediterranean precedents. The latter is perhaps particularly true of the varieties of timber-laced defences culminating in the *murus gallicus* described by Caesar, and it is these that we will examine more closely.

Theoretical considerations

Multifarious considerations – political, economic, cult, legalistic – may have lain behind the decision-making involved in hill-fort construction. Both the selection of the circuit that the defences were to follow and the precise defensive architecture chosen for a particular locality would have had considerable consequences, economic and otherwise, for the community concerned. It is thus undoubtedly simplistic to consider in isolation the forms of defences adopted and to assess them purely in terms of defensive requirements. However, renewed discussion of this factor at a theoretical level may make a useful contribution to the wider consideration of later prehistoric fortifications. Factors directly linked to military requirements, and which may therefore have been given consideration when the structural form of a defence was to be decided, might have included:

a. *Numerical strength and armament of forces likely to be deployed.* Under ideal conditions a set of defences should be constructed to resist an attack by the best-equipped and largest attacking force that can be envisaged.
b. *Resources.* The local availability, quantity and quality of constructional materials (primarily stone, earth, turf and timber) sets obvious limitations on the potential range of defensive architecture.
c. *Time and labour availability.* These are liable to be particularly critical when either is in short supply.
d. *Location.* The particular geographical location and any natural defensive advantages it may have conferred are another important factor.
e. *Convention.* Tradition within a society may exert considerable pressure in the choice of structural types.

It may be instructive to consider the general forms of defence which have been reconstructed on the basis of archaeological evidence, with a view to providing an estimate, at a theoretical level and certainly exceedingly crude, of their defensive potential. Only methods known to have been used will be mentioned; other 'options' may of course remain to be discovered. For the purposes of this exercise, our hypothetical hill-fort will be considered to lie in the middle of a flat plain which offers no natural defensive advantages. In this way, the effects of factor (d) – location – may be minimized. Similarly, to neutralize the effects of differential distribution of, and access to, resources – factor (b) – the main constituents of hill-fort defences will be taken to be of equal availability. By varying the input of factor (a) – the combatants and their armament – some of the perceived differences in the scale of defences may be accounted for.

The simplest form of defence would be required against wild animals or casual banditry. In either of these cases, two principal options suggest themselves: either a delimiting wall or a wooden palisade, perhaps set in the upcast from a small ditch. A third option, a thorn hedge, either living or dead, would be possible, though difficult to detect archaeologically. The appearance of an armed force equipped for hand-to-hand fighting would require the addition of a fighting-platform and breast-work to the wall or stockade. Another element of importance is the entrance, by definition a weak point, and increasing elaboration of the defences at this position is perhaps likely as the postulated level of aggression increases.

The sword and, to a lesser extent, the spear appear to have been the weapons *par excellence* of the European iron age. Slingstones are the most frequently recorded missiles, though the classical authors occasionally mention that stone-throwing was also practised. Archery seems to have been comparatively unimportant for much of the iron age, though metal arrowheads are recorded from both Hallstatt and late La Tène contexts (Mercer 1970; Duval 1970). The use of such missiles might provoke two rather different defensive reactions. The more spectacular would involve the widening of the defensive zone by the construction of a second circuit, or indeed multiple circuits, of ramparts. The alternative would be to increase the height of the wall, perhaps enhanced, though only slightly in defensive terms, by the excavation of a ditch outside the wall-line.

The appearance of cavalry would not be expected to inspire improvements to the main line of defence but rather to promote means of disorganizing an attack by extending the defensive zone outwards. These might include the construction of *chevaux-de-frise*, though constructions of this kind may be assumed to have disrupted foot charges as well. The use of cavalry would also increase the speed of approach, and this might necessitate the construction of watch-towers in order that defenders could be alerted. Undertakings of this kind will have had constructional implications if such superstructures were to be built onto the wall-line.

Another aggressive technique recorded in the archaeological record is the use of fire, to which two very different responses are possible. Any exposed timber in the defences would represent a major hazard, so that minimizing the quantity of timber visible to an attacker, in addition to the selection of more fire-resistant woods, might be expected to have received high priority. Greater precautions to protect unavoidably inflammable features, such as wooden gates, might further contribute to the elaboration of the defensive works around the entrances. It would be expedient to minimize the risk of structures within the fort being set alight, and one solution would involve leaving a zone of the fort interior adjacent to the fortification itself clear of buildings. This might incidentally confer defensive advantages by simplifying access to the rampart. At this stage, the arguments in favour of a radically different defensive formula become persuasive. The alternative defensive arrangement would be to abandon the construction of walls containing timberwork (with vertical external face) in favour of a dump rampart (with sloping external face). As with missile warfare, multivallation, or at least bivallation, might be advantageous, depending on the scale of the primary defence.

Against other more elaborate methods of attack the construction of a large dump rampart would also seem to be the most efficient. Height could thus be obtained and the dangers of collapse inherent in a vertical wall-face avoided. Advanced techniques of attack would embrace those mentioned in *de Bello Gallico*, including the use of battering rams, mining and sapping, artillery and siege-towers, most – though not all – of which probably represented new kinds of threats with the advent of Roman military expertise in Temperate Europe. Resistance to all these techniques would place a premium on additional precautions to render the approach to the defences more difficult, for example by deliberately waterlogging an area outside the fort, or by removing all brushwood and similar material which the attackers could utilize to level up the ditch in order to bring machinery into contact with the walls, and so on.

In all these cases, the alternative solution, that of building a stone-faced, rubble-cored wall, remains a possibility. The height of the defences might need to be increased from previous standards if siege-towers were likely to be employed. Similarly, the wall would need to be made thicker, to resist battering rams. An earthen rampart placed behind the wall would help to absorb the impact of the battering ram and might, incidentally, make the defenders' access to the fighting-platform easier. The division of the wall into compartments by internal timber-lacing (spiked at the intersections of the beams in the most elaborate Continental examples) or internal stone walls (*murus duplex*) might reduce the extent of the disintegration of the rampart core should the external wall-face collapse. This latter consideration would apply whether such internal stone walling ran parallel to (as appears usual in France) or transverse to the line of the wall. But there can be little doubt that both the construction and the maintenance of such a wall would demand greater input of labour and resources than would be required for a dump rampart of equivalent, or greater, defensive capabilities. Even in periods of prolonged peace, the natural decay of internal timberwork would require substantial investments in labour to dismantle the wall before any repair could be effected.

It is thus possible to argue that timber-laced defences, built by craftsmen accustomed to witnessing the decay of woodwork, may have been constructed to counter circumstances which the builders did not believe were going to endure indefinitely. Nor does it appear likely that such defences would have been constructed to counteract an immediate and short-term threat, when a dump rampart would seem to present a more efficient solution, either to refurbish a decayed wall or as an entirely new structure.

Two conclusions emerge from an inquiry of this kind. The first is that the type of defence recorded from a number of protohistoric fortified sites differs considerably from the type which might have been considered, on theoretical grounds, best suited to resist the forms of attack being perpetrated. This contrast can be thrown into high relief by consideration of some of the types of fortification in use during the Gallic War of the mid-first century BC. Julius Caesar described an elaborate variant of the timber-laced wall as the usual type he encountered in the campaigns of 58–51 BC. He speaks highly of its resistance both to fire and to the battering ram. However, archaeological evidence, coupled with at least one reference in Caesar's text, suggests that by the time of the Gallic War the Fécamp variant of the glacis-fronted dump rampart was becoming more common – since its distribution, as presently known, extends beyond the territorial boundaries of the Belgae, to whom Wheeler and Richardson (1957), more particularly followed by Paul-Marie Duval (1959) in his review (*type Belge*) of that work, chose to attribute this particular development. Caesar's text can also be construed to suggest that the Fécamp ramparts also formed a more formidable military obstacle to his armies, as at Noviodunum of the Suessiones (*de Bello Gallico* II, 12), than did the timber-laced walls.

Secondly, it has been argued that defences are constructed as the outcome of decisions involving a complex of factors, some interdependent, some at least partially deterministic. Accordingly, it is perhaps as valid to discuss defences in terms of methods of warfare, a model which would easily accommodate the existence of varying strengths of fortification in a past landscape, as it is to attempt to create a typological sequence based on architectural details of the constructional methods used.

It remains, nonetheless, remarkable that various forms of timber-lacing should appear to be such a persistent feature of Temperate European proto-historic fortifications, as in the Lausitz culture area (Hawkes 1971) and amongst the Dacians (Rossi 1971), as well as in areas further west bordering on France (Graff 1963). Timber-laced ramparts are resource-consuming, demand heavy input of labour for both construction and maintenance, and appear in some circumstances to have been militarily outmoded, while in others they conferred few advantages over dump ramparts, even if substan-tially masked by a protective coating of turf, as has been suggested by at least two very different pieces of excavation and research (Avery *et al.* 1967; Young-blood *et al.* 1978). It is difficult not to believe that the twin goads of convention and prestige were important factors in the decisions to construct the later timber-laced walls.

Timber-laced fortifications in France

One recurrent feature of later prehistoric fortifications in France, as else-where in Temperate Europe, is the use of substantial quantities of timber. Architecturally, if not always chronologically, the culmination of this trend was the construction of the defensive circuits of the massive late La Tène oppida, such as Mont Beuvray in Saône-et-Loire. Such defensive works, with perimeters several kilometres long, are, as Collis has recently argued (1975), the products of societies whose economic base was at least partially industrialized. The defences themselves suggest this, on account of both the large number of uniform lengths of timber and the substantial quantities of iron nails required to fix the timber intersections in the walls of forts enclosed by true *muri gallici*.

Discussion of *muri gallici* has tended to centre on their chronological pos-ition and on the degree of Mediterranean influence which may be exhibited in this form of construction (Dehn 1960; 1969). More recently, Collis and I (1976) have argued in favour of an indigenous Temperate European background to this well-known group of sites, suggesting that the vitrified forts of France may well have formed part of the architectural legacy of the use of timber-work in defences on which the elaborations of the *muri gallici* were based.

Despite MacKie's contention (1976b: 206) that the vitrified forts of Scotland are 'unique in Europe', the 70 or so examples in north Britain are matched by a roughly equivalent number in France, and comparisons between the two sets of monuments have been made intermittently since the nineteenth century (Youngblood *et al.* 1978). In referring to such vitrified forts, we are not directly concerned with the constructional/destructional argument which has come to the fore again recently (Brothwell *et al.* 1974; Nisbet 1974; 1975; MacKie 1976b; Youngblood *et al.* 1978); it is sufficient to remark here that most theories currently propounded seem to be in agreement on the need for considerable quantities of timberwork in the defence. The Appendix to this paper lists all examples of vitrification known to me, mainly from literary sources, as well as defences in which calcined material has been reported. It should be stressed that Nicolardot's recent work in Burgundy and the analyses carried out in conjunction with that programme (Delattre in Nicolardot 1974: 44–5) indicate that calcined material recovered from the neolithic settlement at the Camp de Myard, adjacent to the enclosing wall of that site, was not attributable to the destruction by fire of the defences. Some early identifications of fortifications in which the core has been described as calcined may therefore be suspect, but in general it appears likely that most examples where calcination has been recorded indicate the former presence of internal timberwork in a defence of limestone or similar building stone. I remain unconvinced that vitrification or calcination in most instances is anything other than an indication of the destruction by fire of a timber-laced wall. Accepting that similar defects will

Figure 9. Sites in France reported to be calcined or vitrified (excluding mottes).

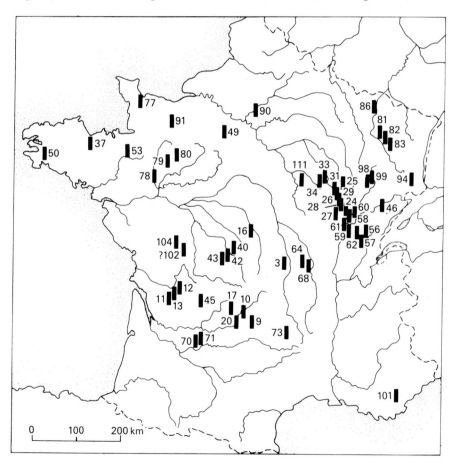

occur in this list as were noted by Nisbet (1975) in her consideration of the Scottish evidence, for example a confusion of some rock types such as conglomerate with vitrification, the overall distribution of calcined and vitrified sites bears a considerable resemblance of that of other types of timber-laced defence, as presently known (figs. 9–11). The distribution maps share a comparative paucity of sites within the Paris Basin and in Provence.

Vitrification may have as wide a chronological range as the use of timber-frameworks in defensive architecture. Thus, in Scotland, we may add late dates for the wall at Mote of Mark, Kirkcudbright (ad 459±42: Laing 1975a) and the slightly-vitrified core of a timber-laced wall at the Green Castle, Portknockie, Banffshire (Ralston 1980) to the end of the series quoted by MacKie (1976b). In France, various mottes which exhibit signs of vitrification may be presumed to represent a later use of structural timberwork in this markedly

Figure 10. Late defences in France: *muri gallici* (lozenges), Kelheim types (open circles), and defences from which nails are recorded (rectangles).

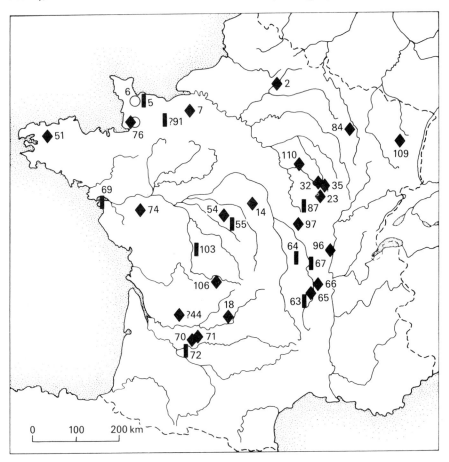

different form of early medieval fortification. The Appendix includes several examples of mottes, which are mapped in fig. 12.

Given the general lack of large-scale excavation or isotopic dating, the chronological range of defences incorporating timber (including vitrified and calcined sites) lacks precision, though at least ten sites appear to have received their defences in later Urnfield or Hallstatt iron age times, including la Crête de la Granède in Aveyron, la Brèche-au-Diable in Calvados, Voeuil in Charente, la Groutte in Cher, le Puy de Sermus in Corrèze, le Châtelet d'Étaules in Côte d'Or, Aubusson in Creuse, and the Britzgyberg in Haut-Rhin; other possibilities include Erquy in Côtes du Nord, and perhaps Camp-Allaric in Vienne. Contrastingly, true *muri gallici* and Kelheim types (Collis and Ralston 1976) remain late in the French sequence, no excavated example clearly pre-dating La Tène III, and they apparently continued into early

Figure 11. Protohistoric timber-laced defences in France, other than those shown in fig. 10: Ehrang type (triangles), ramparts with internal timberwork (squares), and ramparts with burnt internal timberwork (circles).

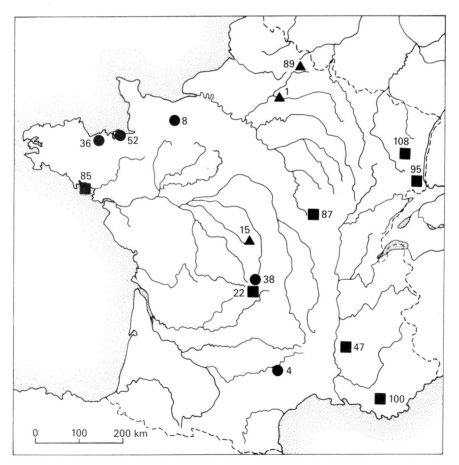

Gallo-Roman ('*précoce*') times, as for example at Vertault in Côte d'Or. Given the recovery of nails from other types of defence in, for example, Calvados and Nièvre, as well as the occasional reference to the recovery of iron from vitrified works, it is perhaps advisable to separate those *muri gallici* identified solely by the recovery of nails from those where a more formal proof exists.

Whilst it has frequently been suggested that there may have been a hiatus in hill-fort construction in France north of Provence for two or three centuries before the spate of fortification construction in late la Tène (Hodson and Rowlett 1974: 187; Collis 1975: 11; Collis and Ralston 1976), the paucity of datable artifacts attributable to these years from settlement sites in general makes this assertion difficult to support, perhaps particularly for western France. In eastern France, recent evidence from excavations, as at La Pierre d'Appel in Vosges (see Appendix), may help to bridge this postulated inter-

Figure 12. Mottes (triangles) and other apparently medieval works (stars) in France, with vitrified material associated.

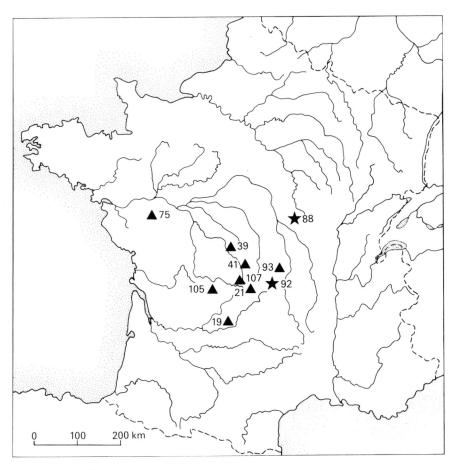

ruption, though, in view of the evidence from elsewhere in Temperate Europe (Collis 1975), there is no *a priori* reason why hill-fort construction and use need have been a continuous process.

However, given the imprecision which prevails at present, it seems preferable to avoid detailed chronological discussion. The distribution maps, with all the shortcomings of their kind, are perhaps the most graphic illustration of the feeling that a considerable expertise in the construction of wood-and-stone defences lay behind the *muri gallici* of mid-first-century BC Gaul.

Appendix: early fortifications in France with evidence of timber recorded from the defences

This appendix represents a preliminary attempt to group information on the use of timberwork in early defences in metropolitan France. Many of the sources on which it is based are old, and the gazetteer is certain to be incomplete. Not the least important reason for this is the survival of the local archaeological society as a major publication agency (for which, see the appendix to *Gallia 23*, 1965). The acquisition of a fuller picture is liable to be a considerable task in view of the lack of a direct archaeological influence on the state mapping agency in France, the Institut Géographique Nationale. In time, the Projet de la Constitution d'une Carte Archéologique de la France (Büchsenschütz *et al.* 1975) may well ameliorate the picture, but for the moment there is still considerable uncertainty about the global total of surviving early fortified sites in France (Büchsenschütz 1971). The most complete national survey remains that of the Commission d'Étude des Enceintes Préhistoriques et Fortifications Anhistoriques, published in a lengthy series of reports in the bulletin of the Société Préhistorique Française in the first three decades of this century. These reports usually take the form of annotated lists arranged by *département* (county) and *commune* (parish). For recent work, the most accessible way of monitoring excavations in France is through the summary reports of the area directors of antiquities, appended to the national archaeological periodicals *Gallia* and *Gallia préhistoire*, which are unfortunately not indexed.

The following list is arranged by *département* and *commune*, after which each entry gives the site names, selected references, and an outline of the nature of the evidence. The same numbering system is used on the maps (figs. 9–12).

1 **Aisne, Montigny-l'Engrain**
Le Châtelet
(Wheeler and Richardson 1957: 129 and 205–6; Cotton 1961: 105–6 and n.13, 113)
Primarily on the basis of Vauvillé's nineteenth-century excavations, Cotton originally considered this to be a timber-laced rampart with iron nails. In 1961, however, she suggested that this camp represented a tribal *chef-lieu* in Gallia Belgica, copying the *murus gallicus*, but without nails.

2 **Aisne, Saint-Thomas**
Vieux Laon/Camp des Romains/Camp de César
(Wheeler and Richardson 1957: 131; Lobjois 1965; Collis 1975: 206)
Classic *murus gallicus*, first recognized by Peter Goessler in 1915, enclosing 32ha. Subsequently reduced in size by the construction of a dump rampart of Fécamp type.

3 **Allier, Bègues**
Un-named site
(Capitan 1913; 1915; 1916)
Calcino-vitrified. Description suggests vertical and horizontal timbers.

4 **Aveyron, Millau**
La Crête de la Granède
(*Gallia 17*, 1959: 410–12; *Gallia 20*, 1962: 550–2; Soutou 1962: 349; *Gallia 32*, 1974: 461–2; Collis and Ralston 1976: 140)
Burnt timber-laced rampart which was constructed, at latest, in the early Hallstatt iron age.

5 **Calvados, Banville**
La Burette
(Wheeler and Richardson 1957: 208–9)
Cotton was able to cite only circumstantial evidence for the presence of iron nails from this 2ha fort in suggesting that it may have possessed a *murus gallicus*.

6 **Calvados, Castillon**
Oppidum de Castillon

(Wheeler and Richardson 1957: 116; Gourvest 1961; *Gallia 20*, 1962: 429–30; Collis and Ralston 1976: 143)

The excavation of one section across the defence of this 35ha oppidum indicated the presence of a Kelheim-type wall (Collis and Ralston 1976: fig. 1). However, quadrangular-sectioned nails came from some of the post-holes for the vertical timbers of the rampart façade.

7 Calvados, Saint-Désir/La Motte

Camp du Castellier

(Wheeler and Richardson 1957: 118 and 203–4)

Massive oppidum enclosing in excess of 150ha and defended by a *murus gallicus*; largely obliterated by the time of the Wheeler expedition in 1938–9.

8 Calvados, Soumont-Saint-Quentin

La Brèche-au-Diable/Le Mont Joly

(Edeine 1966: 247–62; Savory 1971b: 256, 260)

4ha promontory fort, with defence probably of late bronze age date. Edeine (1966: 259) was of the opinion that the traces of charcoal and burnt timber recovered from the excavation of the defences represented the remains of fires set on the clay of the rampart in order to harden the clay.

9 Cantal, Escorailles

Un-named site

(Vazeilles 1936: 85–6)

Vitrified site. Possibly confused with an example in the *commune* of Mauriac.

10 Cantal, Mauriac

Vieux Château at hamlet of Escoalier

(Fournier 1961: no. A2)

Vitrified. Various other sources, including Déchelette (1913: 706), suggest the presence of a second vitrified site here, but it may be that mentioned by Vazeilles (1936: 85–6) in the *commune* of Escorailles.

11 Charente, Mouthiers-sur-Boeme

Un-named site

(Büchsenschütz, pers. comm.)

Calcined.

12 Charente, Soyaux

Camp de Recoux

(Lièvre 1888; Savory 1971b: 259, 260)

Calcined.

13 Charente, Voeuil-et-Giget

Fort des Anglais/Camp de Pierre-Dure

(Lièvre 1888; de la Noë 1892; Pintaud 1956; Savory 1971b: 259)

Calcined. Bersu thought this camp was probably of final Urnfield construction (in Pintaud 1956: 125); there is material of that period from the site, paralleled at Camp Allaric, Vienne (Pautreau 1976: 414).

14 Cher, Bourges

'Avaricum'

(Dumoutet 1863; Wheeler and Richardson 1957: 199–201; Ralston and Büchsenschütz 1975: 10–11)

Dumoutet (1863: 1) makes the only reference to the discovery of a wall conforming to Caesar's description (*de B G* VII, 23); this was located by excavations in the Archbishop's Garden in 1821.

15 Cher, Châteaumeillant

Les Fossés Sarrasins

(Hugoniot and Gourvest 1961; Ralston and Büchsenschütz 1975: 11; Collis and Ralston 1976: 142)

Although it would be possible to account for the absence of iron nails from the timber-laced rampart at the southern end of this 18ha promontory fort by the limited sampling, it may be of Ehrang type.

16 Cher, La Groutte
Camp des Murettes/de César
(Hugoniot and Vannier 1971; Ralston and Büchsenschütz 1975: 12)
The earlier defences of this site show evidence of fire-reddened stones and calcination.

17 Corrèze, Lamazière-Basse/Darnetz
Le Châtelet at La Gane
(Vazeilles 1936: 56–7; Brogan and Frere 1958: 221; Cotton and Frere 1961: 45, n. 38)
One wall is vitrified in a site which has produced evidence suggestive of use in both the iron age and medieval periods. Cotton has suggested that two phases, a vitrified Preist-type wall and a *murus gallicus*, may be represented, but this is unproven.

18 Corrèze, Monceaux-sur-Dordogne
Puy du Tour
(Bombal 1906; Hatt 1941; Wheeler and Richardson 1957: 182–3; Cotton and Frere 1961: 43; Murat and Murat 1967)
The post-war excavators of this c.6ha site did not re-examine the defences, even the line of which must be regarded as uncertain. Bombal's description (1906: 408–10) is somewhat ambiguous, but Cotton (in Wheeler and Richardson 1957) is surely right in suggesting that the lower part of the *murus gallicus* appears to have been rubble-built and to have lacked both the wood and nails recovered higher up. It is possible that a number of post-holes recorded below the rampart represent an earlier defence, but Bombal suggests that they may be evidence of pre-rampart settlement.

19 Corrèze, Monceaux-sur-Dordogne
Le Chastel, Le Puy Grasset
(Rupin 1893)
Vitrified motte.

20 Corrèze, Saint-Geniez-ô-Merle
Puy de Sermus
(Rupin 1893; Raymond 1910; Cotton and Frere 1961: 45; Lintz 1976)
Vitrified promontory fort which has produced a little iron age pottery.

21 Corrèze, Saint-Pardoux-le-Vieux
Château de Confolent
(Vazeilles 1938)
Vitrified motte.

22 Corrèze, Ussel
Camp du Charlat
(Cotton and Frere 1961: 31–42)
Small plateau fort occupied during late La Tène and post-Conquest times; defences of *murux duplex* construction, incorporating horizontal timbers.

23 Côte d'Or, Alise-sur-Reine
Mont Auxois/'Alesia'
(Wheeler and Richardson 1957: 195–8; Collis 1975: 173–4; *Gallia 34*, 1976: 440)
Oppidum enclosed by a *murus gallicus*. Collis (1975: 173) suggests, on the basis of changes of alignment, that there may have been more than one period of construction. A sector of the southern slope of the hill has recently produced indications of *murus gallicus* construction.

24 Côte d'Or, Bouilland
Le Châtelet
(Nicolardot 1975: 92)
Calcined.

25 Côte d'Or, Crecey-sur-Tille
Camp de Fontaine-Brunehaut

(*Gallia préhistoire 15*, 1972: 428–30)
The main defence of this promontory fort appears to be a dry-stone wall; only one sondage produced evidence of calcination. The wall is underlain by Hallstatt material.

26 **Côte d'Or, Êtaules**
Le Châtelet
(Raymond 1910: 3, 22; Guyot 1964)
Promontory fort with rampart of complex structure. The pre-calcined level of the rampart is Hallstatt B/Kimmig Champs d'Urnes III in date.

27 **Côte d'Or, Gevrey-Chambertin**
Château-Renard
(Nicolardot 1975: 92)
Calcined rampart.

28 **Côte d'Or, Flaverignot**
Mont Afrique/camp de César
(Drioton 1905: 50; Raymond 1910: 14; *Gallia 34*, 1976: 441)
Kruta's recent excavations do not seem to have produced further evidence of calcination. Apparently late La Tène in date.

29 **Côte d'Or, Plombières-les-Dijon**
Bois-Brulé
(Drioton 1905: 50–6; Raymond 1910: 3)
Calcined.

30 **Côte d'Or, Lavilleneuve**
Le Bois Vert
(Wheeler and Richardson 1957: 209)
Timber-lacing recovered in the enclosing wall of a barrow. The *Dictionnaire des Communes* lists three Villeneuves in this *département*. Not mapped.

31 **Côte d'Or, Val-Suzon**
Le Châtelet
(Drioton 1905: 50–6)
Calcined.

32 **Côte d'Or, Vertault**
Vicus Vertillum
(Wheeler and Richardson 1957: 198–9; *Gallia 16*, 1958: 308–10; Dehn 1960: 45; Collis 1975: 174)
The most recent investigation of this *murus gallicus*, known since the last century, suggested a post-Conquest date to the excavator, M. R. Joffroy; this depends largely on an assessment of the quality of the stonework, especially in the outer wall-face. Two other unusual features were the short length of the beams employed, and the presence of longitudinal timbers, as well as the beam-ends of the transversals, in the front face of the wall.

33 **Côte d'Or, Villeberny**
L'Haut-Mont
(Nicolardot 1975: 92)
Calcined rampart.

34 **Côte d'Or, Vitteaux**
Camp de Myard
(Nicolardot 1973; 1974; 1975)
Calcined material from directly behind the inner edge of the dry-stone defences is of neolithic date but has been attributed by Nicolardot to a settlement rather than to the wall itself.

35 **Côte d'Or, Vix**
Mont Lassois/Montagne Saint-Marcel
(Wheeler and Richardson 1957: 199; Joffroy 1960: 133; Collis 1975: 174; Joffroy 1975: 71; *Gallia 34*, 1976: 450)

Although previously described as a *murus gallicus*, the presence of vertical timbers in the outer face of the wall suggests that it may more appropriately be classed as Preist-type, or perhaps Kelheim-type. A recent sondage on the south-west edge of the plateau failed to relocate the rampart, but produced six iron spikes, up to 25cm long, of the type used in *murus gallicus* construction.

36 **Côtes du Nord, Erquy**
Cap d'Erquy
(Sancier 1964; Giot *et al*. 1968; Giot and Briard 1969; Savory 1971b: 260)
Substantial promontory fort of 35ha, with outer wall (the Fossé de Pleine Garenne) showing evidence of carbonized transversal and longitudinal timbers. A radiocarbon date of 320±110 bc (GIF-1302) has been obtained (Giot and Briard 1969: 33).

37 **Côtes du Nord, Plédran**
Camp de Péran/Camp Romain
(Daubrée 1881: 21–5; de la Noë 1892; Raymond 1910: 3–5; Wheeler and Richardson 1957: 112)
Vitrified plateau fort. Both Wheeler and Richardson and de la Noë remark on the traces of horizontal timbers in the heavily-vitrified gneiss of the main rampart.

38 **Creuse, Aubusson**
Camp des Chastres
(Léger 1972; *Gallia 33*, 1975: 443)
15ha promontory fort whose main defences incorporate burnt timber-lacing, including a vertical element. A single fibula suggests late Hallstatt construction.

39 **Creuse, Linard**
Chateau Gaillard
(Martin 1905: 51–2; Autorde 1907: 722)
Vitrified material from a motte.

40 **Creuse, Pionnat**
Chateauvieux
(Mayaud 1881; Daubrée 1881; Raymond 1910: 2; Youngblood *et al*. 1978: figs. 5a and 5b, *passim*)
Vitrified.

41 **Creuse, Saint-Dizier-la-Tour**
La butte de la Tour-Saint-Austeille
(de Cessac 1867)
Vitrified material from a motte.

42 **Creuse, Sainte-Feyre**
Le Puy de Gaudy
(de Cessac 1878; Daubrée 1882; Raymond 1910: 2; Youngblood *et al*. 1978: *passim*)
Vitrified contour fort.

43 **Creuse, Thauron**
Un-named site
(Autorde 1907: *passim*; Raymond 1910: 2, 7)
Vitrified.

44 **Dordogne, Coulounieux-Chamiers**
Camp de César/de Périgueux
(de la Noë 1887: 330; Wheeler and Richardson 1957: 207)
First cited as a *murus gallicus* by de la Noë.

45 **Dordogne, Saint-Médard-d'Excideuil**
Castel Sarrazi
(Hardy 1882; Barrière 1933: 16–17)
Vitrified.

46 **Doubs, Myon**
Châtelet de Montbergeret
(Piroutet 1906: 51; 1913: 164)

Calcined.

47 Drôme, Le Pègue
La colline Saint-Marcel
(Hatt 1976)
An earthen bank, at an associated site below the hill ('Chantier de l'École'), contained traces of vertical and horizontal timbers (Hatt 1976: 37–41), and appears to have been in use from late Hallstatt to La Tène II. Whether its purpose was exclusively defensive or was partially designed to protect the site from flood damage is uncertain.

48 Eure, La Fréneuse-sur-Risle/Livet-sur-Authou
La Berquerie
(Coutil 1909: 608)
Previously suggested as calcined, but withdrawn by Coutil. Not mapped.

49 Eure-et-Loir, Sorel-Moussel
Fort Harrouard
(Philippe 1936; 1937; Wheeler and Richardson 1957: 121; Collis 1975: 203–4)
Although Philippe's excavation of the main rampart revealed no details of internal structure, excavations around the perimeter of the promontory indicated the presence of a calcined rampart, with both vertical and horizontal timbers. Philippe considered this to be neolithic in date (1936: 293–8).

50 Finistère, Ergué-Armel
Beg-ar-Castel
(Wheeler and Richardson 1957: 107)
There are patches of burning and indications of vitrification in the rampart of this promontory fort of less than 1ha in area.

51 Finistère, Huelgoat
Le camp d'Artus/d'Arthur
(Wheeler and Richardson 1957: 23–38)
Murus gallicus, lacking rear revetment wall and with vertical timbers (six-post arrangement) in two of the gateways, enclosing an area of approximately 30ha. One of Wheeler's trenches (site E, see Wheeler and Richardson 1957: pl.III) shows a dump rampart, with internal retaining wall; the latter was seemingly not intended to be freestanding, but formed a capping to the main rampart; this second phase is undated.

52 Ille-et-Vilaine, Saint-Coulomb
Ville des Mues/Pointe du Meinga
(Wheeler and Richardson 1957: 113)
Although traces of burnt timber were recorded behind the stone revetting-wall of this 14ha promontory fort, the evidence was felt to be inadequate to classify it as a *murus gallicus*.

53 Ille-et-Vilaine, Vieux-Vy-sur-Couësnon
Oppidum d'Orange
(Collis 1975: 200)
Suggestion of vitrification in the inner rampart.

54 Indre, Levroux (fig. 13)
Les Tours
(Büchsenschütz and Ralston 1975)
Murus gallicus, lacking formal rear revetting-wall, replaced and overlain by a dump rampart.

55 Indre, Meunet-Planches
Le Camp de Corny
(Ralston and Büchsenschütz 1975: 13)
Nails recovered from the rampart of this c. 1ha fort during quarrying operations in the nineteenth century were compared to those from Murcens. Roman finds are recorded from the interior of the fort.

56 Jura, Cernans
Le Grandchamp
(Piroutet 1913: 163)
Evidence of fire in the upper part of the earth-and-stone rampart.

57 Jura, Champagnole
Éperon de Boyise
(*BSPF* 5, 1908: 432–3)
Timber-laced rampart; apparently Merovingian in date.

58 Jura, Chevigny
Un-named site
(Büchsenschütz, pers. comm.)
Calcined. (Almost certainly the same site as Montmirey in the same *département*.)

59 Jura, Mesnay
Roch-Maldru
(Piroutet 1906: 38–42; Millotte 1963: 94)
Calcined defence overlies early bronze age occupation.

60 Jura, Montmirey-la-Ville
Le Mont-Guérin
(Piroutet 1909; 1913: 166; Feuvrier 1913: 692, fig. 2)
Calcined defence overlies early bronze age level.

61 Jura, Rahon
Le Mont-Ceint
(Millotte 1963: 123)
Evidence of burning in a defence compared by Millotte to that of the Wittnauer-horn.

62 Jura, Salins
Camp du Château
(Piroutet and Déchelette 1909; Piroutet 1913: 164–5; 1930; Dayet 1967)
Partially vitrified; this was not apparent in the later excavations of Dayet. (The site is sometimes listed in the *commune* of Pretin, Doubs.)

63 Loire, Chambles
La Ruthe/Le Palais à Essalois
(Wheeler and Richardson 1957: 180–1; Renaud 1962; Preynat 1962; Collis 1975: 179)
Although the 1962 descriptions of this site vary, both Renaud and Preynat oppose the idea that it was defended by a *murus gallicus*. Renaud's excavations produced evidence for *murus duplex* construction, whilst Preynat (1962: 306) argues that the presence of long iron spikes can be related to destroyed wooden structures from the interior of the site.

64 Loire, Saint-Alban-les-Eaux
Châteaulux/Château de Verre de Châteaulus
(Bouttet 1910; Raymond 1910: 2)
Vitrified. Old excavations mention the discovery of iron nails.

65 Loire, Saint-Georges-de-Bariolle
Le Châtelard de Chazi/Le Crêt Châtelard
(Wheeler and Richardson 1957: 181–2; Besset and Périchon 1964: 63–6; Collis 1975: 181)
Promontory fort of 6–7ha in area. When cleared for the planting of vines, the defences produced numerous blocks of stone which did not seem to have formed

Figure 13. Indre, Levroux (site 54), from the south-west. The *murus gallicus* excavated in 1971 lies immediately south of the track encircling the 20ha oppidum (photograph O. Büchsenschütz).

a wall, and amongst which iron nails were found. A *murus gallicus* of 3m overall width seems to have been discovered on the north side of the camp.

66 Loire, Saint-Marcel-de-Félines
Le Crêt Chatelard
(Wheeler and Richardson 1957: 178–80; Besset and Périchon 1964; Collis 1975: 181)
Although the main defence seems to comprise only a dry-stone wall, a *murus gallicus* constructed on an artificially-cut platform has been discovered elsewhere on the perimeter of the site.

67 Loire, Saint-Maurice-sur-Loire
Joeuvre(s)
(Wheeler and Richardson 1957: 206–7; Besset and Périchon 1964: 70–2; Collis 1975: 181)
Only reports of the discovery of iron nails, not certainly associated with a defensive architecture, suggest that there may be a *murus gallicus* here.

68 Loire, Villerest
Le Château-Brulé de Lourdon
(Raymond 1910: 2; Bouttet 1910)
Vitrified.

69 Loire-Atlantique, Vue
Vue
(Wheeler and Richardson 1957: 207)
The only evidence to suggest the presence of a *murus gallicus* seems to be iron nails.

70 Lot, Cras
Murcens/Murceint/Ville des Mues
(Castagné 1874: *passim*; Wheeler and Richardson 1957: 183–5)
A classic *murus gallicus* runs across the isthmus of this promontory. A little calcined material (Castagné 1874: 472) has also been recovered from the site, but much of the perimeter defence seems to be devoid of internal timber-lacing.

71 Lot, Luzech
L'Impernal
(Viré 1913; Wheeler and Richardson 1957: 186–8)
A classic *murus gallicus*, isolating a plateau of about 16ha, was built on the debris which had fallen forward from an earlier calcined rampart.

72 Lot-et-Garonne, Agen
Plateau de l'Ermitage
(Mommèja 1901)
Tentatively suggested as a *murus gallicus* on the basis of nails recovered from the site during excavations in the 1870s.

73 Lozère, La Fage-Montivernoux
Puy de la Fage
(de Lasteyrie 1883: 17–18; Raymond 1910: 2; *BSPF 10*, 1913, lists this site in Cantal)
Vitrified. de Lasteyrie notes that the rampart incorporated a horseshoe.

74 Maine-et-Loire, Fief-Sauvin
Le Camp de la Ségourie
(Wheeler and Richardson 1957: 202–3)
Early records indicate the presence of a *murus gallicus*.

75 Maine-et-Loire, Saint-Hilaire-du-Bois
La Grosse Motte de la Madeleine
(Desmazières 1933)
Vitrified or calcined enclosure for a motte.

76 Manche, Le Petit Celland
Le Châtellier
(Wheeler and Richardson 1957: 38–54; Collis 1975: 200)

Contour fort on a promontory, approximately 20ha in area, defended by a *murus gallicus*. Collis has suggested that a massive vertical timber, located behind the external wall-face in Wheeler's trench A (Wheeler and Richardson 1957: 41, pl.XVII), may represent part of a tower, or some such superstructure, associated with the *murus gallicus*. The approach to the eastern gate displays vertical timbers in Kelheim style.

77 Manche, Saint-Jean-de-Savigny
Le Grand Câtel
(Wheeler and Richardson 1957: 116)
Wheeler and Richardson, following *BSPF 13*, 1916, equate this site with the unlocated La Butte des Romains, Cérisy-la-Foret, which is also said to be vitrified. No evidence of vitrification was seen during the Wheeler expedition. Both Wheeler and P.-M. Duval (1959: 49) suggest that this 14ha promontory fort may have been defended by a *murus gallicus*.

78 Mayenne, Loigné-sur-Mayenne
Loigné
(Büchsenschütz, pers. comm.)
Vitrified.

79 Mayenne, Saint-Jean-sur-Mayenne
Château-Meignan
(Daubrée 1882; Raymond 1910: 3–4)
Vitrified.

80 Mayenne, Sainte-Suzanne
Camp Anglais/de la Motte
(Daubrée 1881; Triger 1907: 68–85; Raymond 1910: 2)
Vitrified.

81 Meurthe-et-Moselle, Champigneulles
La Fourasse
(Beaupré 1902: no. 6, plan; Raymond 1910: 31; Millotte 1965: 65)
Calcined.

82 Meurthe-et-Moselle, Essey-lès-Nancy
La Butte Sainte-Geneviève
(Beaupré 1902: no. 8, plan; Beaupré 1910; Millotte 1965: 77)
The rampart is calcined and shows evidence of timbers.

83 Meurthe-et-Moselle, Messein
Camp d'Afrique at Ludres
(Beaupré 1902: 71–4; Beaupré 1909: 381–4; Raymond 1910: 14)
The inner rampart of two is calcined. (Ludres is listed in the *Dictionnaire des Communes* as a *commune* in its own right.)

84 Meuse, Naix-aux-Forges
Boviolles/Mont-Chalet/Mont-Chaté
(Maxe-Werly 1877; Wheeler and Richardson 1957: 204–5)
Promontory site of approximately 50ha with *murus gallicus*.

85 Morbihan, Bilgroix-en-Arzon
Un-named site
(André 1959: 444)
Small rectangular camp, with evidence of Roman occupation, and evidence of transversal and longitudinal timbers from its enclosing wall. (Arzon is listed as the *commune* name in the *Dictionnaire des Communes*.)

86 Moselle, Lessy
Un-named site
(de la Noë 1892; Coutil 1909: 608)
Calcined. Totally destroyed.

87 Nièvre, Lavault-de-Frétoy
Le Fou de Verdun

(Olivier *et al.* 1969; Harbison 1971: 214–5)
An inland promontory fort with an elaborate defence consisting of a wooden *chevaux-de-frise*, a small ditch and a timber-laced rampart; the latter incorporated both horizontals and verticals, at least near the entrance. According to Harbison, the description of the defences as of Preist type is based on inadequate evidence. The defences have yielded three iron nails. Available dating evidence suggests use in late Hallstatt and late La Tène.

88 **Nièvre, La Machine**
Le Vieux Château de Barbarie
(Barré de Saint-Venant and Poussereau 1906; Raymond 1910: 12)
Vitrified. Apparently medieval.

89 **Nord, Avesnelles/Flaumont-Wandrechies**
Le Chatelet/Camp de César
(de la Noë 1887: 330; Déchelette 1902: 79; Wheeler and Richardson 1957: 132 and 209; Cotton 1961: 113; Collis 1975: 206–7)
Although both de la Noë and Déchelette cited this fortification as an example of *murus gallicus*, it seems safer to classify it as timber-laced, perhaps of Ehrang type.

90 **Oise, Gouvieux**
Camp de César
(Durvin 1962: 44–8)
Vitrified. No clear evidence to support Durvin's contention that the defence consisted of a *murus gallicus*.

91 **Orne, La Courbe**
Chateau Goutier/Les Pierres Brulées/Les Vieux Chateaux
(Daubrée 1881; Coutil 1909: 606–8; Raymond 1910: 2; Wheeler and Richardson 1957: 119)
Partially vitrified. Coutil mentions an iron nail adhering to a piece of vitrified material from this site.

92 **Puy de Dome, Bourg-Lastic**
Un-named site
(Fournier 1961: 90; *Gallia 21*, 1963: 494)
Calcined. No pre-Roman finds.

93 **Puy de Dome, Chateauneuf-les-Bains**
Montagne de Villars
(Vimont and Pommerol 1884; Raymond 1910: 12)
Vitrified motte or tumulus.

94 **Haut Rhin, Hartmannwiller**
Enceinte de Fitzethanne
(Rupin 1893: 184)
Vitrified.

95 **Haut Rhin, Illfurth**
Britzgyberg
(*Gallia 32*, 1974: 368–9; Millotte 1976: 844, with plan)
The middle and late Hallstatt defences of this promontory fort incorporate a palisade and a timber-laced rampart, the latter apparently incorporating vertical timbers in the core of the wall material.

96 **Saône-et-Loire, Macon**
'*Matisco*'
(Barthélemy 1973)

Figure 14. Haute Vienne, Saint-Denis-des-Murs (site 106), from the south-east. The line of trees in the centre of the photograph covers the outermost defence, a *murus gallicus*, which crosses the plateau between the wooded valleys of the Vienne (left) and the Maulde (right, flooded), the confluence of which lies over 4km to the north-west and marks the other end of the oppidum (photograph O. Büchsenschütz).

Recently discovered *murus gallicus*, the main variant feature of which is the presence of vertical timbers in the rear wall-face.

97 Saône-et-Loire, Saint-Léger-sous-Beuvray
Mont-Beuvray/'*Bibracte*'
(Wheeler and Richardson 1957: 190–5)
The main departure from standard practice in the construction of the *murus gallicus* of this contour site is the possible presence of diagonal elements, as well as the usual transversals and longitudinals, in the timber framework of the wall. These were recorded by the earlier excavator, J.-G. Bulliot; his successor, Déchelette, was sceptical about the existence of this irregular feature, though he did not excavate in the defences of the site.

98 Haute Saône, Bourguignon-lès-Morey
Un-named site
(Bouillerot 1905)
Calcined.

99 Haute Saône, Noroy-lès-Jussey
Un-named site
(Bouillerot 1905)
Calcined.

100 Var, Le Luc
La Fouirette
(*Gallia 25*, 1967: 422; *Gallia 27*, 1969: 453–4; Dehn 1969: 166; Collis and Ralston 1976: 140)
One of three towers attached to the external face of a dry-stone wall has transversal and longitudinal timbers.

101 Var, Le Muy
Colle du Rouet
(*Gallia 22*, 1964: 595)
Evidence of vitrification from inner defence.

102 Vienne, Aslonnes
Camp-Allaric
(Pautreau 1976)
Promontory fort of 2ha, defended by a dry-stone wall erected after 610±110 bc (GIF-3008). Calcined material associated with this wall takes the form of a layer overlying tumble from the wall and has been attributed to the destruction of a settlement built against its inner face, though it seems possible to interpret it as collapse from a higher part of the wall.

103 Vienne, Lussac-les-Chateaux
Camp de Cornouin
(Delage 1935; Wheeler and Richardson 1957: 201–2)
Records of the discovery of iron spikes form the main evidence for suggesting that this promontory fort, of c.10ha, was defended by a *murus gallicus*.

104 Vienne, Quinçay
Sénéret
(Chauvet 1926: 13–21; Savory 1971b: 259; Tauvel 1973)
Calcined. The Hallstatt vehicle burial (Chauvet 1926; Joffroy 1958) lay just outside the camp.

105 Haute Vienne, Dournazac
Le Mont Brun
(Lecler 1883: 28–9; Cotton and Frere 1961: 45, lists this site in Corrèze)
Vitrified motte.

106 Haute Vienne, Saint-Denis-des-Murs (fig. 14)
Villejoubert/Camp de César
(Delage and Gorceix 1923; Wheeler and Richardson 1957: 189–90; Cotton and Frere 1961: 42–3)

Massive promontory fort of approximately 350ha, defended by a *murus gallicus*.

107 Haute Vienne, Saint-Julien-le-Petit
Rochein
(Dubois 1900)
Motte with vitrified stonework.

108 Vosges, Etival-Clairefontaine
La Pierre d'Appel
(*Gallia 32*, 1974: 361–2)
This 2.5ha site apparently has four phases of timber-laced defences from La Tène II through to the Augustan period. Much less use was made of wood in the final phase than previously.

109 Vosges, Saint-Dié
La Bure-Tête du Villé
(Tronquart 1976)
Promontory fort of 3.5ha, defended by a *murus gallicus* at its eastern end. This defence seems to have had two phases of construction, marked by a change of alignment in the northern sector.

110 Yonne, Saint Florentin
Mont Avrollo
(*Gallia 32*, 1974: 450–1; Collis 1975: 175; *Gallia 34*, 1976: 462)
Small promontory fort of 3ha, defended by a *murus gallicus*.

111 Yonne, Saint-Moré
Camp de Cora
(Raymond 1910: 2)
Calcined.

Acknowledgments

Many colleagues in France and Britain have assisted me in the collection of information on the hill-forts of France, and I wish to thank them, especially MM. Olivier Büchsenschütz and Guy Lintz, without associating them with the shortcomings of this compilation. I am also grateful to my wife for preparing the maps.

GRAEME GUILBERT

Hill-fort functions and populations: a sceptical viewpoint

The study of hill-fort population figures, so inextricably bound up with that of hill-fort functions, has become a field for serious researchers over the past couple of decades, but we may doubt whether it has yet come of age. The increased scale of excavations inside hill-forts, with the consequent increase in structural information, has done much to foster these branches of hill-fort studies, and a good many people, including the present writer, have warmed to the opportunity of speculating upon a variety of the apparent implications of this new body of evidence. It is, of course, essential to realize that, in its present infancy, our inquiry into the nature of hill-fort interiors has achieved little more than a few glimpses of the potentiality that exists below ground. Mindful of this, I shall here review certain aspects of the twin themes of hill-fort functions and populations rather more coolly than some have done of late, for a feeling of disquiet has increasingly dogged my cogitations about the character of the interiors of two hill-forts where I excavated in the 1970s and thence, inevitably, about hill-forts at large. That I should choose the pages of this volume to discuss, in critical vein, an arena which Dr Hogg has himself entered on occasions says a lot for the measure of esteem in which I hold his open-mindedness, the quality which we ought perhaps to set above all others in an archaeologist.

The types of evidence adduced by those aiming to evaluate the populations of individual hill-forts have been derived from the records of both excavation and surface inspection. We shall examine examples of each in turn.

It may be felt, *prima facie*, that a respectable starting-point for the demographer will lie in the total excavation of a settlement site, provided conditions allow for confidence that all structures have been located, itself a circumstance of considerable rarity, not to say impossibility (Guilbert 1975a: 214–20), and that their sequence of construction is reliably defined. Even then, however, problems will still abound. Above all, the former usage of each structure has somehow got to be established, for in some situations it may not be good enough to prove the function of only a single or even several examples of a recurrent type of structure, still less to analogize with separate sites, no matter if they are contemporaneous and seem comparable at first sight.

Figure 15. Moel y Gaer, Rhosesmor, Clwyd, viewed from the east in 1969, before excavation began (photograph Cambridge University Collection, copyright reserved).

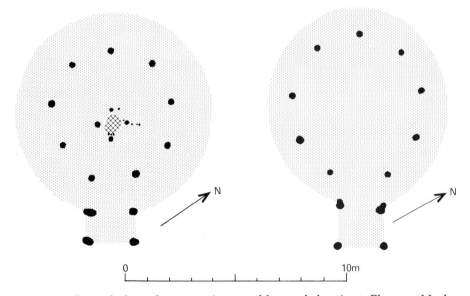

Figure 16. Ground-plans of two post-ring round-houses belonging to Phase 1 at Moel y Gaer, one with and one without a central hearth (cross-hatched) and its attendant post-holes and stake-holes. Stipple covers the probable extent of the floor of each building (see Guilbert 1976: 307).

These are points that can be well illustrated by two of the structural phases revealed by excavation at Moel y Gaer, Clwyd (fig. 15).

Apart from a number of post-hole pairs, and possibly a circle of pits of esoteric purpose, the only structures identified within the excavated proportion, c.5450 of perhaps 30,000sq.m, of the Phase 1 – i.e. mid-first millennium bc – palisaded hill-fort at Moel y Gaer, were post-ring round-houses (Guilbert 1976: 306–9; 1977: 42).[1] The ground-plans of the foundations of many of these round-houses exhibited such similarities as to suggest that they were of a type structurally. Yet there are two reasons for believing that the buildings they embodied were not all of a type functionally.

Of the 29 post-ring round-houses recognized, a few tentatively but most with conviction, only 11 could be shown to have had a hearth, in each case represented by a scorched patch of the undisturbed boulder-clay and situated central to the floor space (fig. 16).[2] The nature of the archaeological evidence must restrain any inclination to assert that the remaining round-houses were without hearths, for there are circumstances in which they need have left no mark on the ground (cf. Guilbert 1976: 309); but there is a further factor to be considered in this instance. Nine of the recorded hearths were flanked on two or more sides by groups of small stake-holes and post-holes whose sooty soil contents reinforce the evidence of their disposition in attesting to some functional connection with the hearths; in contrast, such a setting of soot-filled holes was encountered in just one of the round-houses apparently lacking a hearth. The implications would seem to be that some form of wooden framework was required for whatever activities were associated with these nine hearths and that those particular tasks were not performed in many, if any, of the other post-ring round-houses. While the relative distribution of the round-houses with and without hearths betrays no apparent significance in the area excavated (fig. 17), it may be of interest to note that the detectable hearths occurred in buildings ranging from 8.1 to 11.1m in probable floor diameter, whereas at least eight of the rest measured less than 8m, the smallest being 6.5m, across. It is perhaps doubtful whether our c. 18 per cent sample of this settlement is sufficiently large for much weight to be attached to this possible correlation of a function, albeit unknown, and round-house size, especially since four round-houses of 8m or more in diameter gave no hint of a hearth.

Secondly, the orientation of one of the post-ring round-houses relative to a gap in the enclosure fence indicates that it had probably served the singular role of guard-hut (i.e. that with west-facing porch at top left in fig. 17; see also Guilbert 1977: 47). That so special a usage was not clearly reflected in its ground-plan may come as something of a shock to those who have fondly supposed that some perceptible structural characteristics would distinguish buildings of different functions in the archaeological record. The fact is, though, that even were there no archaeological grounds for disputing it in Britain, ethnographic evidence from abroad readily contradicts that concept (e.g. Denyer 1978: 21–2).

On the other hand, reason has been found in their mode of arrangement to postulate a correlation of building types and functions in the interior of the Phase 2 – i.e. later first millennium bc – ramparted hill-fort at Moel y Gaer (Guilbert 1975a: 205–10). Even so, it is only by demonstrating what particular functions were fulfilled by the zones of stake-wall round-houses and four-posters attributable to this phase in the c.4500sq.m excavated (fig.18), out of a total internal area of c.25,000sq.m, that we can hope to make a start on understanding the part this hill-fort played in the contemporary settlement pattern. On reflection, I would no longer wish to put forward any 'working hypothesis' quite so trite and unsubstantiated as an equation of the round with dwellings and the rectangular with storage units (*pace* Guilbert 1976: 314). Positive evidence relating to the usages of the Phase 2 structures at Moel y Gaer is wanting, but it may be instructive to ponder the consequences of

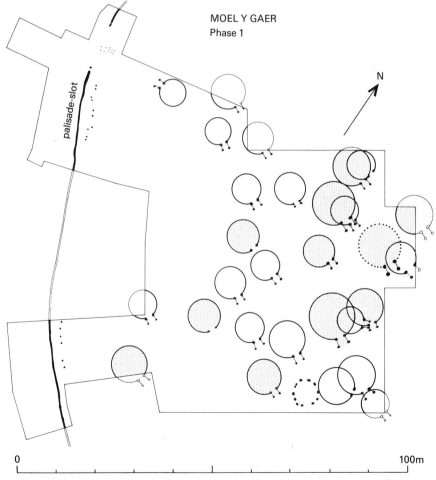

Figure 17. Sketch plan of structures identified in the portion of the Phase 1 hill-fort at Moel y Gaer excavated in 1972–4. The round-houses within which central hearths were recorded are distinguished by stippling.

adopting some of the possible functions advanced by other people for analogous structures elsewhere.

It has to be confessed that the grain-store interpretation of prehistoric four-posters, be they for seed- or consumption-corn, stored in bulk or pre-packed, is the most alluring in many instances; but, to my knowledge, it has yet to be adequately proven in any instance in Britain, either within a hill-fort or on any other type of site. I include in this statement even Rotherley Group III, popularly used as a corner-stone of the theory on account of 'a number of grains of carbonized wheat' recovered from the fill of each of the four 'holes' (Pitt Rivers 1888: 109). Even had those holes been jammed full of the stuff we would surely now need to know more about their condition and circumstances before committing ourselves unreservedly to any proposition of building function. Had the uprights been uprooted or had their buried feet

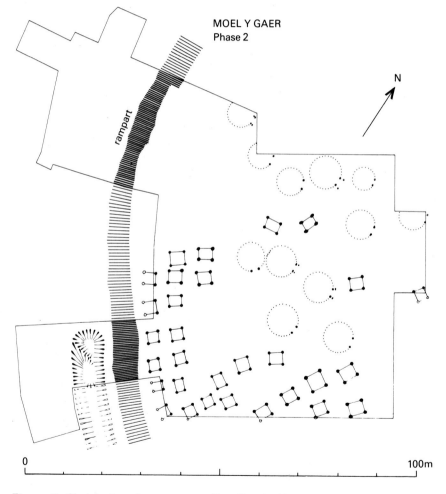

MOEL Y GAER
Phase 2

N

rampart

0   100m

Figure 18. Sketch plan of structures attributed to the Phase 2 hill-fort at Moel y Gaer in the area excavated in 1972–4.

decayed *in situ*? If the former, what is to say that the grains were not among rubbish dumped into the resultant voids, having perhaps been brought from elsewhere on the site and maybe including residual material unearthed from earlier deposits? Or, if the latter, could not the grains have been scattered over the area some time after the building had collapsed and still have found their way into the holes as the four subterraneous stumps rotted? The simple truth is that the function of the four-post structure represented by Group III is as uncertain as is that of each of the other Groups, I-VI, at Rotherley; and the astute General was quite correct to qualify his granary interpretation as 'supposed' (*ibid.*: 55, 57, pl.XCIV). There are others who would have done well to emulate his caution (*pace*, for example, Hawkes 1947: 37, 79; Wainwright 1968: 113–14; Stead 1968: 157–8; Stanford 1970: 110, 112; Challis and Harding 1975: i, 151). Much the same arguments can, of course, also be applied to the so-called 'Granaries A and B' at the Tollard Royal enclosure, also on Cranborne Chase (Wainwright 1968: 112), or to structure G1 at Croft Ambrey hillfort in Herefordshire (Stanford 1974a: 81–2). Indeed, with carbonized grains apparently present in but two of its post-holes, G1B cannot vindicate a granary interpretation even by Stanford's own, previously stated (1970: 110), criteria; and a causal connection between G1C and the grain-laden 'charcoal layer 8' in trench 31 remains unproven, since there must be a chance that that building was dismantled before the deposition of those charred materials. Nor, incidentally, can I see a 'clear connection' between rectangular structures and grain at Meare West Village in Somerset (*pace* Bradley 1978: 43). The short of it is that, wherever it has been claimed, certainty of association of grain and four-post building is lacking.

Supposing, for the sake of argument, the rows of four-posters at Moel y Gaer actually were granaries, could such a large number as we may feel inclined to guess would be disclosed by total excavation really have been needed to garner the yearly yield of a community that inhabited the remaining area of the hill-fort? If not, was that community harbouring the harvest of other farmers, whether as a levy or as a neighbourly contract? Are we in fact dealing with a communal, protected, storage depot or redistribution centre for attendant settlements, much as Cunliffe (1976b: 346–7; 1976d: 209) and Bradley (1978: 121) have conjectured in ostensibly earlier contexts elsewhere?[3]

Or maybe the four-posters were dwellings – a notion championed chiefly by Stanford, in regard of certain hill-forts further south in the Welsh Marches (1970: 110–12; 1971: 47; 1972: 315; 1974a: 124, 230), and Tratman, with particular reference to the iron age village at Glastonbury (1970: 156–60). And if the round-houses were residential too, what do the different structural forms signify? – distinctions in social status? – rich and poor? freeman and slave? officers and enlisted men? young and old? married and single? male and female? Or, to come full circle, perhaps the food supplies were kept in the round (cf. Bradley 1978: 49–50).[4]

Then again, the very assumption that Moel y Gaer was intended for human habitation in Phase 2 may be leading us astray (*pace* Guilbert 1975a: 210). Elaborate entrances notwithstanding (*pace* Guilbert 1975a: 215), those who prefer not to have to envisage stake-rings up to 8.1m in diameter bearing a roof may like to opt for interpretation of the round-houses as animal pens (cf. P. J. Reynolds's sheep-fold reconstruction of a post-ring round-house, 1979: 41–2). Not forgetting byres (e.g. Reynolds P. J. 1979: 81) and pig-sties (Bersu 1940: 97) as possible explanations of four-posters, should we conclude that the iron age economy in this tract of north Wales included a strong and centralized element of meat production? Reynolds's tentative fodder-barn or staddle interpretations of four-, and kindred five-, post structures (1972: 7; 1979: 80–2; cf. Bersu 1940: 97; Coles 1973: 62; Bradley and Ellison 1975: 129, 212) could seem equally appropriate to such a model, while Ritchie's observation (Ritchie A. 1971: 93) that four-post settings could in some cases have been frames for drying and smoking meat might cause us to suppose that the flesh was processed rather than fattened at Moel y Gaer, though the absence of a hearth, such as inspired Ritchie in the first place, in association with any of the 30 four-posters depicted in fig. 18, is clearly an impediment in this instance. Another idea taken from Reynolds's list, chicken huts (1979: 81), could bring to mind a different kind of intensive food production when applied to four-posters laid out in lines as at Moel y Gaer and several other hill-forts (see Guilbert 1975a: 207–9).

The stabling of horses and the garaging of vehicles (after Bradley 1978: 43 and Reynolds P. J. 1979: 81) provide further alternatives for the four-posters which, in these numbers, could again bespeak some very special function for the hill-fort, though the definition of this would, of course, depend upon the type of vehicle involved, cart or chariot.

Such indiscriminate, some might say irresponsible, extension of others' ideas could next induce us to follow Biddle (1965: 234–5) or Piggott (Piggott S. 1968: 61) *re* four-posters and Harding (1972: 62–4) *re* stake-wall round-houses (or Harding 1974: 105–11 *re* both),[5] thus to summon files of stereotyped shrines serried across the hilltop – a grand cult focus for the region? – all ritual offerings having, naturally, disappeared long since in the acidic soil of Moel y Gaer![6] Continuing in romantic mood, and selecting one of several suggestions outlined by Ellison and Drewett for four-posters (1971: 191–2), we might imagine ranks of corpse-exposure scaffolds. Recalling as well the celebrated association of stake-circles with bronze age sepulchral monuments (Ashbee 1960: 60–5), should we picture a massive mortuary? Moreover, let it be said that there was one feature of the Phase 2 rampart, namely the style of the front revetment with its ludicrously closely-spaced timber uprights sandwiching slender stacks of dry masonry (Guilbert 1975b: 110, fig. 1, pl.XIIIa), whose affectation and impracticality may not seem entirely out of keeping in the context of a resort for some sort of ritual.[7]

Far-fetched, even flippant, as some of these alternatives may appear,[8] there is a serious motive in rehearsing them here, for they spotlight the defects in our present ability to appreciate Moel y Gaer in Phase 2, or Phase 1 come to that, much more memorably than would a prosaic sentence or two. Everyone has his own plausible preferences, but until such time as acceptable

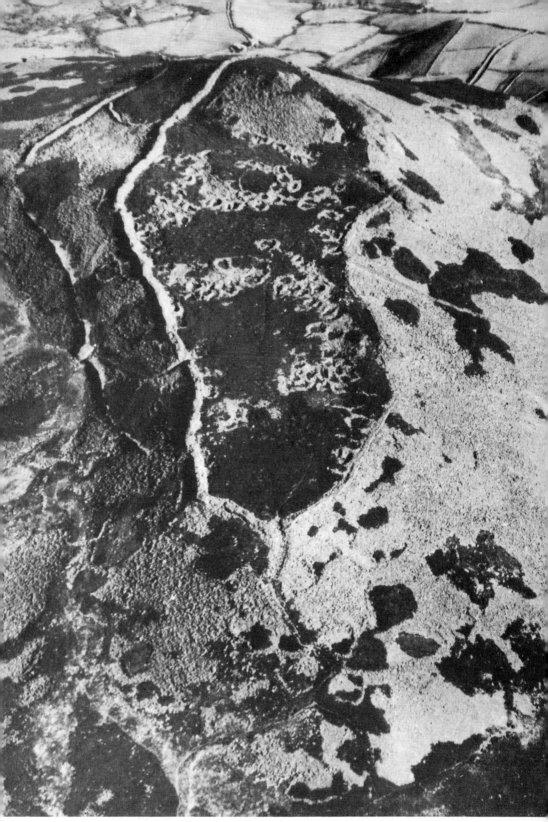

Figure 19. Tre'r Ceiri, Gwynedd, from the south-west. Clusters of stone hut-walls can be seen in the 2ha area enclosed by the main, stone rampart (photograph reproduced by permission of The Controller of H.M.Stationery Office).

proof presents itself we must be prepared to maintain an open mind in these basic matters of function. We know, as opposed to surmise, far too little of how most hill-forts functioned in relation to the surrounding countryside to be in any position to choose between the many possible purposes of their builders, except by our current preconceptions. What is more, the fact that less than one-fifth of the area encompassed by the rampart at Moel y Gaer has been excavated necessarily hinders even speculation; and so it must be for all incompletely excavated hill-forts, for, in the present, inchoate, state of our knowledge, the unexplored acres should not be simply assumed to mirror those parts which have been dissected.

It is these kinds of deliberations that give rise to scepticism about the population estimates sometimes fabricated on the basis of excavated samples of supposed settlement sites and give the lie to simplistic population formulae such as those set out by Naroll (1962) and Casselberry (1974), at least in so far as they could ever be usefully applied to hill-forts and the like. As an example we may adduce the detailed calculations made by S. C. Stanford for the central Marches in the iron age, for these emanate from the apparent density of building-plans uncovered in several relatively small excavations inside selected hill-forts, and the route from excavation record to population figures is littered with suppositions. Two fundamental flaws in Stanford's procedure are (a) the manifest guesswork involved in distinguishing four-post structures of essentially homogeneous form, with respect to their archaeological remains anyway, into so-called 'dwellings' and 'stores'/'granaries' by dint of an odd square metre, or fraction of same, above or below what can only be regarded as an arbitrary threshold of ostensible ground-floor area; and (b) the daring restoration of the total internal plan of the hill-fort, especially of his main example Croft Ambrey, following an arguably inadequate sample (1970: 108–12; 1974a: 122–6).[9] These premises place the dependent assumptions of Stanford's thesis upon a very precarious footing (1972; 1974a: 230–1; 1974b: 45–7).

Even greater difficulties will be incurred when 'guesstimates' of populaton are derived from either the superficial remnants of structures or the artificially levelled platforms, assumed to have been building-plots though often lacking surface signs of any structure, to be seen within some unexcavated hill-forts. Without excavation there can usually be little hope of establishing the coexistence of separate structures or platforms, let alone resolving the other dilemmas that beset even the more informative of excavated sites. Nonetheless, there have been attempts to utilize such suspect and fragmentary evidence for the purpose of gauging the populations of particular hill-forts.

The stone 'hut-circles' which characterize a number of hill-forts in the

Figure 20. Mam Tor, Derbys., from the north-west. The more steeply sloping parts of the 6.4ha enclosed by the bivallate defences are pock-marked by recessed platforms (photograph Cambridge University Collection, copyright reserved).

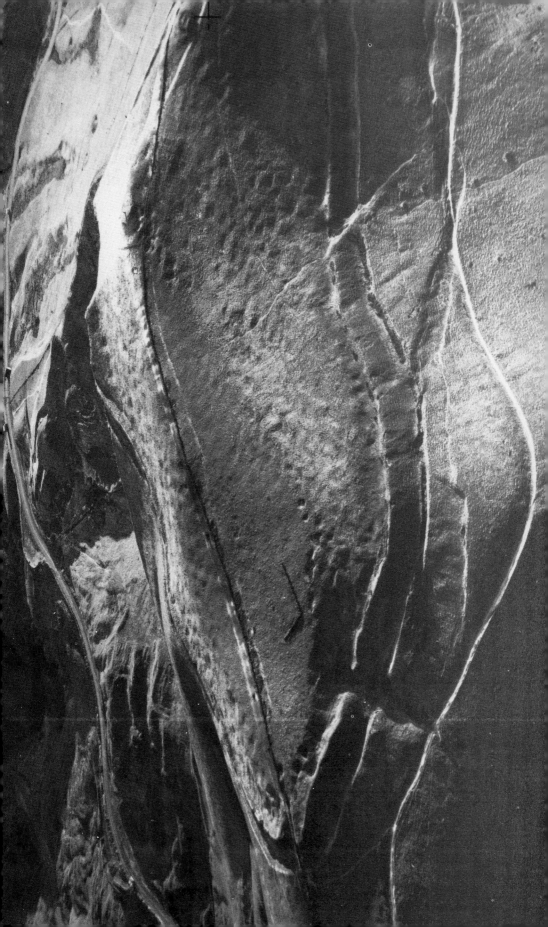

Lleyn Peninsula (e.g. fig. 19) have provided the material for Dr Hogg's own most explicit contributions to this field (1960: 22–3; 1971: 114). The population totals he produced for his principal example, Garn Boduan, have been queried by Alcock (1965: 194) and in turn defended by Hogg (1971: 118), but it is not my intention to juggle the same data again in search of fresh insight – one set of dubious statistics is as good, or as worthless, as another, because the dwelling assumption pervades the whole debate.[10] Besides, the considerable gaps between the recordable structures pose an intractable problem, generally conveniently ignored, for those bent on wresting conclusions from these largely unexcavated sites – were they, for instance, occupied by timber structures which are now undetectable superficially, or were they really the open spaces which at first sight they may seem?

North Wales is not alone in affording visible remains of hut-walls inside hill-forts and, hence, attracting conjectural estimates of population. Thus, for example, Cunliffe (1974a: 254) has made use of the unploughed portion of the interior of Hod Hill in Dorset to arrive at a possible range of figures for the whole of that site. But there is no need to dwell further on this matter here, for the assumptions are the same wherever the hill-fort.

In discussing various lines of inquiry into prehistoric settlement populations, Alcock (1965: 192) and Atkinson (1972a: 64) have each put forward the same hypothesis that the 'total of houses'/'total number of buildings' standing at the height of the period of occupation can, for suitable hill-forts, be assessed merely by counting the scooped platforms so often encountered where much of the enclosed land is sloping (e.g. fig. 20). It ought to be added that neither of them ventured an actual count of heads for any individual site on this basis, though others have been tempted (e.g. Feachem 1966: 79; Hogg 1971: 115; 1976: 9–10).

Before its progressive destruction by quarrying during the past quarter century, the northern and eastern slopes of the domed interior of Dinorben, Clwyd, were bestrewn with recessed platforms of just the sort under discussion (fig. 21). As it happens, there is a strong possibility that, because of the dense vegetation-cover, the total of platforms mapped at Dinorben does not faithfully represent the number that once existed. For this reason, plus the occurrence within the c. 2.3 ha enclosure of some areas of more gentle gradient where terracing would not have been a necessary prelude to building,[11] this hill-fort would not meet the requirements of the Alcock/Atkinson method. Nevertheless, there is one aspect of the platforms at Dinorben which is relevant to their theory and which merits our consideration.

One of the undertakings of the most recent rescue excavations at Dinorben was the stripping of an area of bedrock which sloped naturally by 20–30° and which, before excavation, displayed numerous flattish platforms of curvilinear outline. The final results are adumbrated in fig. 22 where it will be seen that the distribution of rock-cut features, few provably post-holes but many presumed to be so, obeyed no intelligible pattern on the floors of most platforms. Only in the case of that numbered 35 can the features be, hesitantly, interpreted as the ground-plan of a building (Guilbert 1978: 182–3), but it is

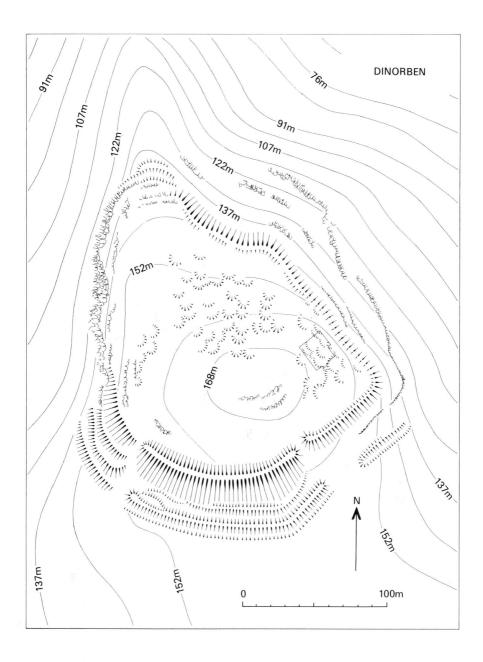

Figure 21. Plan of Dinorben showing hill-fort earthworks and recessed platforms in relation to contours. The area outlined in the eastern part of the hill-fort is that shown in fig. 22. (After Gardner and Savory 1964: figs. 2 and 3, and Savory 1971: fig. 2, with amendments in the south-east corner, by permission of the National Museum of Wales.)

platform 32b which commands attention here, because no features at all were recognized in its floor and we must therefore infer either that no structure had ever stood there or that that which did so left no imprint upon the rock. This writer has been at pains to illustrate from evidence unearthed at Moel y Gaer that a wooden stake-built structure, like that recorded on a clay-cut platform in another part of Dinorben (*ibid.*: 188), would be unlikely to make much impression on a hard rock floor (Guilbert 1975a: 217–19), though this need not have prevented its construction. I have also joined others (e.g. Alcock 1965: 190; Barker 1970; Harding 1974: 52) in acknowledging the very real possibility that timber-framed buildings with walls founded upon ground-level cill-beams could defeat our powers of detection entirely (Guilbert 1975a: 214; 1976: 305–6); and there are other forms of structure employing, say, cob or turf or other perishable materials, or even stone, which could disappear or be removed to leave no tangible trace. Moreover, it must be admitted that the highly-jointed limestone of Dinorben is not the best medium in which to identify even shallow post-holes. So it would be foolhardy to declare that the blank platform 32b had always been structurally barren – rather, what we have here may be more a case of absence of evidence than evidence of absence.

Imponderables of interpretation aside, however, 32b at Dinorben is a graphic reminder that such platforms *may* not all be what we might wish to think, that they *may* not all have been intended to carry buildings.[12] Many outdoor activities would have been facilitated by level ground, and it could well be that, in order to make best use of the steeply sloping areas within many hill-forts, working-platforms were sometimes created, perhaps scattered among building-platforms or perhaps, in some instances, grouped together in a 'working quarter'. The initial input of labour required to quarry platforms would surely have been fully requited with the daily convenience subsequently enjoyed, in a permanently occupied settlement anyway; and the sprinklings of post-holes which cannot be integrated convincingly as building-plans on some platforms at Dinorben and elsewhere (e.g. Forde *et al.* 1963: 145–7; Brewster 1963: 29–43) may be explicable as wind-breaks, work-benches, washing-lines, or whatever.

The identification of superficially featureless platforms with buildings goes back to at least the eighteenth century,[13] but, despite their frequent occurrence in some regions of Britain (e.g. Forde-Johnston 1976: 109–19 which is by no means exhaustive even for southern Britain), surprisingly few have been excavated. There is, however, good evidence from excavations, both inside hill-forts (e.g. Cadbury Castle – Alcock 1972: pl.53; Guilbert 1975a: 215, fig.3) and on unenclosed sites (e.g. Green Knowe – Feachem 1961), and, rarely, from surface indications, in the form of a ring-groove (e.g. Yeavering Bell – Jobey 1965: 32, fig.8) or a stone-footing (e.g. Pen y Gaer, Llanbedr y Cennin – RCAHMW 1956: 101), to show that certain platforms did accommodate buildings; and it is only the prevalent assumption that *all* platforms on supposed settlement sites can be equated with buildings, worse still dwellings, which is impugned here. If a generic name is to be

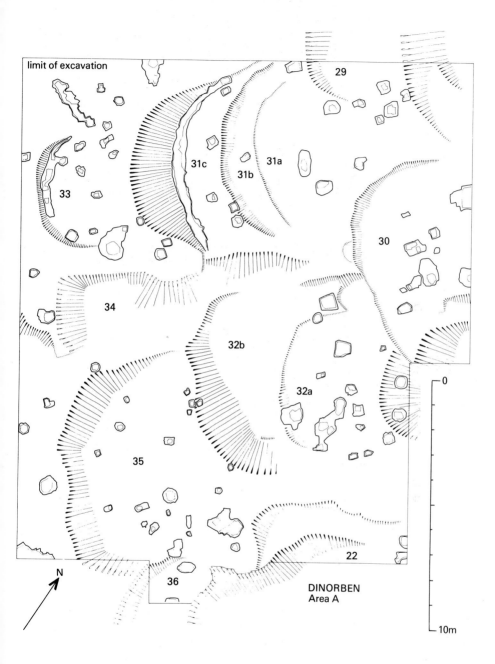

limit of excavation

29

31c

31a

31b

33

30

34

32b

32a

35

0

22

DINORBEN
Area A

N

36

10m

Figure 22. Simplified plan of an area excavated inside Dinorben in 1977–8. Hachures represent the back-scarps of recessed platforms (34 is a relatively recent quarry); rock-cut features are outlined at top and base.

given to examples whose former usage has yet to be determined, a stricter adherence to some such non-committal term as 'recessed platforms' might serve hill-fort studies better than any of the abundance of presumptuous epithets now in common use.[14] We must also learn to live with the unpalatable truth that excavation may often be incapable of demonstrating either the former presence of a building on a platform or its function even if one can be found. At any rate, the conclusion that unexcavated platforms should not be employed as population indices is inescapable.

The ideas and sentiments expressed in this paper are not all original, other writers having previously commented more succinctly, and more abstractly, upon much the same themes (e.g. Atkinson 1972b: 108; Jobey 1974: 17; Cunliffe 1978: 11). But it is not unusual for these and other fundamental constraints to be waved aside so as to clear the way for demographic conjecture on a wider scale. The sole object here has been to air these issues of function more fairly than is generally their lot and thereby to emphasize certain weaknesses inherent in received attitudes towards hill-forts. Doubtless there are people who will choose to dismiss these strictures as a brand of puritanism with no rightful place in the mind of the prehistorian whose province is inference from whatever proportion of the surviving evidence has so far been acquired and about all manner of aspects of the human past. Nobody could deny that prehistory, as we know it, is largely built on inference, and, if I may dare to compare opinions, I, like Wheeler (1954: 3), would as soon collect bus-tickets as excavate and fail to seek meanings. But there is, or should be, a difference between inference and guesswork, and if we cannot reach a conclusion via the former it is mistaken to resort to the latter. In the case in point, guessing at the functions and populations of individual 'settlements' will provide an unreliable base not only for the broader investigation of demography, which, rightly, is held by many to be vital to a proper appreciation of the dynamics of prehistoric societies (e.g. Atkinson 1972b: 107; Stanford 1972: 307; Smith C. 1977: 55–7; Cunliffe 1978: 3,22–4; Renfrew 1973: 114–16), but especially for the elucidation of first-millennium BC, perhaps also to some extent mid-first-millennium AD (Fowler 1971; Burrow 1979a), settlement patterns, which in some parts of Britain currently appear to pivot upon the functions of the hill-forts. Even where there is genuine inference from observed 'facts' (à la Piggott S. 1965: 5) at the root of an interpretation, there is still great danger in the secondary and tertiary inferences whose validity diminishes with increasing remoteness from the hard evidence and increasing dependence upon one another rather than the facts. The evaluation of hill-fort populations normally involves several stages of inference mixed with guesswork.

Due deference to the archaeological evidence inevitably leads to a recognition that, worthy aims as they may be, certain realms of prehistory fall beyond the sound bounds of inference, at least in so far as these are delimited by the present quantity and nature of the evidence. That inference regarding hill-fort functions and populations may some day be made more legitimate by additional evidence and, in particular, by future developments in the scope of the archaeological discipline is ever a possibility. All the same, prehistorians might do well to content themselves in the pursuit of those facets of knowledge and interpretation that lie within their contemporary archaeological grasp. In this I would echo Barry Cunliffe's recent viewpoint (1977) – maybe the time has come to show a greater respect for the limitations of our evidence.[15]

Notes

1. Some people may feel that the term 'hill-fort' is a little strong in the context of a palisaded enclosure but, as I have suggested elsewhere (1977: 47–8), there is no apparent reason to suppose that the stimulus to build this fence was much different from that which gave rise to many a rampart, especially considering the defensible hilltop siting (cf. Feachem 1966: 62; Challis and Harding 1975: i, 101; Avery 1976: 2–4).

2. The excavated portions of three of the post-ring round-houses shown in fig. 17 could not have included a central hearth. So the proportion of round-houses with hearths to those without should be recorded as 11:15.

3. The sites of any local settlements in this or any other way associated with Moel y Gaer remain to be discovered.

4. For the purposes of this paper it should be stressed that the term 'round-house' is a convention and should not necessarily be construed to mean that such structures were residential or, for that matter, exactly circular.

5. In fairness, it should be added that none of these writers, nor many of the others whose ideas are here, for the sake of debate, adduced out of context, proposed any blanket interpretation of these structural types as a whole.

6. The soil at Moel y Gaer has a pH of around 4, acidic enough to dissolve bone and, apparently, metalwork too. And it can be stated that not a single item among the numerous 'domestic' artifacts (including coarse pottery, quernstones, spindle-whorls, whetstones, and other stone implements) recovered by excavation can un-equivocally be counted among the possessions of those who built and maintained, for whatever purpose, the Phase 2 hill-fort.

7. Ritual is not, of course, the only possible explanation of ostentation in hill-fort rampart design. John Collis and Ian Ralston (following many others – e.g. Avery *et al.* 1967: 250–1; Rivet 1971: 189) have both reminded us, on pp. 75 and 84 above, that prestige may have been a powerful factor in some instances.

8. Of all the possible interpretations of particular four-posters that I have seen opined in print, 'fighting-platforms' and 'watch-towers' (Ellison and Drewett 1971: 186–8; Dixon 1973: 8; Jackson and Ambrose 1978: 130–1) and 'guard-huts' or the like (Forde *et al.* 1963: 145; Dixon 1973: 8; Challis and Harding 1975: i, 150) are the only ones that I find it impossible rationally even to contemplate for the rows of four-posters at Moel y Gaer; (and it need hardly be said that their authors would surely agree in this context). Incidentally, I would reject the grounds given by Ellison and Drewett for suggesting that Grimthorpe structures 5 to 8 were probably fighting-platforms – for one thing, the 'settlement-edge location' of the four-posters recorded at Grimthorpe may be illusory owing to the bias of the excavated sample (cf. Cunliffe 1974a: 259) and to the heavy plough-erosion (Stead 1968: 152, 155, 158).

9. Similar reservations have been expressed before (Cunliffe 1974a: 259; May 1974: 398; Boon 1975: 120; Guilbert 1975a: 209). The riskiness of extrapolating the full plan of Croft Ambrey in this way can be readily illustrated by running a templet of the limit of excavation of Croft Ambrey Site F, as seen in Guilbert 1975a: fig. 2, across the plan of the excavated area of Moel y Gaer Phase 2, seen at the same scale in Guilbert 1975a: fig. 1, and observing the variety of results thus attainable.

10. To be fair again, it should be noted that Hogg and Alcock, in company with most others who dabble in population estimates, recognized the assumptions involved in their calculations; also that Hogg has subsequently owned the frequent impossibility of distinguishing structures of diverse function (1973: 17).

11. At Moel y Gaer, ground sloping by up to c. 1 in 16 was commonly used for round-houses without need of terracing; and in certain circumstances a slope of greater than 1 in 10 was tolerated for a round-house or a four-poster.

12. It should perhaps be stated that no positive evidence for any other function was recovered from any of the platforms excavated at Dinorben in 1977–8.

13. Christison (1894: 116–19) described 'foundation-spaces for huts' at Eildon Hill

North in Roxburghshire, citing Milne's identification of 'huts' there in the eighteenth century; but, barring a few isolated examples such as 'hut-sites' at Moel Trigarn in Dyfed (Baring Gould *et al.* 1900: 194, 200), the interpretation did not become common practice for some time, so that even Allcroft made no mention of platforms in his review of 'traces of habitations' (1908: 252–5).

14. A scan of publications cited elsewhere in this paper yields the following variety of terms for unexcavated platforms: 'hut-floors' (Gardner and Savory 1964: 52–3), 'hut-emplacements' (Hogg 1976: 10), 'hut terraces' (Stanford 1974b: 46), 'hut platforms' (Jobey 1965: 36), 'hut-circles' (Cunliffe 1974a: 255), 'huts'/'hut remains' (Forde-Johnston 1976: 109–19), 'house-floors' (Feachem 1966: 79), 'house platforms' (Forde *et al.* 1963: 145), 'house-sites' (Atkinson 1972a: 64), 'houses' (Cunliffe 1974a: 260), 'building platforms' (Guilbert 1976: 303), 'buildings' (Atkinson 1972a: 64), and, even more loaded because they specifically advance a secondary supposition of function for the supposed structures, 'habitations' (Forde-Johnston 1976: 109–10) and 'dwellings' (Alcock 1965: 192). Other variations on much the same lines would not be hard to find.

15. Compare also, for example, Smith M. A. 1955 or Piggott S. 1959: 7–12.

IAN BURROW

Hill-forts after the iron age: the relevance of surface fieldwork

'I have been greatly deceived at times by the external appearance of earth-works...' A. Pitt Rivers, *Excavations in Bokerly and Wansdyke, Dorset and Wilts.* (1892: xi).

Introduction

The assumption that the vast majority of the larger and more complex hill-fort defensive schemes at present known in the British Isles were constructed in the pre-Roman iron age is one which need not be seriously challenged. However, the increasing number of instances in which dates both earlier and later can now be demonstrated for such schemes should at least alert us to the possibility that there may be quantifiable differences between iron age defences and those pre- or post-dating them. It is only by very extensive and long-term survey and excavation programmes that such differences will be finally defined, and the limitations of deductions made on the basis of surface indications alone need not be stressed here. Nevertheless, this paper attempts to discuss ways in which this subject may be approached by non-excavational fieldwork in a limited geographical area, in relation to Roman and post-Roman hill-fort use. The basic assumptions behind the work discussed below are that data relevant to post-iron age activity on hill-fort sites is identifiable in the surface evidence, and that hill-fort studies have not in general been sufficiently concerned with this matter in the past to seek out and analyse this data. The future of the study will depend largely on high-quality survey and description of hill-fort structures; the many detailed analyses of the visible remains of these sites for which A. H. A. Hogg has been responsible are a model for emulation, and they have provided much of the inspiration for the fieldwork on which this paper is based (Burrow 1979b).

Roman and post-Roman hill-fort earthworks

While the evidence specifically related to the *construction* and use of defensive systems of hill-fort type, subsequent to the Roman conquest of the Lowland Zone of Britain, remains small in quantity, indications that hill-fort *sites* continued to be frequented are much more common. In the Roman period the evidence comes largely from unstratified finds in the interiors of sites, and indicates uses ranging from casual visits, through a continuing or revived religious importance, to large-scale and permanent occupation. Evidence for the latter has been most frequently forthcoming in areas where Roman control may have been insecure at various times, in particular in Wales (Simpson G. 1964), or in those parts of Britain lying outside the Roman Province. However, material from sites in the Civil Zone is sufficiently plentiful to indicate that sizeable populations may have continued to live in major hill-forts, although the state of their defences is unknown.[1] In Somerset, the area to be considered in more detail below, 25 per cent of known hill-forts and enclosures have produced Roman material, and in the majority of *excavated* examples there is evidence for activity within the Roman period. It seems probable that hill-forts formed an element in the Romano-British settlement pattern to which more attention might profitably be paid in the future, though it is difficult at present to envisage such sites retaining all their iron age functions, at least in the Civil Zone.

Crucial to any appreciation of the role of hill-forts in the Roman period, and later, is the condition of their defences. Were they refurbished, left to decay, or merely (the most difficult of the three to identify) maintained? In the majority of cases we have no useful data because earlier techniques of examination of hill-fort defences were not capable of recording such information, and it is only with the extensive stripping of lengths of rampart that reliable answers to this question can be hoped for (Guilbert 1975b). Nevertheless some indications of the range of possibilities can be given. Firstly it is clear that outside the Roman Province hill-fort construction continued, both in Scotland (Traprain Law – Jobey 1976) and Ireland (Freestone Hill – Raftery 1969). Within the Civil and Military Zones evidence of this sort is generally lacking, though one may guess that in Wales at least some large hill-forts may have retained very much their iron age appearance and function in the Roman period (Savory 1976b: 282–91).[2]

At the smaller end of the size range, evidence for the continuing occupation and construction of enclosures of 'rath' type is relatively plentiful, quite large-scale defensive works – indistinguishable morphologically from those of iron age date – being recorded at various sites. While the apparently uninterrupted development of the rath tradition in Ireland well into the first millennium AD and later is unremarkable (O'Kelly 1970), the construction of similar sites in areas under Roman control raises a number of questions about the degree to which traditional settlement patterns were affected by the Roman administration which will not be enlarged on here. The best-documented examples come from west and south-west Britain (Wainwright G. J. 1971; Miles and Miles 1974), but it must be wondered how many sites further east, and now surviving only as crop marks, may ultimately produce similar data.

At Kingsdown in Somerset, for example, a small enclosure located in an area containing several villas, close to a major Roman road and only 12km from Bath, was refurbished after AD 133 (on coin evidence – Gray 1930: 66). The defences consisted of a dry-stone wall 2.5m thick fronted by a V-shaped ditch averaging 1.6m deep, the original maximum vertical difference between wall top and ditch bottom being perhaps as much as 4m. Both the technique of defence and the character of the site as a whole indicate the continuity of iron age practices even in such an intensively 'Romanized' area as east Somerset. So it would appear that, even if large hill-forts suffered extensive abandonment and decay, small enclosures may have continued the constructional traditions of iron age defences right through the Roman period. It is evident, however, that even in the south and east of Britain large hill-forts were not wholly abandoned, and modifications to their defences did take place in some instances. The eastern gateway at Maiden Castle, Dorset, was remodelled in association with the fourth- to fifth-century AD re-use of the interior (Wheeler 1943: 77, 120–2), and major refurbishment of the earthworks of Lydney, Gloucestershire, was undertaken, again in a primarily late Roman religious context (Wheeler and Wheeler 1932: 63–5). A possible non-religious example is Garden Hill, Sussex (Money 1974). The weight of present evidence does suggest, however, that even though the interiors of many hill-forts may have been intensively used for various purposes throughout the Roman period their defences were usually allowed to decay, although their defensive potential remained considerable.

Evidence for hill-fort use in the centuries after AD 400 is becoming relatively plentiful, especially from Highland Zone areas, and the material has been summarized elsewhere (Alcock 1971; Fowler 1971; Laing 1975b). The means by which sites have been dated to this period are relevant to the present discussion and must be briefly considered. In a number of cases documentary sources suggest that known locations were in use as fortified settlements at this time. Although the historical references cannot always be securely linked to features now identifiable on the ground, the nuclear forts of Scotland, apparently a regional type, were isolated in this way by Stevenson (1949), and the typology was extended to other sites by Feachem (1955; 1966) with a number of additional types proposed on the basis of artifactual evidence and relative sequences observed in the field. This model is one which the writer's research has sought to develop in a more limited geographical area, the county of Somerset, though similar typological criteria for the identification of post-Roman defended sites in Wales could not be identified (Alcock 1971: 14), and the chances of doing so elsewhere might initially be regarded as equally slight.

Written sources mention a number of sites in the British Isles, but the recognition of the majority of the known post-Roman defended sites has been directly by archaeological means. The number of sites with 'traditional' or legendary associations with the period which have on excavation been shown in fact to have been in use at this time (e.g. Dinas Emrys, Caernarvonshire; Mote of Mark, Kirkcudbright; Cadbury-Camelot, Somerset; Glastonbury Tor, Somerset) does suggest that this type of evidence should not be disregarded (see also Alcock, below).

Direct archaeological evidence has only rarely been found as a result of a deliberate fieldwork campaign. The best-known defended site of this period, Dinas Powys, Glamorgan, was excavated as part of research into the Welsh iron age (Alcock 1963: 6–8); work at Cadbury Congresbury, Somerset, began as an attempt to locate a suspected Roman site (Fowler *et al.* 1970: 9); and the post-Roman character of the defences of High Peak, Devon, was similarly unanticipated (Pollard 1966). Casual finds of the, at present, crucial dating evidence of imported Mediterranean or 'Gaulish' pottery have for the most part provided the first indication that a particular site was used in this period. The discovery of probable post-Roman amphora sherds among the material from Ham Hill, Somerset,[3] demonstrates the need for a systematic search of pottery collections from hill-forts for the identification of new sites.

The present total of known sites is therefore unlikely to be at all representative, and the overall distribution, both geographically and in terms of the types of site, is probably highly misleading. The recognition that the large hill-forts of Cadbury-Camelot and Cadbury Congresbury were in use in this period immediately qualifies Alcock's model of the probable role and size of defended sites after AD 400. He suggested that the generally small size of such sites, as then known, was related to their social function as the residences of local rulers and that their military importance was slight (Alcock 1971: 346–9). The model was developed chiefly to explain data from Highland Zone areas, and it seems probable that no universal pattern of hill-fort usage will in fact be identified in Britain between c. AD 400 and 700. Just as in the iron age, we must anticipate wide regional differences in the purposes to which hill-fort sites were put, the types of site chosen, and the techniques used in the construction or refurbishment of defences.[4]

Even on present evidence it is clear that constructional techniques follow closely those in use in the iron age, and owe relatively little to Roman exemplars (but cf. Alcock 1972: 176–7; Laing 1977). Techniques employed include simple dump construction, probably surmounted by palisades (e.g. Dinas Powys – Alcock 1963: 27–8), stone revetments (e.g. High Peak – Pollard 1966: 43), timber-lacing (e.g. Mote of Mark – Laing 1973a: 122–3; Cadbury-Camelot – Alcock 1972: 175–7), turf-built construction (e.g. Traprain Law – Feachem 1956: 289), and stone walls (e.g. Dinas Emrys – Savory 1960: 21–8). Very few entrances have yet been excavated and fully published, but the elaborate defensive schemes of the larger iron age forts do not seem to be generally repeated.[5]

The fieldwork contribution

It is necessary at this point to consider the character of the data which is being sought from fieldwork. Of the three situations outlined above, refurbishment, decay or maintenance of *existing* defences, only the first is likely to show any surface trace. This might be expected to manifest itself either by abrupt breaks in the surface profile of ramparts, indicating that a decayed structure has been heightened and rebuilt, or by evidence of alterations to specific features such as gateways, or additions to, or major changes of, plan. The identification of *relative sequences* should therefore be a primary aim of fieldwork, hill-forts with complex earthwork defences being the obvious targets for detailed study.

It must be questioned, however, to what extent such evidence as that produced by the postulated refurbishment of existing ramparts will have survived in a recognizable form to the present. Such evidence may only be identifiable by excavation, for much may have been lost to erosion which will render definitions of earthwork types, based on their apparent profiles, of dubious validity.

While it may be that the majority of hill-fort sites producing evidence of Roman or later use will be found to be older sites re-occupied, the instances cited above indicate that completely new sites were constructed also. There is always the possibility that such new enclosures will show features which set them apart from their iron age counterparts – differences of location, size and plan being those which might be identified from fieldwork alone. Research to substantiate such a suggestion seems best directed towards the examination of the data from all the hill-forts within a limited area in order to search for groups of characteristics which seem 'anomalous' against the general background (Hogg 1972a; 1972b).

The crucial factor, that of absolute date, is one which no amount of fieldwork and surface analysis can finally resolve. Any attempt to apply fieldwork techniques to the study of post-iron age hill-fort usage must therefore seek to set the earthwork evidence against as many dated examples as possible, and this dictates to a great extent the choice of the area to be considered in detail.

Somerset hill-forts after the iron age

The region to be discussed here is that of the former county of Somerset, an area of some 4200 sq. km containing a minimum of 89 hill-forts and related enclosures, ranging in size from the 85ha of Ham Hill, to small hill-slope enclosures of less than 0.1ha. It was chosen for study for several reasons. There is definite evidence for the re-use and refurbishment of Cadbury Congresbury and Cadbury-Camelot, and the other post-Roman evidence known up to 1972 had previously been summarized (Rahtz and Fowler 1972). Twenty-six other hill-forts in the area have been excavated, although mostly on a small scale, and Roman finds have been recorded from about a quarter of the total sampled. In addition, Somerset lies within the known area of distribution of post-Roman imported pottery, and new finds of this material can be anticipated.

Against these advantages must be set Somerset's lack of regional coherence. Physically it straddles the boundary between Highland and Lowland Britain; the sandstone uplands of Exmoor, the Brendons and the

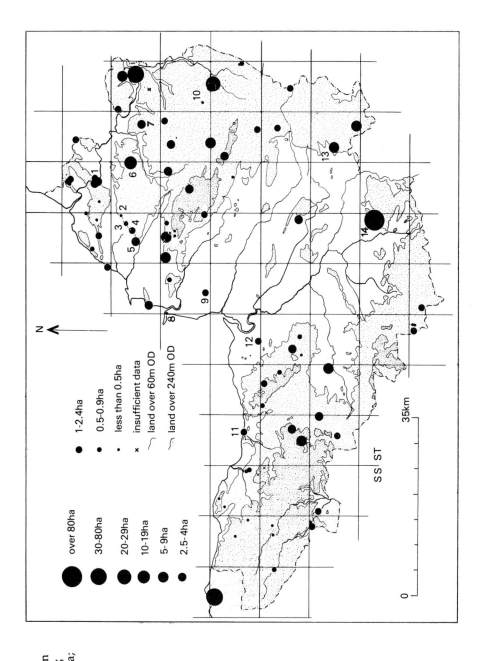

Figure 23. Distri-
bution of hill-forts in
Somerset, showing
size of enclosed area;
sites mentioned in
the text are num-
bered as in the
figure.

1 Clifton Camp
2 Backwell
3 Tap's Combe
4 Cleeve Toot
5 Cadbury Con-
　gresbury
6 Maes Knoll
7 Stantonbury
8 Brean Down
9 Brent Knoll
10 Kingsdown
11 Daw's Castle
12 Cannington
13 Cadbury-
　Camelot
14 Ham Hill

Quantocks being separated by the Somerset Levels from the complex geology and relief of south and east Somerset, areas which are much more fertile and 'lowland' in character. This basic division can, however, be seen as an advantage in that contrasts between the two areas may be viewed as a microcosm of the situation in Britain as a whole. To the west, small enclosures predominate, with a minimum of 30 sites averaging 2.4ha in area. To the east, 53 sites give an average size value of 4.8ha, reflecting the greater preponderance of larger multivallate sites in this area.[6]

Initial consideration of the hill-fort data concentrated on two factors, size and location (fig. 23), in order to identify any groupings or apparently anomalous sitings. In neither case were significant features noted. A plot of hill-fort sizes shows a sharp decrease from the first to the fifth largest sites (from 85ha to 12ha), but beyond this there is a very gradual diminution in size with no sharp break between 'hill-forts' and 'enclosures' at the lower end of the size range; no groupings could be detected. An analysis of the location of sites in relation to geology, relief and soils shows that enclosures of all sizes are overwhelmingly concentrated along the interfaces between different topographical areas, presumably because a greater range of land resources is readily available in such locations. The concentration of hill-forts along the edges of the Carboniferous Limestone plateaux of north Somerset, close to fertile 'head' deposits on the edge of the Levels (whose economic potential was probably also considerable), illustrates this point. With few exceptions, hill-forts avoid extensive upland areas such as Mendip and the hills of west Somerset, and for the exceptions a specialized economic base may be suspected. The observed location pattern therefore leads us to a proposition put forward for another part of Britain (Alcock 1965) – namely, that hill-forts were constructed by communities having a mixed farming economy, with a view to the exploitation of a range of land and soil types within a reasonable distance of a defensible site. This pattern is presumably pre-Roman in origin, but the re-use of a number of these sites at later periods must at least raise the possibility that the same pressures motivated Roman, and more especially post-Roman, hill-fort re-occupations. Such a basic analysis therefore does little other than provide a broad framework against which to consider more detailed evidence.

The procedure next adopted was a simple typological classification of the Somerset hill-forts on the basis of the size of the enclosed area, the form and scale of the defences, and the use made of the local topography. The aim here was to investigate the possibility that some types of site might have a restricted distribution, or be especially associated with Roman or later evidence. Four broad groups were defined for the purpose of this exercise:

Group I   Strongly defended contour hill-forts (e.g. fig. 24), most of them over 1ha in area, are concentrated in the north and east of the area (fig. 23). It is from the 33 sites in this category that evidence of Roman and post-Roman activity is most plentiful.[7]

Group II   These sites share the common characteristic of defences which

Figure 24. Maesbury Camp, Croscombe, Som., from the east: a group I hill-fort on the Mendips (photograph West Air Photography, Weston-super-Mare, copyright reserved).

run up to clifftops at the edges of plateaux. The natural defences provided by cliffs define less than 50 per cent of the enclosed area. Nine sites fall into this category, none of which have been adequately examined by excavation, although one (Clifton Camp, Bristol: fig. 25) has produced Roman material, and an inhumation cemetery, possibly of early post-Roman date, was observed at another (Daw's Castle: fig. 26) in the nineteenth century (Page 1890: 241; Rahtz 1977). Three of the sites (one now destroyed) are within 4km of each other along the north-west flank of the limestone upland of Broad-field Down in north Somerset, two being shown in fig. 26. The device of using the natural defensive potential of a cliff seems an obvious one, but has only been utilized in a handful of cases in the area we are considering. The possibility that they do reflect a specific intrusive element into the general hill-fort pattern must be considered, however unfashionable such a suggestion may be at present. The common features, small-scale defences (the banks of the illustrated examples are 2m or less in height) and clifftop siting, and the close grouping of three of the sites, lend support to this argument. The suggestion that these enclosures have Irish affinities has been made elsewhere (Burrow 1974).

Group III   These are basically promontory forts in which natural slopes provide the main defence. A number of the larger examples of the 18 in this group have produced Roman material. One earthwork, that on Brean Down, was excavated on the hypothesis that its somewhat unusual L-shaped plan and its proximity to a Roman temple complex and sub-Roman cemetery increased the likelihood of a post-Roman date. The refutation of this suggestion by radiocarbon determinations is sufficient warning against drawing such conclusions from surface evidence alone (Burrow 1976).

Group IV   The remaining enclosures are weakly defended and broadly of 'rath' type. Eighteen of the 29 sites are of less than 0.5ha, though five possess outworks defining larger areas (e.g. fig. 27). Two sites have produced evidence of Roman occupation and construction, and two are probably iron age. The simplicity and lack of specialization of the earthworks of these little enclosures greatly limits the application of the approaches under discussion here. If more Roman and post-Roman sites are included among these enclosures, as seems highly likely, they are not distinguishable from iron age examples by any differences of plan or earthwork form.

It is amongst the large sites of group I that results of the greatest potential are forthcoming,[8] and, though the conclusions drawn can only be tentative, it must be considered probable that, in east and north Somerset at least, re-use of the larger hill-forts in both Roman and post-Roman times did occur on a considerable scale.

A start can be made with the earthworks of *Cadbury Congresbury*, which have been briefly described elsewhere (Fowler *et al.* 1970: 7–9). Here the perimeter bank, now shown by excavation to be of fifth/sixth-century AD date, does show distinctive features which can be tentatively identified at one other site. The bank has a flattened top, 3m in average width and about

Figure 25. Clifton Camp, Bristol, from the north: a group II hill-fort (photograph West Air Photography, Weston-super-Mare, copyright reserved).

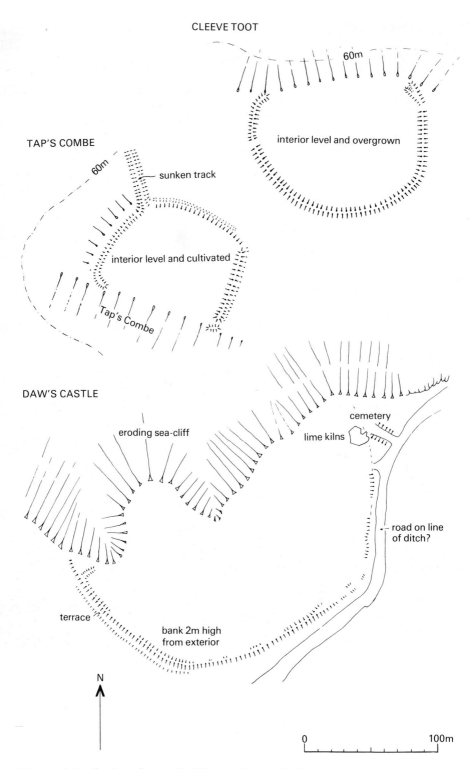

Figure 26. A selection of group II clifftop enclosures in Somerset.

Figure 27. Bury Camp, Selworthy, Som., from the south: a group IV enclosure, with outwork at the west (photograph West Air Photography, Weston-super-Mare, copyright reserved).

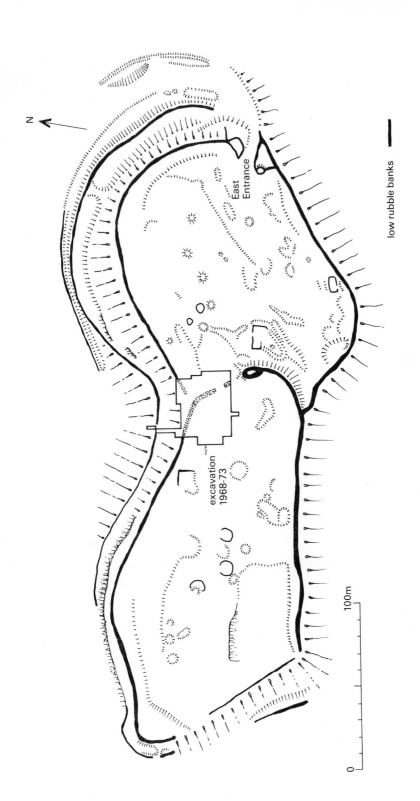

East
Entrance

excavation
1968-73

low rubble banks

100m

0

Figure 28. Cadbury Congresbury, Som. (after Rahtz).

0.5m high, set some 2–3m back from the edge of the steep, wooded slopes that delimit the plateau on all sides except the east (fig. 28). The complex arrangements at the east entrance consist of two irregularly looped enclosures flanking the gap in the bank. The northern enclosure consists of a curving length of bank, apparently added to the front of the perimeter bank, the whole forming a D-shaped structure of about 10 × 5m internally. The enclosure on the south side is more complex. It appears that here the main perimeter bank ends abruptly at the outer end of the entrance passage, in contrast to that on the north side, which is inturned. From the termination of the south bank a slighter bank returns westwards for about 20m and thence runs south to rejoin the main perimeter, thus defining a triangular area measuring 20m long by a maximum of 10m wide. At the western apex of this area is an embanked circle about 5m in diameter.

The total scheme appears therefore to comprise a simple inturn-outturn entrance to which small enclosures have been added in order to increase and emphasize the length of the entrance passage. The slight character of these earthworks, as well as their plan, sets them apart from iron age hill-fort entrances, and similar features might therefore be sought on other Somerset sites.

Only at *Brent Knoll*, 17km south-west of Cadbury Congresbury, has similar evidence been found. This hill-fort (figs. 29–31) is situated on a prominent, isolated Lias hill, rising about 135m above the surrounding Levels. The defences enclose an area of 1.6ha, much disturbed by quarrying in medieval and later times, from which considerable quantities of Roman material, including substantial evidence of a building (perhaps a temple), have been recovered (Skinner). The only visible entrance is on the east side where modifications similar to those at Congresbury appear to have taken place (fig. 30). The front of the inner bank on each side of the entrance appears to have been disturbed subsequent to its construction, the material being pushed outwards to form hollow, 'bastion-like' structures with slight outer banks. The scale of these earthworks and the areas they enclose are closely similar to those at Congresbury, but a major difference between the two sites is the positioning of the additions which were both made to the outer side of the inner bank and on a steep slope at Brent Knoll (fig. 31). If it is assumed that the basic defensive structure of the inner bank of Brent Knoll is of iron age date, in apparent contrast to Congresbury, then the slightly different arrangement can be explained. Despite later quarrying which has obscured the earthworks, it appears from surface indications that the original entrance was inturned, and it would thus have been difficult to construct the slight enclosures at the rear of the entrance without demolishing lengths of rampart in order to utilize the flatter ground in the interior. The construction of the enclosures as they stand was perhaps seen as a more economical alternative. At Brent Knoll it is thus possible tentatively to identify a Roman or post-Roman alteration to a hill-fort by analogy of field indications with a better-dated example. The function of these small added enclosures may be analogous to that of the 'guard-chambers' of iron age forts, but their irregular

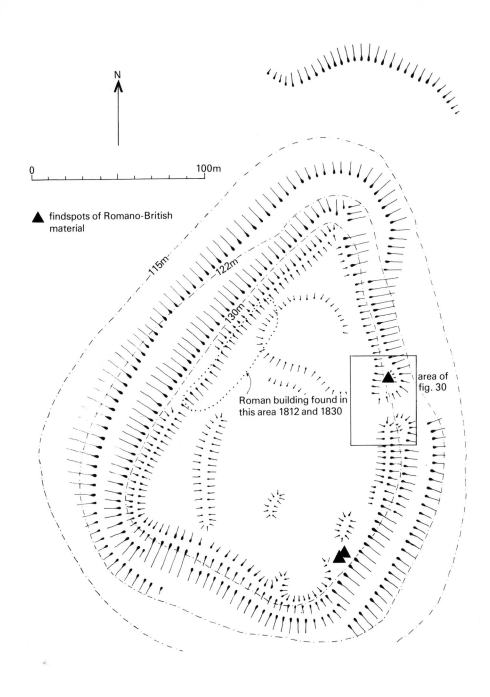

N

0 _____ 100m

▲ findspots of Romano-British
material

115m—

122m

130m

Roman building found in
this area 1812 and 1830

area of
fig. 30

Figure 29. Brent Knoll, Som. The area outlined is shown in fig. 30 (based on Ordnance Survey, Crown Copyright reserved).

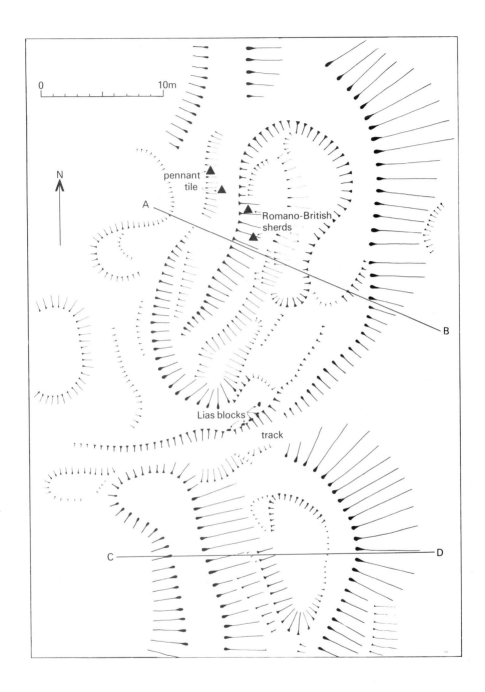

0   10m

N

pennant
tile

Romano-British
sherds

A

B

Lias blocks

track

C   D

Figure 30. Brent Knoll, Som.: the eastern entrance of the hill-fort. See fig. 31 for profiles at A–B and C–D.

shape argues against it. It may even be that the religious use suggested by excavation in the interiors of these sites is in some way reflected in these
entrance arrangements, and may therefore account for their apparently non-
defensive character.

The next site to be considered, *Cannington*, shows a relative sequence
which may extend from late Roman into later centuries (fig. 32). Summary
descriptions of the hill-fort and the adjacent cemetery have been published
elsewhere (Rahtz 1969; Rahtz 1977: 56–9). The hill-fort earthworks are set on
a rocky limestone knoll, the highest of three rising above the surrounding
land near the mouth of the River Parrett. Heavily overgrown, though
apparently bivallate, defences enclose a rocky, uneven interior of c. 1.8ha.
There are two entrances. That on the south emerges on to a gentle slope
measuring about 200m from north to south and running east–west along the
south side of the limestone outcrop. Along this side a third line of defence
protects the entrance (A on fig. 32), and excavations at the rear of this bank
have suggested that it might be a late Roman addition to the iron age scheme
(Rahtz 1969: 64–6).

Cannington is unique in Somerset in having extensive earthworks,
apparently of a settlement, immediately adjacent to its defences, the preservation of which is almost certainly due to the emparking of the area in the
middle ages. One wonders how many similar complexes have been lost to
cultivation elsewhere.

The earthworks consist of a series of enclosures, defined by banks, ditches
and scarps, extending along the slope outside the hill-fort and delimited on
the east side by a bank and slight outer ditch at the top of a steep drop of about
5m. Immediately to the west of this, three small enclosures (C, D and E on fig.
32) run down the slope from the outer bank of the hill-fort. Further enclosures
to the south have been obscured by quarrying. Against the bank on the east
side of C is a small sub-rectangular hollow measuring 10 × 6m overall (F).

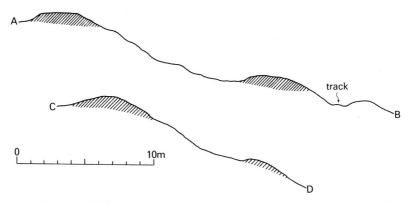

Figure 31. Brent Knoll, Som.: profiles across the entrance enclosures; the alignments
are shown in fig. 30.

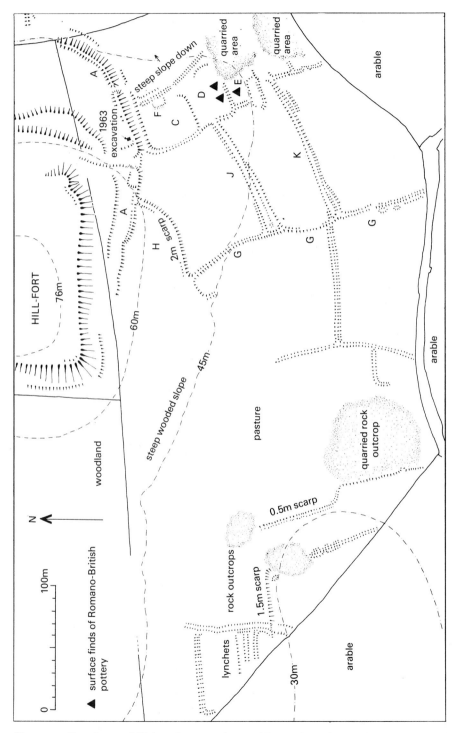

Figure 32. Cannington hill-fort, Som., and part of the earthwork complex to the south.

Areas trampled by cattle in D and E have yielded black-burnished ware and samian, as well as a little iron age pottery. 100m west of these enclosures a continuous bank (G) defines the west side of three further enclosures. These are divided by two complex linear features (J and K) which are interpreted as embanked trackways leading into the eastern enclosures (C, D and E) and those further south. Similar enclosures extend across the field to the west, including a flight of lynchet-like features at the extreme western end, and modern cultivation beyond the present field boundary has probably destroyed much more.[9]

Leaving aside for the moment the interpretation of these features, it is clear from the plan, and even more evident on the ground, that they post-date the construction of the outer bank (A) of the hill-fort. The crucial relationship is the junction between A and the combined scarp and bank (H) which runs up to it on the west side of the entrance. If the outer bank is indeed late Roman, as Rahtz has surmised, then the conclusion that the complex to the south is Roman or later can hardly be avoided. A medieval date, though not impossible, seems unlikely in view of evidence for emparking, the Roman surface finds, and the general form of the earthworks. It might be objected that the finds, for what they are worth as evidence, indicate an early Roman date for the complex, but evidence from Congresbury and elsewhere strongly suggests that Roman pottery, in particular samian ware, was current for many centuries after its manufacture, and a post-Roman date is not therefore impossible (Burrow 1979a).

The earthworks may be interpreted as those of a small settlement, with attendant fields to the west, which was created outside the main entrance to the hill-fort subsequent to the construction of the outer defence. This settlement was probably more extensive than surface indications suggest, as there were structures of late Roman or later date behind bank A also (Rahtz 1969: 64–6). Does this indicate that the hill-fort itself was not occupied, and that the settlement to the south was that of its former inhabitants? This view would, one suspects, be that favoured by many students of the period, and one piece of evidence may support it. At the outer (southern) end of the hill-fort entrance passage a sharp drop of about 30cm continues the line of the front of bank A. It is possible that this scarp has been produced by ploughing of the enclosure immediately to the south, and, if so, it would imply that this entrance to the hill-fort was not in use at that time. In view of the evidence from behind the rampart, however, the possibility of continuing occupation in the hill-fort cannot be ruled out.

Hill-forts are only rarely incorporated into post-Roman linear earthwork schemes. Fox (Fox C. 1955: 81–3) indeed argued that Offa's Dyke deliberately *avoided* the hill-fort of Pen-y-Gardden, and postulated that this was because the latter was in Welsh control at the time. The western defences of Llanymynech hill-fort were incorporated into the dyke, as were Old Oswestry on Wat's Dyke (*ibid.*: 249–50) and Chisbury on the Bedwyn Dyke (Fox and Fox 1960: 18–20). Despite the work of Fox and later research the precise function and historical context of these immense linear earthworks remains obscure, and thus the significance of the inclusion of hill-forts in their lines is difficult to assess. Fox postulated that the most likely motive was the value of the hills on which these hill-forts are located as vantage points from which the lines of the dykes could be set out, and that the pre-existing hill-fort defences were merely used to economize on labour and were not refurbished (Fox C. 1955: 158–9; Fox and Fox 1960: 32). The possibility must at least be entertained that the role of the hill-forts was more important than this minimal view would suggest. Current views of the military capabilities of migration period societies preclude the use of these sites as permanent forts for a patrolled frontier after the manner of Hadrian's Wall, but it may be wondered whether the considerable workforce required to construct the dykes did not make use of the considerable strength of existing hill-forts as protection in what, by definition, was an insecure border area. Such temporary occupation would probably leave little archaeological trace, unless the defences were refurbished. The historical evidence we possess suggests that these linear boundaries were constructed under the auspices of territorial rulers, and C. Thomas (1971: 33) has pointed out that hill-fort sites were probably regarded as in some way the property of these individuals. This may provide a historical context against which to set any archaeological data relating to the use of hill-forts in association with dykes.

West Wansdyke, running for 14.5km from the Jurassic Ridge south of Bath (where it crosses the Fosse Way) westward across undulating country south of the Somerset Avon, incorporates two large and complex hill-forts in its line. The previous accounts of the relationship between the dyke and the hill-forts (Fox and Fox 1960: 26–8, 30–2; Tratman 1963) can be challenged on a number of points, though the crucial question as to the use to which the hill-forts were put at the time of the construction of the dyke cannot be resolved.

The historical context of West Wansdyke, and its relation to the Wiltshire Wansdyke, have been discussed on several occasions (Myres 1964, with references). The pagan Saxon origin normally accepted is not considered by this writer to be the most probable, and a sub-Roman context in the fifth or sixth century is favoured. The only direct evidence of date, however, is a *terminus ante quem* given by a tenth-century charter.[10]

It can clearly be seen at *Stantonbury* that the complex earthworks of the hill-fort pre-date those of West Wansdyke (fig. 33).[11] Previous descriptions of the site have been inaccurate and misleading, due to the dense vegetation which was cleared only in 1974. The Fox study suggested that Wansdyke was not even physically joined to the hill-fort, but this is quite incorrect as it meets the earthworks of the latter at both the north-west and north-east corners and seems to have made use of the defences along the north side. The hill-fort itself, which is situated on a prominent east-west Oolite ridge rising some 60m above the surrounding land, consists of two enclosures. Only the western enclosure, of about 2ha, has been considered in earlier descriptions of the hill-fort. This is defined on the west and south by a bank very much obscured from the interior by ploughing, but possibly consisting of a massive dry-stone wall, on the evidence of the large Oolite blocks visible in places. The eastern side of this enclosure is delimited by a broad shallow ditch with a low, much spread, bank on its *east* side. There is no sign of a bank on the inner, western, side except at the north end. It seems probable that the bank here has been ploughed into the ditch. The defences on the north side are still prominent from the interior, the bank rising about 1m from the quarry hollow. On the exterior the bank drops about 5m to a flat terrace about 5m wide. This has a short length of bank on its outer edge immediately north of the point at which the ditch on the east side of the enclosure reaches the northern slope of the hill.

It seems clear that the western enclosure is primary in the sequence of visible earthworks. This is demonstrated particularly by the behaviour of the northern defences at the junction between the eastern and western enclosures. At this point there is a marked outward bulge and a drop of some 50cm in the main bank of the eastern enclosure, strongly suggesting that it here runs across the pre-existing eastern ditch of the western enclosure.

The eastern enclosure itself seems to be unfinished. On the south the hillside may have been artificially steepened for some distance but this does not join up with the defences of the western enclosure. Along the north side the defences are of the same profile as those of the western enclosure, although in places disturbed by quarrying, and have a well-defined quarry hollow at the rear for most of their length. About 50m from the junction with the western enclosure the ground is disturbed and the line of the 'quarry hollow' turns south-westwards to run across the summit plateau. There is a slight bank on the north-west side. These complications could conceivably be related to an intermediate stage of the extension of the western enclosure, but it seems more probable that a later trackway has made use of and enhanced the quarry hollow, before diverging from it to run across the hill to the south-west.

What is the relationship of Wansdyke to these two main enclosures? On the north-west it is evident that the dyke is secondary to the western enclosure. Wansdyke here is at its most impressive, being about 4m high and fronted by a ditch and counterscarp bank. It runs up the spine of the hill to meet the hill-fort's northern defences at an obtuse angle. Here the ditch and counterscarp bank end, and the crest of Wansdyke is some 50cm below that of the corner of the hill-fort. The visual impression is that Wansdyke runs up to a pre-existing feature at this point.

The relationship is not so clear at the north-east end. Here it at first appears that Wansdyke runs continuously along the hilltop from the eastern slope as far as the western enclosure. There is no change of scale in the earthwork at any point, although the counterscarp bank does fade out below the slight banks forming the eastern side of the eastern enclosure. An initial hypothesis might be that banks 1, 2 and 3 on fig. 33 were designed to run up to the pre-existing bank of Wansdyke, perhaps with an entrance passage formed between it and the bank terminals. If this were the case then we should have here an example of hill-fort type defences contemporary with or later than a post-Roman linear earthwork.

143

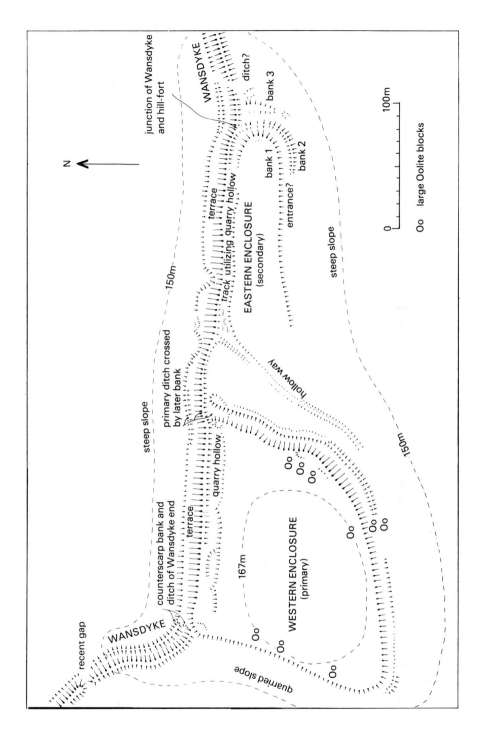

Figure 33. Stantonbury (*Merces Burh*), and Wansdyke, Som. (based on Ordnance Survey, Crown Copyright reserved).

Attractive though this idea is, it must be rejected for two reasons. In the first place it can be seen on the plan that there is a slight but definite change of direction where the Wansdyke bank converges on bank 1, suggesting that two periods of construction are involved. Secondly, although the use of the area immediately south of the Wansdyke bank as a track has severely degraded banks 2 and 3 of the eastern enclosure, bank 2 can be seen to be continuous and to determine the curve of 'Wansdyke' on the north side of the hill.

Wansdyke therefore appears to join a pre-existing earthwork at both the eastern and western ends of Stantonbury, but there is a possibility that the northern defences of the eastern and western enclosures were also refurbished at the time of its construction (Fox and Fox 1960: 32). The profile is strikingly similar along the whole length of the northern defences, and there may have been some additional scarping and refurbishment when Wansdyke was brought up to the hill-fort. The termination of the ditch and counterscarp bank of the dyke at the junction with the hill-fort would, however, suggest that the treatment of the pre-existing earthworks was, for some reason, different, if the suggestion that the builders of Wansdyke did modify them is accepted.

Thus, although it is possible to postulate a relative sequence at Stantonbury, and even to envisage some modification to the pre-existing earthworks, we cannot argue that the hill-fort itself was a major part of the Wansdyke scheme. One piece of documentary evidence may, however, reflect a greater importance for the site than might otherwise be allowed. Stantonbury is one of the few hill-forts mentioned by name in Anglo-Saxon charters, being recorded as *Merces Burh* in 941 (Sawyer 1968: no. 481). The first element is the OE *mearc* 'boundary', and, although the fort is used as a reference point on the charter bounds, which in itself is perhaps sufficient to account for the name, it must be considered probable that in the tenth century the hill-fort was thought to be linked in some way to the huge *mearc* formed by the *Ealdan Dic* of Wansdyke.

The western termination of Wansdyke was almost certainly on the plateau of Dundry Hill south of Bristol, despite documentary references which may imply a continuation westwards (Fox and Fox 1960: 37; Collinson 1791: 140). The hill-fort of *Maes Knoll* (figs. 34 and 35) lies at the eastern end of Dundry Hill, its enclosed area of c. 12ha being separated from the rest of the plateau by the large earthwork called the Tump. Along the western side any defences formerly extant have probably slumped down the unstable slope. A slight bank survives on the north side where the land falls away steeply, and the irregularity of the ground below indicates instability here also. At the south end there are at least two lines of defence, the innermost curving back northwards to form an inturned entrance, behind which iron age sherds were recovered in excavation (Rahtz and Barton 1963).[12] Along the east side of the hill-fort the arrangement of the earthworks is less easy to work out. Fox and Fox inexplicably described Wansdyke, approaching the hill-fort from the east-south-east, as ending some 75m from the eastern scarp of the hill-fort. The line of the ditch of the dyke is continued, in their view, by a 'typical hollow way' which runs up to the scarp and then turns northwards up the northern slope of the hill.

Neither Tratman (1963) nor the present writer accept this view. Careful examination of the ground beside the 'hollow way' reveals slight traces of a bank on the south side, and there seems every reason to believe that Wansdyke was in fact continued right up to the hill-fort, as at Stantonbury. Tratman argued that Wansdyke had been originally continued around the northern slope of the hill and terminated by the construction of the Tump. He also suggested that the line followed by the dyke on the east side was a new one which cut across pre-existing hill-fort defences and left an isolated length of bank and ditch to the north-east.

This hypothesis is not wholly satisfactory as it fails to explain why the builders of Wansdyke changed its alignment so markedly in the vicinity of the hill-fort. If it was intended to utilize the northern scarp of the fort it would seem more logical to have run the dyke directly towards it up the hill from the east. Moreover, it can be suggested that the line of north–south bank and ditch interpreted by Tratman as Wansdyke is in fact a northward continuation of the much ploughed-down scarp which runs as far as the south end of the fort. The plan of the area in which the Wansdyke ditch meets this scarp (fig. 35) suggests that Wansdyke was here brought up the existing (?)iron age defences. The bank and ditch of the dyke were taken across the hill-fort counterscarp, and the dyke ditch run along that of the hill-fort for a short distance and then terminated, the existing partly-silted hill-fort ditch being deemed sufficient beyond this point.

Both hill-forts on Wansdyke appear therefore to have had their still sizeable defences incorporated into the linear boundary. In neither case can it be suggested that the defences, other than those needed on the northern side to take the place of the dyke, were in any way refurbished or the interiors reoccupied. Any idea that the dyke was garrisoned must at this stage be firmly abandoned. So too must suggestions that any continuous patrolling of the dyke was intended. Were this so, one would imagine that unimpeded access along the rear and summit of the bank would have been required. The hill-fort earthworks of Stantonbury and Maes Knoll lie athwart any such required access and present an obstacle to movement along the back of the dyke which its constructors could readily have cleared away had they been so minded. The conventional view, that dykes were simply an emphatic expression of territoriality, does therefore seem to be supported by the way Wansdyke relates to these two hill-forts.

Conclusions

The hill-fort earthworks of Britain are a vast archaeological resource to which far more detailed attention can profitably be paid in the future. Until many more have received detailed examination and survey it is probable that generalizations about the identification by fieldwork of hill-fort usage in the

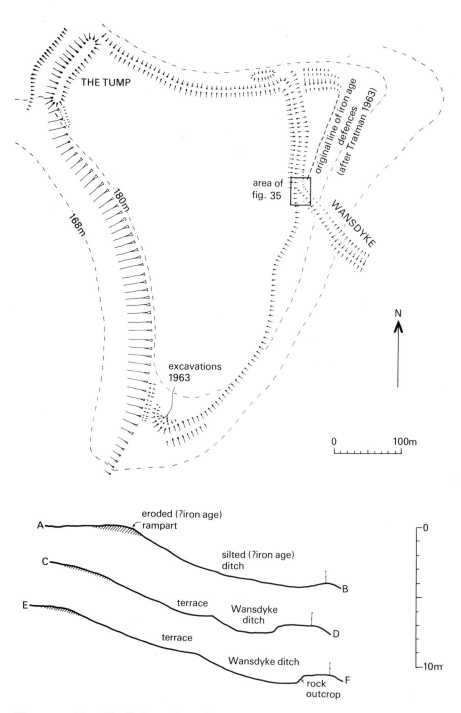

Figure 34. Maes Knoll, Som. (based on Ordnance Survey, Crown Copyright reserved), with profiles across the junction of the hill-fort and Wansdyke; the alignments are shown in fig. 35.

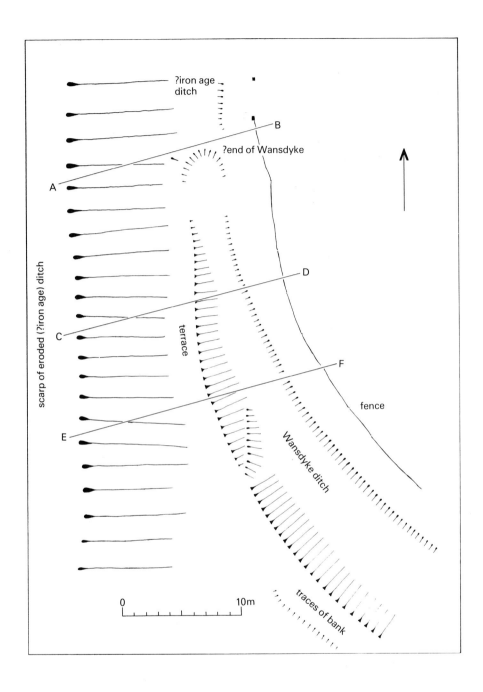

Figure 35. Maes Knoll, Som.: the junction of Wansdyke and the hill-fort.

centuries after the iron age would be premature in the extreme. This may seem pessimistic, but a close knowledge of the earthworks of smaller regions, and of the geological and archaeological framework in which they are set, may at this stage produce more useful results. Somerset is one area in which considerable archaeological work related to these problems has already been undertaken. It is also one in which the hill-forts themselves are particularly well preserved. Whether the approach outlined in this paper can be applied more generally might be questioned, but the regional treatment of the subject of Roman and post-Roman hill-fort use is being followed up at the time of writing (1978) in the adjacent area of Gloucestershire[13] and the results will make an interesting comparison with those presented here.

Notes

1. See the distribution map in Fowler (1971: fig. 39), which chiefly indicates the frequency with which Roman material occurs in hill-forts in western England.

2. For example, Tre'r Ceiri, Gwynedd (Hogg 1960). The question of the possible refurbishment of the defences of Dinoben remains problematic (Gardner and Savory 1964; and *ex inf*. G. Guilbert, excavations 1977–8).

3. By the writer in 1974, and examined by Dr D. P. S. Peacock, University of Southampton.

4. The word 'defences' is used merely as a convenience. It is possible that the works enclosing many sites were not in fact primarily defensive in purpose.

5. The excavated evidence from Cadbury Congresbury indicates that the entrance was of very slight construction. More elaboration is reported at the Mote of Mark (Laing 1973a: 123). The timber gatehouse at Cadbury-Camelot remains unique.

6. Six sites have no size information available.

7. There is undoubtedly a bias here because, of 26 hill-forts and enclosures excavated in Somerset, 15 are sites of group I. Even so, surface finds of post-iron age material are more common from group I sites than others.

8. All the known hill-forts in the county were examined on the ground in 1973 and 1974; new surveys were made of selected sites.

9. Aerial survey of Cannington under suitable crop and soil conditions might be rewarding.

10. Sawyer no. 711 (963 AD).

11. The sequence outlined here was worked out on site with the assistance of Dr P. J. Fowler and Mr K. Gardner, to whom I am grateful.

12. Roman sherds have been reported from the interior of Maes Knoll (Branigan 1977: 162).

13. By Janice Klein, University of Birmingham.

LESLIE ALCOCK

Early historic fortifications in Scotland

Dedicatory Dark Age history and archaeology have always been among AHAH's interests, and it is therefore fitting that this volume should include some papers which deal with the post-iron age use of hill-forts. Indeed, he was the discoverer of one of the forts discussed below, *Colodaesburg* (Hogg 1945). The present essay is offered in gratitude for a quarter of a century of stimulating site visits in his company.

Introduction

This paper deals with those hill-top fortifications in Scotland which may be placed in the centuries between the formal end of Roman Britain, and the introduction of medieval methods of castle-building, along with other Norman ideas, in the twelfth century AD. 'Early historic' is a convenient term to use for a time-span otherwise known as the dark ages, the migration period, or the early Christian period, because it emphasizes the availability for the first time of local – as opposed to Mediterranean – historical sources. Some of these are in Latin, but many are in vernacular languages. Their importance for dating is supreme: indeed, it must be affirmed that in an historical period, literary evidence takes precedence over all other forms of chronological evidence.

The term 'early historic fortifications' can be interpreted in two ways. In the wider sense, it could refer to all fortifications which may be dated from the fifth to the eleventh centuries AD on any grounds at all: historical, typological, radiometric, or whatever. If this meaning were followed here, it would lead us to some very fascinating sites. One of these would be Craig Phádraig (Small and Cottam 1972), a typical prehistoric vitrified fort, whose defences were re-occupied, without any apparent refurbishing, in the fifth to seventh centuries AD, according to the evidence of pottery of Class E (p. 155 below), a mould for a hanging-bowl escutcheon (Stevenson 1976), and radiocarbon dates. Another leading example would be the massive multivallate promontory fort of Burghead with its timber-laced ramparts, which had been fastened in places with iron spikes or nails. This gives radiocarbon dates of ad 390 ± 110, ad 390 ± 115 and ad 610 ± 105 (Young H. W. 1891; 1893; Small 1969). Another timber-laced fort, this time very tiny, is Mote of Mark, which yields important evidence for dark age metalworking, as well as pottery, glass, and a radiocarbon date which is consistent with the archaeological evidence (Curle 1914; Laing 1975a). Along the west coast, a number of the small but heavily enclosed forts known as duns have also yielded pottery and metalwork of the period: notable examples are Dun Fhinn (RCAHMS 1971: no.203), Kildalloig (*ibid*.: no.219) and Kildonan (Fairhurst 1939).

The list of forts dated on archaeological and radiometric grounds is already extensive (Laing 1975b), and it will expand further as a result of research in the archaeological literature, in the museums and on the ground. Rather than entering such an open and ill-defined field, the present study takes a second, narrower meaning of 'early historic', as referring to those sites whose date and identification are inferred from historical sources. Because these sources are largely known, and no major expansion of them is to be expected, early historic fortifications in this sense are a more or less finite field. Of course, some new documents may be found; and more particularly, new places will be identified in the documents and on the ground. (In compensation, some old identifications may come to be rejected.) In theory, then, a definitive list of early historic fortifications could be drawn up, and useful comparisons could be made, both within the class, and with other types of fort. It should be emphasized at once that this paper does not present such a final list. It is little more than a preliminary statement matured to some extent through presentation at various public lectures and conferences.

It begins by introducing the historical sources – not indeed at a level which would commend itself to the critical eye of historians, but at least in a form which may serve to acquaint archaeologists with some of the potential sources and some of their problems. It then considers the more accustomed techniques of archaeological dating, which serve to confirm the identifications inferred from historical sources. The core of the paper is a survey-gazetter of identified sites, including some excavated examples. Some dubious examples are also discussed, to expose the problems. A final section briefly synthesizes the evidence, and attempts some generalizations.

Methodology

1 *The historical sources*

The principal sources for our purpose have been gathered and translated by A. O. Anderson (1922). General comments on some of the relevant historians may be found in Gransden (1974); but more detailed comments, often with recent translations, are to be found in H. M. Chadwick (1949); in Bannerman (1974) for the documents of Dalriada; in F. T. Wainwright (1955b) and M. O. Anderson (1973) for the Pictish and later Scottish material; in Jackson

(1963) for the northern British sources; and in Whitelock (1955) for Anglo-Saxon texts. Other commentaries, relevant to particular fortifications, are referred to in the individual site accounts. The most recent general history of the period, which furnishes an integrated background to the case-studies offered here, is by Duncan (1975).

Most of the sites listed are mapped by the Ordnance Survey in *Britain in the Dark Ages* (1966) and *Britain before the Norman Conquest* (1973). An alternative cartographic presentation, with valuable supporting texts, is in McNeill and Nicholson (1975). Finally, mention must be made of Graham's pioneering attempt (1951) to extract archaeological evidence from the dark age literary sources.

It is impossible here to give a detailed account of all the available sources, and their historical strengths and weaknesses; but for the sake of non-historians, a sketch may be attempted. Among the available sources, a rough hierarchy of reliability may be established, based on such factors as the con-temporaneity or otherwise of the source, the quality of the manuscript, and the specificity of the site details. Best of all is the incidental topographical ref-erence by a contemporary writer, such as we have for Alt Clut, Castle Rock, Dumbarton (pp. 157–9 below), in Bede's *Ecclesiastical History*. Bede is writing about a place fortified in his own day; the location is specific – beyond the western end of the Antonine Wall, and beside the Clyde; and we have an abundance of good early manuscripts of the *Ecclesiastical History*. This then is an ideal source, but we should contrast it with Bede's mention of Giudi. All the same criteria apply except that, as we shall see (pp. 175–6 below), the loca-tion itself has been disputed.

An excellent source is provided by contemporary annals – that is, the con-temporary record of events, compiled year by year as they occur, most fre-quently, if not invariably, in a monastery. Examples of these would be the *Annals of Ulster* and other Irish annals and the *Anglo-Saxon Chronicle*. The value of these depends, in theory, on the closeness of contact between the monastery and the events it records, and on our confidence that the record is indeed contemporary. Unfortunately, in no relevant case do we have early manuscripts; in the case of the Irish annals they are very late indeed, and it is certain that interpolations, of dubious historical value, have occurred. More encouraging for our purpose is the demonstration that the *Annals of Ulster* incorporate annals which had been compiled at Iona in the seventh and eighth centuries (Bannerman 1974). These provide a good source for events in Dalriada, and, to a lesser extent, over a wider area of Scotland. They refer to many events – sieges, burnings and destructions – at fortified places; but un-fortunately a large number of these cannot be identified today.

The *Old Scottish Chronicle* is preserved in a fourteenth-century manuscript, which appears to be a copy of a chronicle originally composed in the late tenth century. This in turn was based partly on oral traditions, partly on an earlier written source, but it is not possible to determine whether this was contem-porary with the events it describes (Anderson M. O. 1949).

Another group of documents comprises the Scottish and Pictish Regnal

Lists. In essence, these are simply lists of kings giving the lengths of their reigns, but the lists sometimes contain useful notes about where a king died or was killed, and, more rarely, other information as well. They may represent a twelfth-century writing down of oral traditions (Anderson M. O. 1973), and consequently they may indicate places that were considered important in the twelfth century, rather than in the eighth to tenth centuries.

Other dynastic records, containing much incidental historical information, include the Anglian (especially Northumbrian) genealogies contained in the so-called *Historia Brittonum*. This appears to have been compiled in the early ninth century, though most of our manuscripts are of the eleventh to thirteenth centuries. A detailed examination of the northern British material in *Historia Brittonum* has suggested that it is based on a northern chronicle which was compiled more or less contemporaneously with the events which it records (Jackson 1963; for a more pessimistic view, Dumville 1977).

Occasional references to fortified places occur in saints' lives. Sometimes these are embedded in miraculous events which display the saint's power. For instance, Columba visited Brude, king of the Picts, in his fortress; the gates were barred, but sprang open when the saint made the sign of the cross and laid his hand on the door. Likewise when Wilfrid was imprisoned by Ecgfrith, king of Northumbria, at Dunbar, the iron fetters miraculously fell from his limbs. In each case, the location, which is crucial for us, is only incidental to the biographer. Its encapsulation in a miracle-tale in no way weakens its validity. Normal canons of source criticism therefore apply. Wilfrid's life was written, within a decade of his death, by Eddius Stephanus, who had been his companion. Columba's biographer, Adomnán, was writing rather more than a century after the events he describes; but, since he was abbot of Columba's own monastery, he would have had strong tradition for his source. In these two cases, at least, we can credit the existence of the royal strongholds of Brude and of Ecgfrith. Many saints' lives, on the other hand, are so late that they inspire little belief.

A final source is that of early vernacular poetry. The earliest mention of the fortress of Edinburgh, *Din Eidyn*, appears to be that in the Old Welsh battle poem, *The Gododdin*. But such references to actual identifiable sites in Scotland are rare. The main interest of *The Gododdin* lies in what it tells us of the weapons and tactics of the time. Here, there is a strong contrast with our other historical sources, for these are generally so terse as to tell us only that a stronghold was besieged, or burned, or destroyed. There are no tactical details, and, given the flimsy fabric of early Scottish history, we infer the political or strategic purpose of such attacks at our peril.

In concluding this outline of the available historical sources, some mention must be made of the terms actually used for fortified sites. In Irish sources, even if the language used is Latin, the normal word is *dun*; the comparable Welsh (British) term is *din*. These may imply nothing more than a small hill, especially a craggy one, which looks suitable for defence (cf. Doon Hill, Aberfoyle, p. 175 below). But the normal meaning is 'fort', and the descent of *dun* from the final element of prehistoric fort-names, such as

Camulodunum, is evident. But not all places which now have *dun* in their names were necessarily either forts or craggy hills, for it seems that Dunblane was originally *Dulblaan,* the Valley of Blane (Anderson M. O. 1973: 250, n. 128). In Latin sources, *urbs* is commonly used. In Classical Latin, this would mean a city or walled town, but in our period we may note that the *urbs* where Wilfrid was imprisoned was *Dynbaer,* from a British form **Dinbarr,* where the fort element is clear; that Bede's *Coludi urbs* (Coldingham) was *Colodaesburg* in the Life of Wilfrid (p. 162 below); and that the *urbs* of Clyde Rock was also called *civitas munitissima* by Bede, and *arx,* 'citadel', in the *Annals of Ulster.* (For a recent discussion, see Campbell 1979.)

More unusual words are *munitio,* used by Adomnán of a Pictish king's stronghold; *castellum* of Ecgfrith of Northumbria's strongholds (Colgrave, VW: c.39) and of an unidentified Pictish fortress near Scone (Anderson M. O. 1973: 178); and *oppidum* of Dunottar and Edinburgh. Finally, our sources give us one instance of the use of *rath* for a fort, in the form of *Rathinveramon, Rait inveramon* (p. 177 below). In Irish, *rath* appears to mean specifically a fort with a dug fosse, from which material was thrown up to form a bank (O'Kelly 1970).

2   *Archaeological dating*

An outline of archaeological methods of dating in the earlier centuries of our period is given by Alcock (1971). Although this is biassed towards southern Britain, much of it is applicable to Scotland as well. Laing's account (1975c) is wider in both chronological and geographical range, but it is marred by inaccuracies and by poor illustrations. Very broadly, the potential evidence may be divided into coinage, fine metalwork and pottery. To these should be added various techniques dependent on the physical sciences.

No coinage was minted in our area by the Britons, the Picts or the Scots. From the late seventh century, coins were used in Northumbria, and some of these spread into Scotland. From the ninth century, coins appear more widely, especially in the north and west, in hoards deposited by Viking raiders, traders and settlers (Graham-Campbell 1976), though the evidence does not suggest a money economy. In any case no coins have yet been found on fortified sites.

Fine metalwork is altogether more common. Even more useful in some ways as site-finds are the moulds in which it was cast. These tell us exactly where particular classes of object were made, and they localize art styles. Most important, whereas a richly-ornamented brooch may have been treasured, for centuries, a broken mould has no further life except in an archaeological layer. In other words, whereas with jewellery there may be a considerable discrepancy between age of manufacture and age of deposition, this is unlikely with mould fragments. In the long run, therefore, we are more likely to build a sound chronology, both for fine metalwork and for the sites where it occurs, on the basis of moulds than of finished objects. Meanwhile, we may have difficulty in agreeing the date of a piece within a couple of centuries. Some of the chronological dissension which arises is well explored by Stevenson in his discussion of early Pictish metalwork (1976).

In the early part of our period, pottery imported from the Mediterranean or from Gaul gives hope of a tighter chronology (Radford 1956; Thomas C. 1959; 1976). Three classes are involved. Class A comprises fine red-slipped bowls and dishes, sometimes with stamped ornament, in a late Roman tradition (Hayes 1972). It can be dated fairly precisely on the basis of exact analogues found in coin-dated contexts in the Mediterranean, and appears to belong to the late fifth and sixth centuries. Unfortunately, it is very rare in Scotland. Class B comprises a range of two-handled storage jars or amphorae, used to import wine. No doubt the needs of the Church played a large part in the importation, but vessels (and presumably the wine they had contained) commonly found their way to secular strongholds. The dating evidence again comes from coin-dated levels in the Mediterranean, and a time-span from the late fifth to the early seventh century is indicated. Thirdly, Class D consists of both culinary vessels (especially mortaria) and drinking bowls, certainly imported from the Bordeaux region (Rigoir 1968), perhaps along with wine in cask. There is no clear evidence for dating in Gaul, but British associations point to the late fifth, sixth and even, perhaps, seventh centuries.

A fourth group, Class E, is sometimes grouped with these, but its status as an import is more doubtful. It consists of very serviceable kitchen ware – cooking pots, bowls, flagons and beakers – in a rather rough stoneware. In the absence of convincing Continental parallels (Hodges 1977), it can only be dated by its occurrence on historical forts such as Dunadd, where the seventh and eighth centuries are indicated. A further problem is that, even at the level of hand-lens examination, Class E is difficult to distinguish from some Norman-period wares (Laing 1973b:187).

Apart from the imported wares, most of Scotland, at least in the areas which concern us at present, appears aceramic. In parts of the Hebrides, on the other hand, derivatives of the pottery styles of the iron age broch/ wheelhouse cultures may have persisted (Young A. 1966). At one site at least, the Udal in North Uist, a long stratified sequence is under study, which may reveal ceramic changes at the time of the Norse settlement, and also at an earlier, rather enigmatic phase (Crawford and Switsur 1977). Ultimately, we must hope that the excavation of historic sites will provide a dated sequence for areas and periods which at present lack pottery.

Another material potentially susceptible to close dating is glass. Fragments, ultimately of Merovingian origin, have long been recognized on sites in western Britain (Harden 1956b: 148–52). It is generally agreed that they are present as cullet, that is, broken glass intended to be used as raw material for making beads, bangles and ornamental inlays (Alcock 1963: 52–3, 178–88). It is 20 years since a comprehensive attempt was made to date the Anglo-Saxon glasses from which these must derive (Harden 1956b). Even if Harden's dating is still acceptable, it is not clear how closely the date of deposition of scrap glass could be tied to the original chronology. More work here would be profitable. On the other hand, it seems unlikely that any precise chronology will be derived from the study of bone combs and pins, which are common site-finds in areas with suitable preservation conditions.

In a historic period, with the possibility of precise and accurate dating from documentary sources, radiocarbon dating is of less value than in earlier periods. The reasons for this are explored, in a slightly earlier historic context, by Campbell, Baxter and Alcock (1979). Some of the problems may be rehearsed here for the benefit of readers who are not fully conversant with the method. For statistical reasons, a radiocarbon date is expressed in the form ad 650 ± 70. Here, ± 70 represents a bracket of 140 years, within which there is a 2:3 chance of the date lying. To narrow the chance to 19:20, it would be necessary to quote a bracket of 280 years. This reflects only that element in the error which can be calculated in the dating laboratory. Other potential sources of error include both secular and short-term variations in the global radioactivity which forms the basis for the method; and the possibilities that the sample chosen for dating has been contaminated by older or younger material, or that its stratigraphical context has been mistaken by the archaeologist. So far as secular variations in radioactivity are concerned, an attempt is made to compensate for these by reference to samples from the long-lived bristlecone pine tree. But it is not certain that these results, from high altitude trees in western America, are really applicable in western Europe. We must await the completion of a correction curve based on west European oak trees before we can feel confidence in the dendrochronological calibration of our insular radiocarbon dates (Pilcher and Baillie 1978).

Given that the stratification of his sample has been correctly observed by the archaeologist, that the sample is not contaminated, and that all the radiocarbon calculations have been correctly made, what is it that is dated, to a bracket that is unlikely to be less than ± 50 years? If, for instance, the sample comes from a structural timber of a building or a rampart, which has been burned *in situ*, then the earlier date of the C14 bracket is the earliest possible date for the cutting of the original timber. In fact, if the timber is from the heart of a large tree, then its cutting might well be a couple of centuries later than the C14 date, simply because of the difference in age between the inner and outer rings of the tree. This particular source of error can be narrowed if we have thin branches, for instance in the form of hurdling, since the age range of these is likely to be in years rather than decades or centuries. Finally, of course, the timber may have been re-used over a long period before it became incorporated in the structure in which it was found. Even from this simplified account, it is evident that radiocarbon dating can only be used with extreme caution on historic sites. Indeed, in a sense, the radiocarbon dates are up for trial, or at least for calibration, before the historical dates.

Other methods dependent on the physical sciences will eventually become available, to be tested against historic dates, or to fill in the details of a long sequence, when only part is tied to a documentary chronology. They may include the magnetic dating of hearths or other areas of burned soil; and the dating of pottery by the thermoluminescence technique. Since, on some of our forts, the defences have been so fiercely burned that their rubble has fused or vitrified, a technique for dating this major physical change is conceivable. Some experiments have been made on these lines, but as yet a degree of accuracy suitable for a historic period has not been attained (Alcock 1976: 113).

Gazetteer of sites

See fig. 36 for the locations of the sites, fig. 38 for plans of certain examples.

Aberte Dunaverty   NR 6807

The *Annals of Iona* record the siege of *Aberte* in AD 712, probably in the course of some dynastic struggle in Dalriada. The site is normally identified with Dunaverty, a precipitous headland of conglomerate on the southern tip of Kintyre (Bannerman 1974: 16, 113; RCAHMS 1971: 157–9). The headland has a flat top, about 16m by 10m, and below this on the north-west is a lower terrace. A neck, narrowed by steep gullies, joins the promontory to the mainland. The natural defences are thus very strong; but traces of artificial work of the eighth century are altogether lacking. Evidence of occupation might, indeed, be found by excavation on the terrace, but the summit itself appears to be totally denuded.

Dunaverty immediately overlooks a gently shelving sandy beach, which is the nearest landfall in Dalriada for voyagers from Ireland. It is tempting therefore to think that it played a strategic role in the foundation of the kingdom of Dalriada.

Alt Clut Castle Rock, Dumbarton   NS 4074

The range of evidence from this site, historical, archaeological and radiometric, has been discussed by Alcock (1976), and so it requires only summary treatment here. The site was identified circumstantially by Bede in AD 731 as 'a strongly defended political centre of the Britons up to the present day' (Colgrave and Mynors, HE I: 1 and 12). Non-contemporary references, in Muirchu's *Life* of Patrick, and in Adomnán's *Life* of Columba, carry the tradition that 'the Rock of the Clyde', Castle Rock, Dumbarton, was a seat of the Strathclyde dynasty back, respectively, to the fifth and sixth centuries. Symeon of Durham's statement, in the early twelfth century, that it was captured by an alliance of Northumbrians and Picts in AD 756, may rest on contemporary Northumbrian annals. Finally, the *Annals of Ulster* record, probably contemporaneously, that the citadel was besieged, and ultimately destroyed and plundered, by two Irish Vikings, Olafr and Ivarr, in 870–1.

The archaeological evidence is consistent with this. Pottery of Class B, and Merovingian glass, probably take the occupation back to the late fifth century, and certainly into the sixth. Sherds of Class E belong to the century or so before Bede, and give archaeological substance to his statement that the Rock had been defended up to his own day. An iron pommel-bar from a Viking sword, and a lead weight embellished with a fragment from an Irish glass bangle, may be referred to the depredations of Olafr and Ivarr.

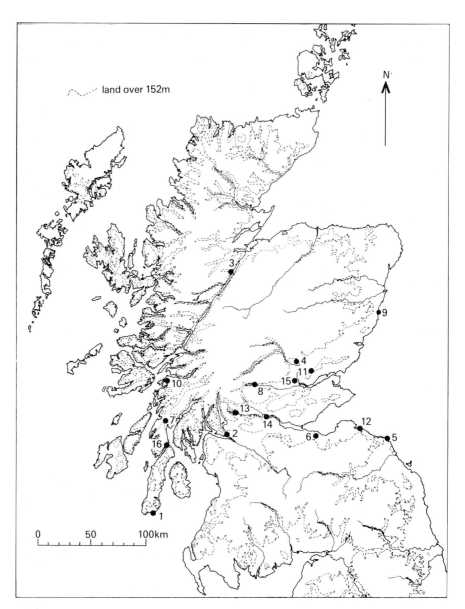

land over 152m

N

0   50   100km

1 **Aberte**, Dunaverty
2 **Alt Clut**, Dumbarton
3 **Brudei munitio**, ?Urquhart
4 **Cluana**, Clunie
5 **Colodaesburg**, Coldingham
6 **Din Eidyn**, Edinburgh
7 **Dun Att**, Dunadd
8 **Dun Durn**, St Fillan's

9 **Dun Fother**, Dunottar
10 **Dun Ollaigh**, Dunollie
11 **Dunsion**, Dunsinnan
12 **Dynbaer**, Dunbar
13 **Eperpuill**, Aberfoyle
14 **Giudi**, Stirling
15 **Rathinveramon**, Inveralmond
16 **Tairpert Boitter**, Tarbert, Loch Fyne

Figure 36. Early historic fortifications in Scotland.

Apart from the formidable natural defences, only slight evidence for fortifications was discovered in excavations in 1974–5. These took the form of an
earth-and-timber terrace or fighting platform, which overlooked the tidal
isthmus linking the Rock to the mainland. Radiometric dates from the oak
beams of this fortification are: UB 2060, ad 485 ± 40; UB 2061, ad 540 ± 30;
UB 2062, ad 655 ± 40. Since UB 2062 is statistically later than the other two
dates, it may be that the earlier ones refer to the original building of the
defences, and that UB 2062 marks a later repair. But it is at least as likely
that all three are dates for a unitary work, the two earlier ones coming
from heart wood, and the later one from the outer rings, of large trees
such as would be needed to provide the beams for an earth-and-timber
defence. In any case, these dates are entirely consistent with Bede's
statement, but they do not enable us to determine whether the Rock was
already fortified in the time of Patrick or Columba.

The site itself is tactically very strong: a volcanic plug, divided into twin
summits by a natural cleft, occupying an isthmus between the Clyde and the
Leven, which is said to have been tidal as late as the sixteenth century (fig. 37).
The crags are truly precipitous; indeed, it is not frivolous to remark that they
provide the severest of tests for the modern rock climber. Only occasional terraces, especially around the eastern hill, and the cleft between the summits,
can have provided much ground for building. It is difficult therefore to com-
prehend where Bede's *urbs* or *civitas* (as opposed to the *arx* of the Ulster
Annals) was located, unless it was at the foot of the rock, on ground that is not
now available for excavation; or unless, alternatively, no weighty significance attaches to the terms used by Bede.

The strategic importance of the Rock lies in its potential for controlling the
Clyde waterway. Before the channel was artificially deepened at the
Dumbuck ford to enable sea-going ships to reach Glasgow, the Rock was at
the highest navigable point of the Clyde. Its strategic importance in our
period is demonstrated by the sequel to its destruction by Olafr and Ivarr: in
the following year, they returned 'to Dublin from Scotland with 200 ships and
a very great booty of Englishmen, Britons and Picts taken off to slavery in
Ireland'. After a period of eclipse, the Rock became the site of an important
medieval and Hanoverian castle, and retained a military role into the 1939–45
war.

Brudei Munitio   Urquhart Castle (?)   NH 5328
During Columba's first (or only) mission to Brude of the Picts, he visited the
king in his fort. There are passing references in the saint's *Life* to the *regis
munitio* (Anderson and Anderson, VC: 40a, 80a); and also to the king's hall
(*aula regia*, *ibid*.: 80b) and the house (*domus*) of Brude, which appears to have
been near the River Ness (*ibid*.: 79b). There is also a longer account of the
miracle in which the two-leaved door (*valvae*) of the gates (*portae*) of the fort
sprang open for the saint (*ibid*.: 82b). Even if we accept some basis of historical
fact behind the miracle-tale, the wording of Columba's biographer,
Adomnán, does not allow us to infer anything about the *munitio* to which the

gate gave access: whether it had a timber palisade, an earthen rampart, or a wall of dry-stonework, timber-laced or not.

Inevitably, attempts have been made to identify Brude's *munitio* on the ground. Henderson (1975) has entered a claim for Inverness itself, but has offered no evidence other than the topographically-vague statements of Adomnán. A long-favoured candidate is the small vitrified fort of Craig Phádraig (Anderson and Anderson 1961: 83). Excavation here has produced finds which bracket the period of Columba's mission (p.150 above). Despite these archaeological pointers, it seems unlikely that Craig Phádraig was indeed the royal stronghold of the northern Picts. Firstly, according to the excavator, the defences, which were first built in the fourth century bc, were not repaired or refurbished in the early historic period (Small and Cottam 1972: 48). If so, then there could have been no *portae* or *valvae* to be opened by St Columba. Secondly, Adomnán implies that Brude's house was close to the Ness. It is difficult to see Craig Phádraig meeting this specification, because it is some 2km from the river, and separated from it by broken terrain.

In fact, a case can be made that Brude's fort is buried beneath the medieval walls of Urquhart Castle (Simpson W. D. 1951; 1964). This stands on a rocky

Figure 37. Alt Clut, Castle Rock, Dumbarton, from the River Clyde, showing the confluence of the River Leven to the left. The earth-and-timber fighting platform was on the right-hand skyline of the Rock (from a nineteenth-century print).

promontory by the shore, not indeed of the River Ness, but of Loch Ness. Since Adomnán elsewhere specifically mentions the lake, *Nisae fluminis lacus* (Anderson and Anderson, VC: 114b), and since he places Brude's *domus*, and by implication his *munitio*, close to the river, this may be thought to rule out Urquhart Castle. On the other hand, it is a fine discrimination between *Nisae fluminis lacus* and *Nesae fluvius*, and it may be doubted whether Adomnán's knowledge of Pictish geography can be pressed so far.

The positive indicators are threefold. First, Urquhart Castle is claimed to be the find-spot of a terminal broken from a silver penannular brooch of Pictish workmanship and seventh- or eighth-century date (Small, Thomas and Wilson 1973: 90). There is, unfortunately, an element of doubt as to whether the provenance is precisely at the castle, or more vaguely in Glen Urquhart. Second, on the highest part of the castle promontory, the so-called motte, clearance by the Office of Works has revealed that the medieval stone-work overlies a timber-laced fort, evidenced by the discovery of vitrified rubble (fig. 38.3). There is, of course, good evidence to show that timber-laced forts were being built in the early historic centuries (*Alt Clut*, p. 159 above; Burghead, pp. 150–1 above; Dundurn, p. 168 below). Finally, the form of the promontory, craggy overall, with a higher boss suitable for a citadel at the western end (the 'motte'), and fairly level terraces below it, seems eminently suitable for an early historic *arx*, *urbs* or *munitio*.

Failing the recognition of some other fortification beside the river itself, the claim of Urquhart Castle to encapsulate Brude's *munitio* must rank very high. It could, indeed, be tested quite economically. A trench, extending across the top of the 'motte' and down one or both of the long sides might provide datable artifacts, radiocarbon dates for the beams of the timber-laced fort, and magnetic dates for its vitrification.

Cluana Clunie   NO 1144

According to the *Old Scottish Chronicle*, in the reign of Kenneth, son of Alpin (AD 843–58), *Danari vastaverunt Pictaviam ad Cluanan et Duncalden*, 'the Danes ravaged Pictland up to Clunie and Dunkeld' (Anderson M. O. 1973: 250). The mention of Dunkeld serves to identify the Clunie in question as that by Loch of Clunie, in the Lunan valley between Dunkeld and Blairgowrie.

The site is a steep-sided, flat-topped hillock, possibly glacial, beside the lake. On the summit are the scanty and incomprehensible ruins of the masonry castle from which David I, among other kings of Scots, issued charters. There are traces of a rampart round the lip of the hill, which may mark the curtain of the medieval castle. On the north-west side, however, where the slope is gentler than elsewhere, there are four close-set scarps and terraces which suggest multiple ramparts of earthwork (fig. 38.4). The topmost of these has a battered revetment of mortared rubble, but it is impossible to say whether this is original or secondary. Certainly, the multiple close-set ramparts look quite un-medieval, and may mark the defences of a ninth-century political centre, whose administrative importance continued into the twelfth and later centuries.

Colodaesburg, Urbs Coludi   Kirk Hill (?), Coldingham   NT 916687
The earliest reference to this fortification appears to be in Eddius's *Life of Wilfrid*, chapter 39, where he tells of the Northumbrian king and queen coming to the monastery *quod Colodaesburg dicitur*, 'which is called "Colod's fort"' (Colgrave 1927). Bede, writing rather later about the double monastery of St Abb, calls it *Coludi urbs* in both the *Ecclesiastical History* (iv, 19; iv, 25) and in his *Life of St Cuthbert*. The implication would seem to be that the monastery had been founded in what had originally been a fortified place – *burg* in Old English, *urbs* in Latin – which had been made over to the Church for the purpose. Reculver in Kent, Bradwell-on-Sea in Essex and Burgh Castle, Norfolk, are other Anglo-Saxon examples of this practice which come immediately to mind, while in Ireland, St Mochaoi's monastery at Nendrum, Co. Down, is an outstanding example of a religious foundation set within an earlier fortification (Lawlor 1925).

It seems likely that the original fort would have been a British, not an Anglo-Saxon, work. There is little evidence for an English interest in hill-forts or other fortified places until the *burh*-building of late Saxon times, and certainly no evidence at all that the early Anglo-Saxons built fortifications (Alcock 1978). Against this it might be argued that the *Anglo-Saxon Chronicle* for the year AD 547 gives a quite circumstantial account of the building of Bamburgh by Ida, the first Anglian ruler of Bernicia. This, we are told, was first defended with a hedge or palisade, and subsequently with a wall. But Hunter Blair long ago pointed out that the account of Ida building Bamburgh is 'a tradition where existing MS evidence is not older than the eleventh century', and adduced other reasons for scepticism (1954: 147–9). On the other hand, the ninth-century *Historia Brittonum*, which in this case may incorporate earlier north British sources (Jackson 1963), provides a British name for Bamburgh: *Dinguoaroy*. The *din*-element clearly implies a fort; and from this it is a reasonable inference that Bamburgh was a pre-Anglian, British promontory fort which was seized by Ida or granted to him at a formative stage in the Bernician dynasty.

Returning to *Colodaesburg*, we may reasonably believe that this likewise was a pre-Anglian, British, fort. It does not help to suggest that Colod or Colud is the personal name of its builder, since we appear to have no record of such a person. Crawford suggested that *Colodaesburg* was a translation of a British form *Caer Golud* (Crawford 1934), which he had found in the *Book of Taliessin*. He therefore considered this to be a reference going back to the late sixth or early seventh centuries. In fact, it occurs along with several other *Caer* names which appear to represent the Celtic Otherworld (Jackson 1959b: 15–16), so it is irrelevant to the world of historical fact.

If we accept that *Urbs Coludi* was originally a British fort, we have here a preliminary clue about the kind of site we should be seeking. Our literary sources add further hints. The sea-shore must be sufficiently accessible for Cuthbert to have gone down at night to immerse himself in the sea, as Bede tells us that he did in his *Life* of that saint. Moreover, the fort must have been

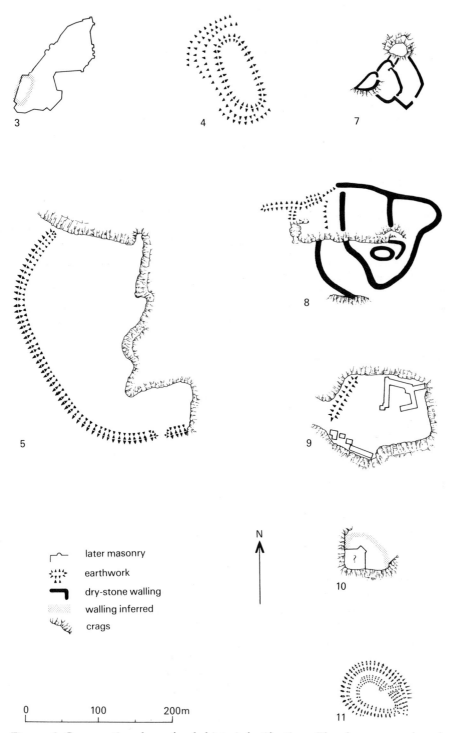

Figure 38. Comparative plans of early historic fortifications. The plans are numbered as in fig. 36: 3 Urquhart; 4 Clunie; 5 Coldingham; 7 Dunadd; 8 Dundurn; 9 Dunottar; 10 Dunollie; 11 Dunsinnan.

large enough to have enclosed the structures of a double monastery. Bede again refers to its lofty buildings, *aedificia illius sublimiter erecta* (Colgrave and Mynors, HE: iv, 25), which appear to have included both public and private ones. There would certainly have been a church, or one or more oratories. Bede mentions also individual cells and beds, *singulorum casas et lectos*, as well as 'little houses, which were made for praying or reading', *domunculae quae ad orandum vel legendum factae erant*. Admittedly this description is embedded in a miracle-story, and one may suspect a strong element of literary convention. Nonetheless, Cramp finds here a valid account of a seventh-century monastery combining communal buildings and individual cells (Cramp 1976: 206–7). It is reasonable to expect that, although the monastery was largely deserted as the result of a fire in AD 679, some traces of the monastic layout should still be visible at *Colodaesburg*.

In recent discussions, the favoured location is a promontory fort on St Abb's Head, centred on NGR NT 911694. Here, in 1934, O. G. S. Crawford reported a mortared wall defending the promontory, and enclosing at least two buildings. The major building now visible, which is of mortared local rubble, appears on the OS 1:2,500 plan as 'St Abb's Nunnery, remains of'. It has long been considered to be a chapel of the seventh or later centuries (Mac-Gibbon and Ross 1896–7: I, 437). But the most obvious features of its plan are a fireplace recess in the upper gable, and a curious projecting wing, perhaps to accommodate a stair-landing, in the lower gable. There can be little doubt that this is a later- or post-medieval hall; and its masonry carries with it the wall across the neck of the promontory. It should be added that the headland has little level ground to hold the buildings of a double monastery.

Aidan Macdonald has pointed out to me that an altogether more likely site for *Colodaesburg* was discovered about 1944 by A. H. A. Hogg himself (Hogg 1945). This is on Kirk Hill, centred on NGR NT 916687, where, on the edge of a 60m high sea cliff, stand a medieval church and graveyard. Inland of the cliff is a fairly level area, demarcated roughly by the 60m contour. Away from the sea, this plateau plunges off steeply on all sides, creating a naturally defended area. At the break of slope, the whole circuit is marked by clear traces of a rampart backed by an internal quarry ditch, with entrance gaps beside the cliff on the north-west and south-east (fig. 38.5). This rampart is so denuded that Hogg considered that it did not appear to be defensive; but given the natural strength of the hill, quite a slight artificial work would have produced a very formidable barrier. The greater part of an area of 3ha is available for buildings, and the occurrence of dense patches of nettles (otherwise rare or absent on the cliff-top) argues for intensive occupation. On two grounds – the proven ecclesiastical connection, and its size and convenience – Kirk Hill is clearly an excellent candidate for the site of St Abb's double monastery. Moreover, Cuthbert could have reached a convenient cove in less than five minutes from the south-east entrance.

It is equally evident that the situation and form of the enclosing rampart are in keeping with a pre-Anglian, British, cliff-castle. Some of the occupation suggested by the nettles may belong to this rather than to the Anglian monastery. Significant here is Hogg's discovery of a Romano-British coarse ware rim, apparently datable to AD 150–250, on Kirk Hill. This makes it possible that we have here not an early historic fortification, but a work of the pre-Roman or Roman iron age, which was already derelict when St Abb founded her monastery. Certainly these suggestions require testing by excavation, as does the hypothesis that the so-called St Abb's Nunnery site is a secular building of much later date.

Din Eidyn, Etin Edinburgh   NT 2573

In the early Welsh poem, *The Gododdin*, and its annexed lays, there is frequent mention of *Eidyn*, or *Din Eidyn*, or *Eidyn Gaer*. *The Gododdin* is a series of elegies on warriors who came, for the most part, from what is now south-east Scotland, and met their death in battle at the hands of the Angles at *Catraeth*, most probably Catterick in Yorkshire. From the individual elegies we can reconstruct the story of the gathering together of an expeditionary force by Mynyddog Mwynfawr, ruler in *Din Eidyn*; of the feasting of the band in the hall, or in the stronghold of *Eidyn*; of its launching against the Northumbrian kingdoms of Bernicia and Deira; and of its annihilation, all save the poet Aneirin, at the hands of the Angles. Jackson (1969), following I. Williams (1938), has argued that the political context of the expedition, as well as linguistic considerations, points to a date shortly before AD 600 for the oral composition of the poem. This dating has been questioned (MacCana 1971; Dumville 1978) but not seriously shaken (Jackson 1973). We can take it as certain, therefore, that *Din Eidyn* was already an important political centre, and specifically a stronghold or fortified town, by the late sixth century.

Watson (1926: 340–1) argued that *Din Eidyn* was Edinburgh, and Jackson reinforces this attribution (1969: 75–8). Edinburgh is noticed also in the Iona annal for AD 638, in the laconic form *obsesio Etin*, and this may well be when it passed into Anglian hands, along with much of the southern shore of the Firth of Forth (Jackson 1959a). In the reign of Indulf (AD 954–62), according to the *Old Scottish Chronicle, opidum Eden vacuatum est ac relictum est Scottis*, 'Eden town was abandoned [by the Angles] and left to the Scots' (Anderson M.O. 1973: 252). Watson took *opidum Eden* to be Edinburgh, and this has rightly been accepted.

There can be little doubt that *Din Eidyn* stood on the summit of what is now Castle Rock, Edinburgh. The tactical advantages of the site are obvious: precipitous on three sides, more gentle to the east, and probably with a flattish top suitable for building. Its early strategic importance lay in its situation where the Roman route from the south reached the Firth of Forth (RCAHMS 1951: xxxv). Once it ceased to be the northernmost stronghold of Northumbria, it came eventually to acquire a pre-eminent position in the kingdom of the Scots.

No trace of early work can now be discerned beneath or among the medieval and later fortifications which overlaid it. It is permissible to speculate that St Margaret's chapel now occupies the remains of a boss of rock which formed the nucleus of Mynyddog's stronghold. But given, on the one hand, the varied and informal layout of early historic fortifications, and on the other, the cutting down of bed-rock and other alterations within the castle, such speculation is vain. It might be hoped that building work within the castle, or external clearance, might occasionally produce relics of early date. With this in mind, in 1977, material collected from high on the south-west slope of the Castle Rock was laboriously wet-sieved and then hand-picked. A very large haul of nineteenth- and twentieth-century artifacts was obtained, but the earliest material comprised four fragments only of sixteenth-century pottery (*ex inf*. E. J. Talbot). It may yet be that at the foot of the Rock there are rich early middens to be found, overlaid by the detritus of each successive century. Quite certainly, any disturbance of the ground in, or around, the castle must be regarded as a potential source of new evidence.

Dun Att Dunadd   NR 8393
The Iona *Annals* record *obsesio Duin Att* (and also 'siege of Dundurn') in AD 683. In 736, they relate that the Pict, Oengus, son of Fergus, captured Dunadd. Although there is no continuous oral tradition to support the attribution, it is generally considered that the site is a craggy hill, with clearly marked defences, which stands up from *Mòine Mhór*, the Moss of Crinan, on the Crinan isthmus of Argyll. It is at once the best known and the most distressing of the early historic fortifications of Scotland. It has sometimes been regarded as capital of the Scottic kingdom of Dalriada, but it is preferable to see it as the chief seat of one of the three kindreds into which the early Scots were divided, perhaps the Cenél Loairn (Bannerman 1974: 112–13).

It appears in the historical record in connection with the conflicts between the colonizing Scots and the native Picts in the late seventh and early eighth centuries. In 683, the two sieges of Dunadd and Dundurn may be seen as reflecting the swinging fortunes of these conflicts. The capture of Dunadd by Oengus, king of Picts, in 736 must have come close to crushing the Scottic colony out of existence.

The defences currently visible at Dunadd were partly exposed by excavations in 1904 (Christison 1905: 292–322) and 1929 (Craw 1930: 111–27). They comprise a roughly pear-shaped citadel, enclosed by a dry-stone wall, and set on a dominant boss of rock; a quite massive dry-stone bank or wall, which encloses a wide terrace to the east of the citadel; flimsier walling, often in short stretches linking together outcrops of rock, and dividing the main enclosure into smaller compartments (fig. 38.7; Christison 1905: 297, fig. 20; Hogg 1975: 197, fig. 61); and more doubtful traces of another stone bank below the main terrace (Stevenson 1949: 192–4; Feachem 1955: 81–2, fig. 8). Minor features include a well (not necessarily ancient) in the north angle of the terrace; other walls, probably of relatively recent buildings, towards the main entrance at the south-east corner of the terrace; and a flight of built steps leading from the upper compartment of the terrace to the citadel. Some of these walls and other features have become dilapidated since they were uncovered, and their deterioration continues.

The excavations of 1904 and 1929 yielded the greatest collection of loot –

the word is used advisedly – of any early historic site in Scotland. This included pottery of Class D (Craw 1930: fig. 10, nos. 12, 19 and 21) and Class E (*ibid.*: remaining sherds). Indeed, this is the type-site for the Dunadd bowl (*ibid.*: 9), and the supposed chronology of Class E pottery rests largely on the historical dating of Dunadd. Fine metalworking is attested by 'sketch-pads' (Christison 1905: figs. 30 and 31), moulds (*ibid.*: fig. 35; Craw 1930: fig. 7), crucibles, including handled examples (Christison 1905: figs. 36–40; Craw 1930: fig. 8), and rare finished products such as pins (Christison 1905: figs. 49–50) and a bronze disk with interlaced ornament (Craw 1930: fig. 4). Scrap glass from some Germanic source (Harden 1956b) is also consistent with jewel-making, because it provides the raw material for vitreous inlays and enamels. The very wide range of iron objects includes, quite unusually, spears and swords (Christison 1905: figs. 55–8; Craw 1930: fig. 5) as well as knives and tools (Christison 1905: figs. 51, 52, 59, 60). Bonework includes composite bone combs (*ibid.*: fig. 48), while among a range of stone objects a large number of rotary querns is noteworthy (*ibid.*: fig. 29).

There is no record of stratification or association for any of the rich haul of artifacts, which has been briefly summarized here. None the less, it clearly deserves to be published in a fully illustrated catalogue. There is no reason to think that this will produce anything that is not already known from the illustrations in the excavation reports; but the importance of the collection clearly demands proper publication. At present, all that can be said is that nothing is known from Dunadd which could not have reached the fort in the seventh or eighth centuries AD.

One other group of features requires special mention. On a bare rock surface immediately below the citadel, among other graffiti of recent date, are some which certainly go back to the early historic period. A deeply carved human footprint, the more lightly pecked outline of a foot, and a hemispherical bowl, are thought to relate to royal inauguration ceremonies (Thomas F. W. L. 1879). They constitute a principal reason for the idea that Dunadd was capital of Dalriada. More enigmatic are an Ogam inscription, and the incised outline of a boar. Jackson (1965) has shown that the inscription can be transliterated, but cannot be read intelligibly. It is gibberish, and it is therefore likely to be Pictish. The boar is also comparable with Pictish animal art, and it is regarded as a token of Oengus's capture of Dunadd in 736. This may be so, but it is difficult to understand why the boar and the Ogam were not obliterated when the Scots regained control of mid-Argyll. In the present study, these features must remain enigmatic.

A comment is nevertheless justified on our need to seek information about the construction and chronology of the defences of Dunadd. None of these were sectioned in the excavations of 1904 and 1929. This is particularly critical in view of the suggestion, notably by Feachem (1966: 85), that 'Dunadd and Dundurn represent Early Iron Age hill-forts, the defences of which may have been repaired or improved' as late as the seventh century AD. A variant on this hypothesis is that the rampart of the terrace is indeed of the early iron age, but the citadel and minor compartment walls were inserted later, most probably in the sixth century AD. From surface appearances, the variant hypothesis would have much to recommend it. At Dundurn, on the other hand, an early iron age date has been decisively disproved by excavation (see below). At Dunadd it could be tested by sectioning the citadel wall and the terrace rampart. This economical operation would enhance greatly our knowledge of this important early Scottic stronghold.

Dun Durn   St Fillan's Hill   NN 7023

The Iona annal for AD 683 follows its record of the siege of Dunadd with *et obsessio Duin Duirn*. This has long been identified with a craggy pyramidal hill, otherwise known as St Fillan's Hill, which overlooks Strathearn where it starts to open out below Loch Earn (fig. 39; Christison 1898). There is a second reference to Dundurn in the Regnal Lists, which tells us that Girg, son of Dungal, died there (in 889) (Anderson M. O. 1973: 267, 274, 283).

St Fillan's Hill has clear traces of massive, but very ruined, dry-stone walls, which enclose terraces around the summit boss (fig. 38.8). Slight traces of walling may also be seen on the south side of the boss, so that the overall plan is that of a citadel with dependent enclosures: in Stevenson's terms (1949), a nuclear fort. Excavations in 1976 and 1977 demonstrated that the summit boss had originally been defended by a wall of dry-stone, stabilized by hazel wattling and oak beams, nailed together with massive iron spikes in a manner reminiscent of the reported defences of Burghead (pp. 150–1 above). This nailed-timbered defence was destroyed by fire, and its ruins were overlaid by a dry-stone wall which may have been timber-laced, but which was certainly not nailed. Contemporary with the second phase of the citadel was the enclosing of the terraces with walls up to 8·0m thick, built of dry-stone but apparently without timber-lacing. Within the limited scope of the excavation, it was not possible to establish whether there had been an earlier terrace wall, contemporary with the first citadel; but certainly in this phase there had been timber buildings on the upper terrace. The depths of deposit here suggest that occupation may go back even before the construction of the citadel, and if so, the earliest defences may have been wooden.

Ten radiocarbon dates have been obtained for Dundurn. They are set out in table 2, from which it will be seen that they agree well with a historical reference in the late seventh century AD. We may ask, however, whether a closer correlation is possible. The siege of AD 683 = 1267 BP should provide a date before which the earliest defences were constructed. On stratigraphical grounds, samples 001, 002, 003, 006, 009 and 010 should all antedate the siege. The first three are, indeed, directly relevant to the construction dates of the early citadel, because they come from structural timbers. When the dates are calibrated to the bristlecone pine curve (in this case, following Damon *et al.* 1974), the 1-sigma brackets for 002 and 003, respectively AD 625–795 and AD 575–745, are fully consonant with the historical date. By contrast, 001 falls after the historical date at the 1-sigma level, but is consistent at the 2-sigma bracket, AD 610–950. In short, within the limits of the counting errors, and making no allowance for unquantifiable error-sources, the radiocarbon dates for Dundurn are in full agreement with the historical evidence.

Finds of relevance to the historical dates include a base silver strap-end with zoomorphic ornament; a virtuoso glass boss with blue and white spirals reminiscent of some of the bosses on the Nigg, Ross-shire, cross slab; other glass fragments; a mould for a boss-ornamented pin; a highly decorated leather shoe; and an iron knife with sharply angled back in the late Saxon/Viking manner. Objects of a domestic character include a barrel padlock, rotary querns, and well-preserved animal bones. A noteworthy feature of the defences is that, for the most part, they were not built of rock quarried on the hill, but of split boulders brought up from the valley bottom; and more remarkably of slabs and blocks of red sandstone quarried some 15km away. This suggests that whoever ordered the construction of the fort commanded wide resources.

In strategic terms, Dundurn appears capable of blocking a major west–east route through the southern Highlands – a line of communication and of hostility between the power centres of the Scots at Dunadd and Dunollie and the

Figure 39. Dun Durn, St Fillan's Hill, from the west, looking down Strathearn. The upper terrace is immediately right of the rock boss of the citadel (cf. fig. 38.8) (photograph L. Alcock).

Purpose of date	Phase	Relevant features	Samples submitted	Site ref.	Lab. ref.	Date ± 1σ in years bp	Calibrated date AD
Date after which terrace wall was reinforced	IIIB	106	Charcoal twigs, 50g	004	HAR 2003	1220±70	750±85
			Mixed charcoal, no visible twigs, 129g	005	HAR 2518	1190±60	780±80
		406	Mixed charcoal, incl. 7g twigs, 75g	007	GU 1040	1330±60	640±65
Date after which terrace wall was built	IIIA	415	Mixed charcoal, incl. twigs, 30g	008	GU 1041	1365±65	605±65
AD 683 HISTORICAL DATE: SIEGE TERMINATING PHASES I AND II						1267 BP	683
Date after which early citadel was constructed	II	012	Charcoal, hazel twigs, 59g	001	HAR 2000	1190±70	780±85
		013+014+017A+017B	Charcoal, hazel twigs, 37g	002	HAR 2001	1260±70	710±85
		013	Charcoal, oak beams, 200g	003	HAR 2002	1310±70	660±85
Date of intensive timber phase on terrace	II	426	Unburnt hazel twigs, 330g, divided between Harwell and Glasgow	009	GU 1042	1510±60	460±65
				006	HAR 2519	1390±60	580±65
Date of earliest known occupation	I	427	Animal bones, 215g	010	GU 1043	1435±65	535±70

Table 2. Dundurn C14 dating. Calibrated dates after Damon et al. 1974.

Picts at Forteviot and Scone. As such, it sprang into importance during the time of Scotto-Pictish confrontation, the seventh and eighth centuries, when it was built, destroyed, and rebuilt. But after Kenneth's union of the kingdom it had no further significance, and so it was soon abandoned.

Dun Fother   Dunottar   NO 8883

The *Annals of Iona* record *obsessio Duin Foither* in AD 681; and again in AD 694, *obsesio Duin Fother*. The *Old Scottish Chronicle* tells us that in the reign of Donald, son of Constantine (AD 889–900), *opidum Fother occisum est a gentibus* (Anderson M. O. 1973: 251) 'was destroyed by the gentiles, i.e., the Vikings'. The place-name is generally regarded as referring to Dunottar, near Stonehaven (Watson 1926: 510–11).

Figure 40. Dun Fother, Dunottar Castle, from the south. The supposed earthwork defence of the early historic fort forms the left-hand skyline of the castle (cf. fig. 38.9) (photograph Cambridge University Collection, copyright reserved).

The site is a formidable headland of pudding-stone, overlaid by a medieval and later castle (figs. 38.9 and 40; Simpson W. D. 1941; 1968). On the landward edge of the promontory, overlooking a daunting cleft, is a massive earthwork. In its present form, this is a defence against artillery bombardment from the mainland, but it seems at least likely that its core is the rampart of a promontory fort attributable to the seventh to ninth centuries AD, if not to earlier centuries as well. This could be tested by excavation.

If it is permissible to seek a strategic purpose for the historical significance of this particular headland, it surely lies in its position athwart the narrowest gap between the Grampian mountains and the sea (fig. 36): the narrow corridor which linked the two major areas of Pictland.

Dun Ollaigh Dunollie   NM 8531
Dunollie is particularly interesting from the point of view of historical methodology. The Iona *Annals* record that it was built (*construitur*) by Selbach, ruler of Lorn – if not indeed of all Dalriada – in AD 714. If this entry stood alone, we would take it as giving a firm date for the foundation of the site. Unfortunately, it had already been mentioned in the annals as destroyed by Selbach in 701. Prior to that, it had been burned in 698, and perhaps even earlier in 686, though this last entry is somewhat confused. The *Annals* also record that, during the Scotto-Pictish conflict of the 730s, Talorcan, son of the Pictish Drustan, 'was taken and bound near Dunollie' in 734. The exceptional frequency of references to Dunollie in the Iona *Annals* may reflect the fact that the fort overlooks Oban Bay, the major mainland landfall from Iona, rather than any intrinsic importance. At the same time, it may be suggested that it has as good a claim as Dunadd to be the *caput regionis*, the 'chief place of the region' where St Columba met sailors from Gaul (Anderson and Anderson, VC: 30a–31a).

It was no doubt the bay itself which provided the strategic reason for Dunollie. Sheltered behind the island of Kerrera, it gave a secure base from which to control the coastlands and islands of Dalriada. At the north end of the bay, Dunollie occupies a precipitous headland of lava (fig. 41). Much of the level top of the promontory is taken up with a medieval tower house and bailey, the seat of the MacDougall family. To the north and east of this, at the head of slopes which are steep, but by no means precipitous, are earthwork banks and ditches which appear to have no relevance to the masonry castle (fig. 38.10). Limited excavation in 1978 demonstrated that the headland had indeed been occupied at the turn of the seventh–eighth centuries, on the evidence of pin- and ingot-moulds similar to those from Dunadd; and, more decisively, a Class E beaker comparable to that from the Buston crannog (Munro 1882: fig. 250; Thomas C. 1959: fig. 43, c and d). In the earliest phase, the perimeter of the headland was not defended, though there was intensive activity on an upper terrace below the summit. Subsequently, the edge of the terrace was protected by a massive dry-stone wall. This structural sequence may be compared with that at Dundurn (p. 168 above). It is tempting to attribute the construction of the terrace defence to Selbach in 714, but such an attribution is necessarily unprovable. After a long abandonment, the early historic fortifications were overlaid by defences of stone rubble and turf, which may themselves be two centuries earlier than the tower house.

Dunsion Dunsinnan   NO 2131
Some versions of the Regnal Lists, after recording the slaying of Kenneth, son of Malcolm, at Fettercairn (about AD 995), by the treachery of Finella, daughter of the earl of Angus, add that Finella's only son had previously been killed by Kenneth *apud Dunsion, Dunfinoen* or *Dunismoen* (Anderson M. O. 1973: 275, 284). Fordun, in his *Chronicle*, identified this with the hill-top fortification of Dunsinnan, which surmounts an outlier of the Sidlaw Hills at an altitude of about 300m. The visible remains are of a small multivallate fort, with three ramparts penetrated obliquely by a narrow entrance passage (fig. 38.11; Hogg 1975: 202–3). Careful examination shows that all three banks have external dry-stone revetments.

Because of its traditional fame, Dunsinnan was trenched in the late eighteenth century, and again in 1854. No proper account of the excavations was

Figure 41. Dun Ollaigh, Dunollie Castle, looking north up the Firth of Lorn. This nineteenth-century print brings out the character of the headland; the early historic defences lie behind, and to the right of, the tower house (cf. fig.38.10).

ever published, and it was left to Christison, in 1900 (Christison 1900: 85–91), to attempt a synthesis on the basis of a MS record of the 1854 excavation, controlled in part by his own observations. The tentative conclusions from this work are that there may originally have been a timber-laced fort on the site, which was partly burned and vitrified. This was superseded by a stone wall, with vertical inner and outer faces of dry-stone work, surrounded by two earthen ramparts. There may have been no entrance through the wall at ground level, as seems also to have been the case at Castle Law, Abernethy (Hogg 1975: 170–1, with references) and Castle Law, Forgandenny (*ibid.*: 171–2, with references). In the interior there appear to have been rectangular buildings, their walls of stone bound with clay. The scanty finds, which were subsequently lost, tell us nothing about the date of occupation.

It is difficult to know what to make of this. A small stone-walled hill-top fort might well be pre-Roman in this area, and even the outer banks are vaguely reminiscent of Forgandenny or the White Caterthun (Hogg 1975: 288–9, with references). Alternatively, the multivallations may recall the multiple terraces at Clunie (p. 161 above), except that Clunie is a valley bottom site whereas Dunsinnan is emphatically on a hill-top. The relevant part of the Regnal Lists was probably compiled a century or more after the events; and even if there were oral traditions behind it, this is long enough for the growth of a spurious attribution of Kenneth's slaying of Finella's son to this prominent hill-fort. Indeed, we may well consider that A. O. Anderson was right to question Fordun's identification of *Dunsion* with Dunsinnan (1922: 513, n.4). We should hesitate before assigning a late tenth-century date either to the defences or to the internal buildings. There is, however, ample scope for testing the date of Dunsinnan by excavation, for, according to the plan (Christison 1900: 88, fig. 42), only about one-third of the interior was despoiled in 1854.

Dynbaer, Dunbarre   Dunbar   NT 6779

In AD 680, King Ecgfrith of Northumbria, angered by the intransigence of Bishop Wilfrid, ordered him to be imprisoned in the royal town (or stronghold) of Dunbar, *in urbem suam Dynbaer* (Colgrave, VW: c.38). Watson pointed out that 'Dunbar is "summit-fort", probably taken over [i.e. into Gaelic] from British *din-bar* with the same meaning' (1926: 141); Jackson confirms this by saying that it is 'doubtless from Primitive Cumbric *din barr*' (1953: 320). It is clear, then, from the etymology that even if we translate *urbs* as town, the idea of 'fortification' is present in the *din*-element of the place-name; so that *Dynbaer* is relevant to our present study. Our other early historic reference, in the *Old Scottish Chronicle*, is that in the mid-ninth century Kenneth, son of Alpin, in the course of a series of invasions of *Saxonia*, i.e. Anglian Northumbria, *concremavit Dunbarre* (Anderson M. O. 1973: 250).

There is at present no archaeological evidence for the site of Ecgfrith's *urbs* of Dunbar, and we are therefore dependent on onomastic evidence to locate it. It is inherently probable that medieval Dunbar continued the site of early historic Dunbar, so the problem is to find somewhere that satisfies the likely meaning of Primitive Cumbric *din barr*. In modern Welsh, the second element means 'top, summit', while in Gaelic toponymy, for instance in Argyll, the cognate *barr* is widely used for isolated hillocks. In Dunbar itself, the most likely site for the seventh-century *din* or *urbs* is the pair of stacks, some 12 to 15m high, which were utilized by the medieval and later castle and battery. This is not at all implausible, for the surface area of the castle stack is six times as great as the summit area of Dunaverty, and almost twice that of the citadel of Dunadd. At Dunbar, the medieval and later work is likely to have obliterated all trace of earlier defences, so that, failing the chance discovery of seventh- to ninth-century artifacts, there can be no archaeological proof of the identification advanced here. Professor Jackson kindly informs me that he sees no reason why a seventh-century Briton should not have used the term *din barr* for what a modern archaeologist might call a stack fort.

Eperpuill Aberfoyle   NN 5200

The *Life of St Berach* tells how Berach came to a fort belonging to Aedan, son of Gabran (AD 574–608), and after various miracles, Aedan offered the fort to Berach, that is, Eperpuill, a monastery of Berach's in Alba (Watson 1926: 225, 463).

There is agreement that Eperpuill is Aberfoyle in the Trossachs. It is also agreed that the early form of the name suggests that it is not a late invention. We may therefore have an early tradition about a monastic community founded by Berach or dedicated to him. According to local tradition the annual April and October parish fairs were held in a field called Féill Bearchán, meaning Fair of Berchán, a diminutive of Berach (Watson 1926: 194, 225).

It has been claimed that Aedan's fort was on Doon Hill (MacNair 1973: 2), which stands about 60m above the flood plain of the River Forth, to the southeast of Aberfoyle. It is reasonable to suppose that Doon is an anglicization of Gaelic *dun*, and that the name was given to the hill in the popular belief that it was crowned by a fort. It is true that around the summit of the hill the Old Red Sandstone conglomerate outcrops in scarps which could look artificial and defensive to an untutored eye. But the archaeologist can detect no trace of built defences on Doon Hill. This seems a clear case of *dun* meaning not 'fort', but rather 'a hill which looks fortified, or suitable for fortification'. Since this suggestion is unpalatable to linguists, I shall document it more fully on another occasion. Meanwhile, it must be added that, even if the form Eperpuill looks early, the *Life of St Berach*, as we have it, is considered to be late, and is not based on early texts. Aedan's fort at Aberfoyle should probably be discarded.

Giudi, Iudeu Castle Rock, Stirling   NS 7993

In his topographical description of northern Britain, Bede mentions *urbs Giudi* as lying *in medio* of the eastern inlet of the sea – that is, the Firth of Forth – in such a way as to suggest that it balanced *Alt Clut*, Castle Rock, Dumbarton (p. 157 above) on the western inlet (Colgrave and Mynors, HE I: 12). The name is considered to be the same as *Iudeu*, which occurs in *The Gododdin* as 'the Sea of Iudeu', and also in the *Historia Brittonum* as 'the town [*urbem*] which is called Iudeu'. This figured in a campaign in the 650s, in which Penda of Mercia, in alliance with British kings, most probably from Wales, pursued Oswy of Northumbria to *Iudeu*, and forced him to surrender certain booty in the 'Restitution of Iudeu' (Wade-Evans 1938: 82). One reading of the *Historia Brittonum* account of the conflict of Oswy and Penda suggests that *Iudeu* was in *Manau* (Anderson A. O. 1922: 15), a region around the head of the Firth of Forth which included the modern Clackmannan and Slamannan (Jackson 1969: 72–5, esp. 72 n.1).

Reverting to Bede: a literal translation of *in medio* would place *Guidi* on an island in the Forth. Other suggestions, taking the meaning as 'in the middle of the south shore of the Forth', have been the Roman forts of Inveresk or Cramond. Curiously enough, in view of Bede's balancing of *Giudi* and *Alt Clut*, Edinburgh does not seem to have been considered. Indeed, the fact that it has its own name, *Din Eidyn* (pp. 165–6 above), should rule it out.

In 1959, Graham proposed to identify *Giudi* with Stirling, partly on the grounds that this strategically important and tactically strong position was otherwise lacking from the map of northern Britain in the dark ages. The identification has been generally accepted, notably by Jackson (1963: 36–8; 1969: 72 n. 1), but it has also been criticized by Rutherford (1976). His attack turns largely on the claim that the Firth of Forth could not be considered as the 'Sea of Stirling', and, hence, the existence of the name 'Sea of *Iudeu*' rules out the location of *Iudeu* at Stirling. By the same logic, of course, the Severn Sea could not possibly be called the Bristol Channel. In fact it seems quite natural that a bay should take its name from an important *urbs* at its highest tidal reach. Given that Bede's geographical knowledge of this – for him – rather remote region was somewhat vague, Stirling could well appear as the centre-point of the Firth of Forth; hence his term *in medio*. At present, therefore, Graham's identification holds the field.

If *Giudi* was indeed located at Stirling, then clearly *urbs Giudi* must be Stirling Castle Rock. This is a precipitous crag of columnar basalt. There are no visible traces of an early fortification beneath the medieval and later castle, but the example of *Alt Clut* (pp. 157–9 above) demonstrates that something might yet be recovered by judicious (or fortunate) excavations. The strategic importance of Stirling lies in its position by the highest tidal point and, perhaps, the lowest crossing of the Forth, where the Forth, the Teith, and the Allan Water provide access routes through the outliers of the southern Highlands. A Roman road had crossed the Forth here on the way to Strathallan and beyond, and there was a bridge here in the middle ages; but it is uncertain whether or not there was either a natural ford or a built causeway in the intervening centuries. The castle itself bears witness to the continuing strategic significance of the site; and this is reinforced by the tally of battles fought in and around the Stirling Gap – not least, of course, Bannockburn.

Rathinveramon   Inveralmond   NO 0926

The Regnal Lists tell us that Donald, son of Alpin, died *in Rathinueramon* in AD 862 (Anderson M. O. 1973: 267); and that Constantine, son of Culen, was killed by Kenneth, son of Malcolm, *in Rathinueramon* in AD 995 (*ibid.*). The name means the 'rath or fort at the mouth of the Almond', presumably where it flows into the Tay. If we interpret 'rath' in the general sense of fort, the Roman fort of Bertha (Callander 1919), hard by the confluence, might seem to be the best candidate, re-occupied as an administrative centre centuries after its original use. This identification was indeed advanced by Crawford in 1949 (59–61), and careful excavation may yet prove him correct. Despite heavy ploughing, it might be possible to demonstrate, for instance, a post-Roman refurbishing of the rampart similar to that at the Brecon Gaer (Wheeler 1926: 11–16; Casey 1971).

It should be added that the investigation of *rath*-derived place-names in Scotland is a minor neglected field in its own right. In many cases, no doubt, the word is of ultimately Irish origin, through Scottish Gaelic, and the Irish usage, referring to circular earthworks of ditch-and-bank construction, is very relevant (O'Kelly 1970). But it must not be overlooked that the word was present in the British language too, on the evidence of *Ratae*, the Roman name for Leicester, which appears to come from British *ratis* (Rivet and Jackson 1970: 78).

Tairpert Boitter   Tarbert, Loch Fyne   NR 8668

The Iona annal for AD 712 records *combustio Tairpirt Boitter*; and again in 731, we learn that *Tairpert Boittir* was burnt by Dungal, son of Selbach. The first element in the name clearly refers to one of the many Tarberts or Tarbets – meaning a portage. No suggestion is available about the qualifying force of Boitter. Fortunately the reference in 731 to Dungal, son of Selbach, implies that this particular burning was an incident in the internal power struggle of Dalriada; and this in turn allows us reasonably confidently to identify *Tairpert Boitter* with Tarbert, Loch Fyne.

The strategic importance of the site is obvious, overlooking a fine natural harbour, and controlling the mile-long portage between East and West Loch Tarbert. Its importance is endorsed by the placing there of a royal castle, probably as early as the thirteenth century (RCAHMS 1971: 179–84). This occupied a rocky knoll above the East Loch Tarbert harbour, which could have been a tactical strongpoint in the seventh and eighth centuries as well. But whether the place burned by Dungal was here or elsewhere in the vicinity, no trace of it can be recognized today. In the absence of the term *dun*, or some similar expression, we cannot even be certain that it was a fortified place.

Conclusions

Of the 16 sites described above, the great majority have long been known on the ground, and most of them have been recognized as being identifiable with early historic forts. Despite this, not one of them has been examined extensively by modern techniques of excavation. As a result, little can be said about the character of their defences, and nothing useful about their internal buildings, or about the character, permanence or intensity of settlement. None the less, some general comments are possible, from surface evidence alone, about size and location, and there is some basis for comparison with both earlier and later defended sites.

There is, unfortunately, no ready source of general information about forts of the early iron age in northern Britain. In terms of size, they range from well under 1ha, to 16ha at Eildon Hill North and Traprain Law, and even as much as 40ha on the Mull of Galloway (Hogg 1975: 251–2). Feachem maps 24 'minor oppida' of 6 acres (about 2.5ha) or more (1966: fig. 13). One of these, Burghead, at the minimum of this size range, is probably the largest known fort built in the early historic period, though *Colodaesburg* may run it close. Otherwise, the largest of our examples is Dundurn, at about 1.8ha. Outside our area, this may be compared with Bamburgh, at about 2ha. In other words, even sites important enough to be called *urbs*, and to be attributed explicitly to royal possession, were below the size range of the supposed *oppida* of the iron age.

There is also an evident difference in altitudinal range. Supposedly iron age forts are frequently found at over 250m OD (as well as at lower altitudes), and may be as high as 400m (Eildon), 430m (Arbory) or even 550m (Tap o'Noth). Only one early historic fort is at any height, and that is the disputable example of Dunsinnan at 300m OD. The next highest is Dundurn at 150m; but this statement conceals the fact that Dundurn rises from a valley floor at about 100m. In fact, one typical situation for a fort in our period is an extremely craggy hillock rising from a valley floor (Dunadd, or Dundurn) or a precipitous crag-and-tail hill (Edinburgh, Stirling). The former situation in particular lends itself to the citadel-and-outworks plans classed by Stevenson (1949) as 'nuclear forts'. Iron age forts, by contrast, tend to be on more rounded features, often on the summits and spurs of hill-ranges. Again, coastal promontory forts are relatively rare and restricted in their distribution (map in Rivet 1966), whereas in our period sea-cliffs, headlands and other strong coastal features are used by Dunaverty, Dumbarton Castle Rock, *Colodaesburg*, Dunbar, Dunottar, and Dunollie. At present we can only speculate that seaborne trade was a determining influence in this.

In stressing these contrasts in size and situation between forts built after about AD 400 and those of earlier date, I am expressly rejecting the view that the forts listed in the previous section had early iron age precursors. The opposite hypothesis has, of course, been proposed by Feachem (1966: 85) in relation to Dunadd and Dundurn (pp. 167–8 above), but the radiocarbon dates from Dundurn make it possible to reject decisively Feachem's interpretation of that site (p. 168 above). Dunadd, and perhaps some other sites as well, must remain in doubt, but as a group, the forts considered here seem to represent a new distribution of military power, turning their back on earlier centuries. By contrast, no fewer than 10 out of the 16 are also the sites of medieval (and sometimes later) castles. In this sense, they foretell a new military, political and social order.

Consistently with this, many of them, as we have seen, display a recognizable strategic purpose. The hazards of attributing strategic intent to pre-Roman hill-forts are evident (Alcock 1965: 184–5), and it is significant that the word 'strategy' does not occur in the index of Hogg's survey of the hill-forts of Britain (1975). But later battles in the vicinity underline the strategic importance of Dunbar and Stirling; the destruction of Castle Rock, Dumbarton, opened up the whole of North Britain to Viking slave-raiding; Edinburgh and Dunottar may both control low-level routes between the hills and the sea; and even if we do not know enough about contemporary military organization to understand precisely how it worked, we can hardly deny to Dundurn the role of blocking movement along a major trans-Highland route. Furthermore, whereas the military use of iron age forts has been questioned, many of our sites appear in the historical record purely as a result of a military action, a siege, capture, burning or destruction.

This is not to say that we can discern the details of these actions behind the cryptic phrases *obsesio Duin Att* or *concremavit Dunbarre*. In a literate period we might hope to learn something about tactics and weapon-play. Indeed, it says much for contemporary organization and discipline that sieges could be mounted at all. Here we have confirmatory evidence from south of the Border, such as the besieging of Hussa at Lindisfarne. But our most extensive account of contemporary warfare, *The Gododdin*, depicts a rather irregular form of pitched battle in the open, certainly not a set-piece siege or assault on a fortified place. In our area, very decisive battles might be fought in the open, as is proved by the destruction of the army of Ecgfrith of Northumbria at Nechtansmere in AD 685 (Wainwright F. T. 1948). Certainly, open warfare is largely the pattern revealed by historical sources in southern England (Alcock 1978). Battles were frequently fought at river-crossings; and it is interesting in this connection to see that, according to the *Old Scottish Chronicle*, about AD 995 Kenneth, son of Malcolm, *vallavit ripas vadorum Forthin*, 'fortified the banks of the Fords of Frew', one of the major north–south crossings of central Scotland (Watson 1926: 52–3, 349–50; Anderson M.O. 1973: 252–3).

If the historical sources, with their mention of sieges and captures, demonstrate the military use of our sites, they also hint at non-military functions as well. In contrast to *arx*, 'citadel', terms like *civitas* or *urbs*, used by Bede and others, appear to have political and administrative implications which defy precise translation. Royal halls (*aula*) are referred to at Din Eidyn and at Brude's fort. Eddius describes Ecgfrith making a progress, with pomp and feasting, through 'cities and fortresses', *civitates et castella* (Colgrave, VW: c. 39). In this we can recognize an administrative organization based on the collection of taxes-in-kind at royal centres, where they would be utilized by the king and court in periodic circuits. Other royal functions, notably the dispensation of justice and of hospitality, would have been performed at the same time. Hunter Blair has drawn attention to the fact that, at the time of Wilfrid's imprisonment, Dunbar was the seat of a *praefectus* (perhaps an earl), who may have had responsibility for a wide area between the Lammermuir Hills and the Firth of Forth (1954: 169–70). Barrow has further argued that the administrative arrangements represented by an *urbs* such as Dunbar, and the district around it, survived into the shires and thanages of medieval Scotland (1973: 66–7). Here again, therefore, early historic sites appear to anticipate medieval arrangements, but it would be very unwise to extrapolate such an organization back into the first millennium BC.

Finally, we must ask how representative our sites are of the overall settlement pattern of the period. The answer is, not at all, at the level of the primary producers who furnished the taxes-in-kind which kept the king, his court and army in being. Inevitably, peasant houses and villages are hard to detect, but among the southern Picts at least we are beginning to see hints in the clusters of oval and sub-circular houses adjacent to souterrains (Wainwright F. T. 1963; Watkins 1979). But even at royal level, fortified hills were not the only form of settlement. At present, the chronological status of certain large timber buildings in eastern Scotland is in doubt. Formerly they were thought to be royal or thegnly halls of the Britons or the Picts (Hope-Taylor 1966; Reynolds N. 1980), but the evidence of both finds and radiocarbon dates would put them back to the fourth millennium BC. Dismissing these, we can still assert that literary evidence for the importance of Scone and Forteviot in the ninth and later centuries demonstrates that some royal sites might be on level ground, defended, if at all, by timber stockades.

Archaeologically, nothing is known of Scone, and until recently the only evidence for the palace attributed to Forteviot by the Regnal Lists was a splendidly carved arch-fragment from a major building of the ninth century (Allen and Anderson 1903: 325 with fig. 336). Recently, however, air-photographs of Forteviot have revealed, amid a concentration of ritual and burial enclosures of prehistoric date, clear signs of rectangular buildings which could well hint at a Pictish palace complex. Apparently an early Christian graveyard lies adjacent. Faced with evidence of this kind, we might even ask whether the importance we now attach to fortified sites is not a reflection of twentieth-century archaeological activity, and of the ease of recognition of hill-forts, rather than of any over-riding significance in early times. This, of course, is a very valid question to ask of the pre-Roman iron age as well. Fortunately, in the early historic period, our documentary sources provide the necessary control to enable us to assert that, at the royal level, the fortified hill-top was the dominant form of settlement, and the major centre of political, social and military organization.

Acknowledgments

The fieldwork which forms the basis of this paper was made possible by generous grants from the Carnegie Trust for the Universities of Scotland, the Hunter Archaeological Trust, and the University of Glasgow.

Many individuals have helped in both the archaeological and historical fields, notably E. A. Alcock, M. O. Anderson, H. Burton, R. B. Gourlay, K. H. Jackson, A. Lane, A. Macdonald, M. Miller and E. J. Peltenburg.

Bibliography

Note Places of publication are given only for those works published outside the United Kingdom.

Adomnán, *Life* of Columba. See Anderson and Anderson, 1961.

Alcock, L., 1963. *Dinas Powys, an Iron Age, Dark Age and Early Medieval Settlement in Glamorgan.*

Alcock, L., 1965. 'Hillforts in Wales and the Marches', *Antiquity* 39: 184–95.

Alcock, L., 1971. *Arthur's Britain: History and Archaeology AD 367–634* (also Penguin Books 1972).

Alcock, L., 1972. *'By South Cadbury is that Camelot . . .' The Excavation of Cadbury Castle 1966–1970.*

Alcock, L., 1976. 'A multi-disciplinary chronology for Alt Clut, Castle Rock, Dumbarton', *PSAS* 107: 103–13.

Alcock, L., 1978. *'Her . . . gefeaht wiþWalas*: aspects of the warfare of Saxons and Britons', *Bull. Board of Celtic Studies* 27: 413–24.

Allcroft, A. H., 1908. *Earthwork of England.*

Allen, D. F., 1961. 'The origins of coinage in Britain: a re-appraisal', in Frere 1961: 97–308.

Allen, J. R. and Anderson, J., 1903. *The Early Christian Monuments of Scotland* (2 vols).

Anderson, A. O., 1922. *Early Sources of Scottish History AD 500 to 1286* (2 vols).

Anderson and Anderson, VC. Anderson, A. O. and Anderson, M. O. (ed. and trans.), 1961. *Adomnan's Life of Columba.*

Anderson, M. O., 1949. 'The Scottish materials in the Paris manuscript, Bib.Nat. Latin 4126', *Scottish Hist.Rev.* 28: 31–42.

Anderson, M. O., 1973. *Kings and Kingship in Early Scotland.*

André, J., 1959. 'Les enceintes quadrilatérales du Morbihan', *Ogam* 11: 441–54.

Anglo-Saxon Chronicle. See Earle and Plummer 1892, 1899.

Applebaum, S., 1934. 'An early iron age site at Holwell, Hertfordshire', *Ant.J.* 14: 383–8.

Applebaum, S., 1949. 'Excavations at Wilbury Hill, an iron age hillfort near Letchworth, Hertfordshire, 1933', *Arch.J.* 106: 12–45.

ApSimon, A. M., 1968. 'The bronze age pottery from the Ash Hole, Brixham, Devon', *Procs Devon Arch.Soc.* 26: 21–30.

ApSimon, A. M., Rahtz, P. A. and Harris, L. G., 1958. 'The iron age A ditch and pottery at Pagan's Hill, Chew Stoke', *Procs Univ. Bristol Spelaeological Soc.* 8.ii: 97–105.

Ashbee, P., 1960. *The Bronze Age Round Barrow in Britain.*

Ashbee, P., 1970. *The Earthen Long Barrow in Britain.*

Atkinson, R. J. C., 1956. *Stonehenge.*

Atkinson, R. J. C., 1972a. 'The demographic implications of fieldwork', in *Field Survey in British Archaeology*, ed. E. Fowler: 60–6.

Atkinson, R. J. C., 1972b. 'Burial and population in the British bronze age', in Lynch and Burgess 1972: 107–16.

Atkinson, R. J. C., Piggott, C. M. and Sandars, N., 1951. *Excavations at Dorchester on Thames*, I.

Autorde, F., 1907. 'Les forts vitrifiés de la Creuse: étude sur la structure des murs et l'origine des vitrifications', *Compte-rendu, Congrès Préhistorique de France 3*: 721–50.

Avery, M., 1976. 'Hillforts of the British Isles: a student's introduction', in Harding 1976a: 1–58 and 361–5.

Avery, M. and Close-Brooks, J., 1969. 'Shearplace Hill, Sydling St Nicholas, Dorset, House A: a suggested re-interpretation', *PPS 35*: 345–51.

Avery, M., Sutton, J. E. G. and Banks, J. W., 1967. 'Rainsborough, Northants., England: excavations 1961–5', *PPS 33*: 207–306.

Babes, M., 1974. *Das Gräberfeld von Les Jogasses* (Saarbrücker Beiträge zur Altertumskunde, Bd 13; Bonn).

Bamford, H., 1976. 'Briar Hill: first interim report', *Northants. Archaeol. 11*: 5–11.

Bannerman, J., 1974. *Studies in the History of Dalriada*.

Baring Gould, S., Burnard, R. and Anderson, I. K., 1900. 'Exploration of Moel Trigarn', *Arch. Camb.*, 5th ser., *17*: 189–211.

Barker, H. and Mackey, J., 1963. 'British Museum natural radiocarbon measurements IV', *Radiocarbon 5*: 104–8.

Barker, P., 1970. 'Some aspects of the excavation of timber buildings', *World Archaeol. 1*: 220–35.

Barré de Saint-Venant, J. and Poussereau, L.-M., 1906. 'Les fouilles du Vieux Château de Barbarie, commune de la Machine, Nièvre', *BA 24*: 91–106.

Barrett, J. C., 1976. 'Deverel-Rimbury: problems of chronology and interpretation', in Burgess and Miket 1976: 289–307.

Barrett, J. C., 1978. 'The EPRIA prehistoric pottery', in Hedges and Buckley 1978: 268–88.

Barrett, J. C., 1979. 'Later bronze age pottery in southern Britain', *Current Archaeol. 6*: 230–1.

Barrière, P., 1933. 'Les oppida des Pétrucores', *RA*, 6th ser., *1*: 13–23.

Barrow, G. W. S., 1973. *The Kingdom of the Scots*.

Barthélemy, A., 1973. 'L'oppidum de Matisco', *RAECE 24*: 307–18.

Barton, K., 1962. 'Settlements of the iron age and pagan Saxon periods at Linford, Essex', *Trans. Essex Arch. Soc.*, 3rd ser., *1*: 57–104.

Beaupré, J., 1902. *Les études préhistoriques en Lorraine en 1899 à 1902 et aperçu sur les époques gallo-romaines et merovingiennes dans le Département de Meurthe-et-Moselle* (Nancy).

Beaupré, J., 1909. 'De l'emploi du double vallum dans la fortification préhistorique', *BSPF 6*: 381–8.

Beaupré, J., 1910. 'L'oppidum de Sainte-Geneviève, Essey-lès-Nancy', *Mémoires de la Soc. Archéologique de la Lorraine*: 265–90.

Bede, *Ecclesiastical History*. See Colgrave and Mynors 1969.

Benoit, F., 1975. 'The Celtic oppidum of Entremont, France', in Bruce-Mitford 1975: 227–59.

Benson, D. and Miles, D., 1974. *The Upper Thames Valley – An Archaeological Survey of the River Gravels*.

Bersu, G., 1940. 'Excavations at Little Woodbury, Wiltshire. Part I: The settlement as revealed by excavation', *PPS 6*: 30–111.

Besset, F. and Périchon, R., 1964. 'Contribution à l'étude des quelques sites fortifiés du Département de la Loire', *Celticum 9*: 63–75.

Biddle, M., 1965. 'Excavations at Winchester, 1964. Third interim report', *Ant. J. 45*: 230–64.

Biddle, M., 1972. 'Excavations at Winchester, 1970', *Ant. J. 52*: 93–131.

Birchall, A., 1965. 'The Aylesford-Swarling Culture: the problem of the Belgae reconsidered', *PPS 31*: 241–367.

Birley, E., Dobson, B. and Jarrett, M. (eds), 1974. *Roman Frontier Studies 1969: 8th International Congress of Limesforschung*.

Bishop, M. W., 1971. 'The non-Belgic iron age in Surrey', *SyAC 68*: 1–30.

Boardman, J., Brown, M. A. and Powell, T. G. E. (eds), 1971. *The European Community in Later Prehistory: studies in honour of C. F. C. Hawkes*.

Bocquet, A., 1976. 'Les civilisations de l'âge du bronze dans les Alpes', in Guilaine 1976: II, 483–94.

Bombal, E., 1906. 'Rapport sur les fouilles operées au Puy-du-Tour, commune de Monçeaux (Corrèze) en . . . 1906', *Bull. de la Soc. des Lettres, Sciences et Arts de la Corrèze 28*: 405–19.

Bonnamour, L., Mordant, C. and Nicolardot, J.-P., 1976. 'Les civilisations de l'âge du bronze en Alsace', in Guilaine 1976: II, 601–17.

Boon, G. C., 1975. Review of Birley *et al.* 1974, *Arch. Camb. 124*: 117–20.

Bosch-Gimpera, P., 1939. 'Two Celtic waves in Spain', *Procs British Academy 26*: 25–148, plus maps and plates.

Boserup, E., 1965. *The Conditions of Economic Growth*.

Boudou, J., Arnal, J. and Soutou, A., 1961. 'La céramique incisée à méandres symmétriques du Pont du Diable (Aniane, Hérault)', *Gallia 19*: 201–18.

Bouillerot, R., 1905. 'Quelques notes sur des camps de construction néolithique dans la vallée de la Saône supérieure', *Bull. de la Soc. Grayloise d'Emulation 8*: 115–32.

Bouttet, S., 1910. 'Les enceintes vitrifiées du Département de la Loire', *Revue préhistorique, annales de palethnologie*.

Bowen, H. C., 1975. 'Air photography and the development of the landscape in central parts of southern England', in *Aerial Reconnaissance for Archaeology*, ed. D. R. Wilson: 103–18.

Bradford, J. S. P., 1942a. 'An early iron age site on Blewburton Hill, Berkshire', *Berks. Arch. J. 46*: 97–104.

Bradford, J. S. P., 1942b. 'An early iron age site at Allen's Pit, Dorchester', *Oxoniensia 7*: 36–60.

Bradley, R., 1971. 'Economic change in the growth of early hill-forts', in Hill and Jesson 1971: 71–83.

Bradley, R., 1978. *The Prehistoric Settlement of Britain*.

Bradley, R. and Ellison, A., 1975. *Rams Hill – a Bronze Age Defended Enclosure and its Landscape*, BAR 19.

Bradley, R. and Richards, J., 1978. 'Prehistoric fields and boundaries on the Berkshire Downs', in *Early Land Allotment in the British Isles*, ed. H. C. Bowen and P. J. Fowler, BAR 48: 53–60.

Bradley, R. and Richards, J., forthcoming. 'The excavation of two ring-ditches at Heron's House, Burghfield, Berkshire', *Berks. Arch. J.*

Brailsford, J. and Jackson, J. W., 1948. 'Excavations at Little Woodbury, Wiltshire (1938–39), Part II and Part III', *PPS 14*: 1–23.

Branigan, K., 1977. *Gatcombe: the excavation and study of a Romano-British villa estate, 1967–76*, BAR 44.

Bretz-Mahler, D., 1961. 'Musée d'Épernay: catalogue de la céramique des cimetières de l'époque de La Tène I', *Mémoires de la Soc. d'Agriculture, Commerces, Sciences et Arts de la Marne* (Châlons-sur-Marne) 76: 7–60.

Bretz-Mahler, D., 1971. 'La Civilisation de La Tène I en Champagne: le faciès Marnier', *Gallia*, 23rd suppl.

Brewster, T. C. M., 1963. *The Excavation of Staple Howe* (East Riding Archaeological Research Committee).

Brisson, A. and Hatt, J.-J., 1953. 'Les nécropoles hallstattiennes d'Aulnay-aux-Planches (Marne)', *RAECE 4*: 193–233.

Brisson, A. and Hatt, J.-J., 1966. 'Fonds de cabanes de l'âge du bronze final et du premier âge du fer en Champagne', *RAECE 17*: 165–97.

Brisson, A. and Hatt, J.-J., 1967. 'Fonds de cabanes de l'âge du bronze final et du premier âge du fer en Champagne (suite et fin)', *RAECE 18*:7–51.

Britton, D., 1968. 'The bronzes', in Cotton and Frere 1968: 204–13.

Brogan, O. and Frere, S. S., 1958. 'Camp du Charlat, Corrèze', *Ant. J. 38*: 218–22.

Brothwell, D. R., Bishop, A. C. and Woolley, A. R., 1974. 'Vitrified forts in Scotland: a problem in interpretation and primitive technology', *J. Arch. Science 1*: 101–7.

Bruce-Mitford, R. (ed.), 1975. *Recent Archaeological Excavations in Europe*.

Büchsenschütz, O. E., 1971. 'État de la recherche sur les oppida en France, particulièrement dans le Centre', *Archeologické Rozhledy 23*: 406–16.

Büchsenschütz, O. E., Dorion, J. and Querrien, A., 1975. 'Pour une carte archéologique de la France', *RA*: 319–32.

Büchsenschütz, O. E. and Ralston, I. B. M., 1975. 'Découverte d'un murus gallicus à Levroux (Indre)', *Gallia 33*: 27–48.

Burchell, J. P. T. and Frere, S. S., 1947. 'The occupation of Sandown Park, Esher', *Ant. J. 27*: 24–46.

Burgess, C., 1968. 'The later bronze age in the British Isles and north-western France', *Arch. J. 125*: 1–45.

Burgess, C. 1974. 'The bronze age', in Renfrew 1974: 165–232.

Burgess, C., 1979. 'A find from Boyton, Suffolk, and the end of the bronze age in Britain and Ireland', in Burgess and Coombs 1979: 269–83.

Burgess, C. and Coombs, D. (eds), 1979. *Bronze Age Hoards: some finds old and new*, BAR 67.

Burgess, C. and Miket, R. (eds), 1976. *Settlement and Economy in the Third and Second Millennia BC*, BAR 33.

Burrow, I. C. G., 1974. 'Possible Irish earthworks in Somerset', *Procs Royal Irish Academy 76c*: 228–9.

Burrow, I. C. G., 1976. 'Brean Down hillfort 1974', *Procs Univ. Bristol Spelaeological Soc. 14.ii*: 141–54.

Burrow, I. C. G., 1979a. 'Roman material from hillforts', in *The End of Roman Britain*, ed. P. J. Casey, BAR 71: 212–29.

Burrow, I. C. G., 1979b. 'Aspects of hillfort and hilltop settlement in Somerset, AD 0–700' (Ph.D. thesis, University of Birmingham).

Burstow, G. P. and Holleyman, G. A., 1957. 'Late bronze age settlement on Itford Hill, Sussex', *PPS 23*: 167–212.

Bushe-Fox, J. P., 1915. *Excavations at Hengistbury Head, Hampshire, in 1911–1912* (Society of Antiquaries of London, Research Report 3).

Calkin, J. B., 1947. 'Romano-British jugs from Gallows Gore, Worth Matravers', *PDNHAS 69*: 42–4.

Calkin, J. B., 1948. 'The Isle of Purbeck in the iron age', *PDNHAS 70*: 29–59.

Calkin, J. B., 1951. 'Prehistoric Pokesdown', *Procs Bournemouth Nat. Science Soc. 40*: 79–89.

Calkin, J. B., 1953. 'Kimmeridge coal money', *PDNHAS 75*: 45–71.

Calkin, J. B., 1962. 'The Bournemouth area in the middle and late bronze age, with the "Deverel-Rimbury" problem reconsidered', *Arch. J. 119*: 1–65.

Calkin, J. B. and Piggott, C. M., 1939. 'Iron age "A" habitation site at Langton Matravers', *PDNHAS 60*: 66–72.

Callander, J. G., 1919. 'Notes on the Roman remains at Grassy Walls and Bertha, near Perth', *PSAS 53*: 137–52.

Callow, W. J., Baker, M. J. and Hassall, G. I., 1966. 'National Physical Laboratory radiocarbon measurements IV', *Radiocarbon 8*: 340–7.

Callow, W. J., Baker, M. J. and Pritchard, D. H., 1963. 'National Physical Laboratory radiocarbon measurements I', *Radiocarbon 5*: 34–8.

Callow, W. J. and Hassall, G. I., 1968. 'National Physical Laboratory radiocarbon measurements V', *Radiocarbon 10*: 115–18.

Campbell, J., 1979. 'Bede's words for places', in *Names, Words and Graves: early medieval settlement*, ed. P. H. Sawyer: 34–54.

Campbell, J. A., Baxter, M. S. and Alcock, L., 1979. 'Radiocarbon dates for the Cadbury massacre', *Antiquity* 53: 31–8.

Campbell, J. A., Baxter, M. S. and Harkness, D. D., 1978. 'Radiocarbon measurements on a floating tree-ring chronology from North-East Scotland', *Archaeometry* 20: 33–8.

Capitan, A., 1913. 'Bègues, Allier', *BA 31*: cli-clii.

Capitan, A., 1915. 'Bègues, Allier', *BA 33*: lx-lxiii.

Capitan, A., 1916. 'Bègues, Allier', *BA 34*: lxxxiv-xcii.

Case, H., 1963. 'Notes on finds and ring ditches in the Oxford region', *Oxoniensia 28*: 19–52.

Case, H., Bayne, N., Steele, S., Avery, G. and Sutermeister, H., 1965. 'Excavations at City Farm, Hanborough, Oxon.', *Oxoniensia 29*: 1–98.

Casey, J., 1971. 'Excavations at Brecon Gaer, 1970', *Arch. Camb. 120*: 91–101.

Casselberry, S. E., 1974. 'Further refinement of formulae for determining population from floor area', *World Archaeol. 6*: 117–22.

Castagné, M., 1874. 'Mémoire sur les ouvrages de fortification des oppidum gaulois de Murcens, d'Uxellodunum et de l'Impernal (Luzech) situés dans le Département du Lot', *Congrès Archéologique de France 41*: 427–538.

Catherall, P. D., 1971. 'Henges in perspective', *Arch. J. 128*: 147–53.

de Cessac, P., 1867. *Rapport sur les fouilles exécutées dans les buttes de la Tour-Saint-Austrille* (Paris).

de Cessac, P., 1878. 'L'Oppidum du Puy-de-Gaudy près Guéret (Creuse) et sa muraille vitrifiée', *Mémoires XLII Session Congrès Scientifique de France* (Autun).

Chadwick, H. M. 1949. *Early Scotland. The Picts, the Scots and the Welsh of southern Scotland*.

Chadwick, S., 1961. 'Longbridge Deverill Cow Down', in Frere 1961: 18–20.

Challis, A. J. and Harding, D. W., 1975. *Later Prehistory from the Trent to the Tyne* (2 vols) BAR 20.i and 20.ii.

Champion, T. C., 1975. 'Britain in the European iron age', *Archaeologia Atlantica 1*: 127–45.

Champion, T. C., 1977. 'Some decorated iron age pottery from Chinnor', *Ant. J. 57*: 91–3 and 98.

Chauvet, G., 1926. 'Deux sépultures à char en Poitou', *BA 44*: 1–23.

Chertier, B., 1973. 'Les gobelets de La Tene I du Musée Archéologique de Châlons-sur-Marne', *Celticum 13*: 552–70.

Chertier, B., 1976. 'Les Nécropoles de la civilisation des champs d'urnes dans la région des Marais de St-Gond (Marne)', *Gallia préhistoire*, 7th suppl.

Childe, V. G., 1948. 'The final bronze age in the Near East and Temperate Europe', *PPS 14*: 177–95.

Chisholm, M., 1962. *Rural Settlement and Land Use*.

Christison, D., 1894. 'The prehistoric fortresses of Treceiri, Carnarvon; and Eildon, Roxburgh', *PSAS 28*: 100–19.

Christison, D., 1898. *Early Fortifications in Scotland, Motes, Camps and Forts*.

Christison, D., 1900. 'The forts, "camps", and other field-works of Perth, Forfar, and Kincardine', *PSAS 34*: 43–120.

Christison, D., 1905. 'Report on the Society's excavations of forts on the Poltalloch Estate, Argyll, in 1904–5', *PSAS 39*: 259–322.

Clark, J. G. D., 1936. 'The timber monument at Arminghall and its affinities', *PPS 2*: 1–51.

Clark, J. G. D. and Fell, C. I., 1953. 'The early iron age site at Micklemoor Hill, West Harling, Norfolk, and its pottery', *PPS 19*: 1–40.

Clark, R. M., 1975. 'A calibration curve for radiocarbon dates', *Antiquity 49*: 251–66.

Close-Brooks, J., 1968. 'Considerazioni sulla chronologia delle facies arcaiche dell Etruria', *Studi Etruschi 35*: 323–9.

187

Coles, J. M., 1973. *Archaeology by Experiment*.
Coles, J. M. and Jones, R. A., 1975. 'Timber and radiocarbon dates', *Antiquity 49*: 123–5.
Colgrave, V W. Colgrave, B. (ed. and trans.), 1927. *The Life of Bishop Wilfrid by Eddius Stephanus*.
Colgrave and Mynors, HE. Colgrave, B. and Mynors, R. A. (ed. and trans.), 1969. *Bede's Ecclesiastical History of the English People*.
Collinson, J., 1791. *History and Antiquities of the County of Somerset*, III.
Collis, J. R., 1971. 'Functional and theoretical interpretations of British coinage', *World Archaeol. 3*: 71–84.
Collis, J. R., 1975. *Defended Sites of the Late La Tène in Central and Western Europe*, BAR S2.
Collis, J. R. (ed.), 1977a. *The Iron Age in Britain – a Review*.
Collis, J. R., 1977b. 'An approach to the iron age', in Collis 1977a: 1–7.
Collis, J. R., forthcoming. *Oppida: earliest towns in temperate Europe*.
Collis, J. R. and Ralston, I. B. M., 1976. 'Late La Tène defences', *Germania 54*: 135–46.
Cordier, G., 1972. 'I.Étude archéologique', in Cordier *et al.* 1972: 31–92.
Cordier, G., Riquet, R., Brabant, H. and Poulain, Th., 1972. 'Le site archéologique du dolmen de Villaine à Sublaines (Indre-et-Loire): première partie (néolithique, âge du bronze)', *Gallia préhistoire 15*: 31–135.
Cornwall, I. W., 1953. 'Soil science and archaeology with illustrations from some British bronze age monuments', *PPS 19*: 129–47.
Cotton, M. A., 1961. 'Relationships between iron age earthworks in France and England', *Celticum 1*: 99–113.
Cotton, M. A. and Frere, S. S., 1961. 'Enceintes de l'âge du fer au pays des Lémovices', *Gallia 19*: 31–54.
Cotton, M. A. and Frere, S. S., 1968. 'Ivinghoe Beacon excavations, 1963–65', *Records of Bucks. 18*: 187–260.
Coutil, L., 1909. 'Essai d'inventaire des mottes et enceintes du Département de l'Orne', *Compte-rendu, Congrès Préhistorique de France 5*: 599–620.
Cowen, J. D., 1951. 'The earliest bronze swords in Britain and their origins on the Continent', *PPS 17*: 195–213.
Cowen, J. D., 1955. 'Eine Einfuhrung in die Geschichte der bronzenen Griffzungenschwerter in Süddeutschland und den angrenzenden Gebieten', *36. Bericht der Römisch-Germanischen Kommission*: 52–155.
Cramp, R., 1976. 'Monastic sites', in *The Archaeology of Anglo-Saxon England*, ed. D. M. Wilson: 201–52.
Craw, J. H., 1930. 'Excavations at Dunadd and at other sites on the Poltalloch Estates, Argyll', *PSAS 64*: 111–46.
Crawford, I. and Switsur, R., 1977. 'Sandscaping and C14: the Udal, N.Uist', *Antiquity 51*: 124–36.
Crawford, O. G. S., 1934. 'Coludes Burh', *Antiquity 8*: 202–4.
Crawford, O. G. S., 1949. *Topography of Roman Scotland*.
Crumley, C. L., 1974. 'Celtic social structure: the generation of archaeologically testable hypotheses from literary evidence', *Museum of Anthropology, Univ. of Michigan, Anthropological Papers 54* (Ann Arbor).
Cunliffe, B. W., 1964. *Winchester Excavations 1949–60*: I (City of Winchester Libraries and Museums Committee).
Cunliffe, B. W., 1966. 'Stoke Clump, Hollingbury and the early pre-Roman iron age in Sussex', *SAC 104*: 109–20.
Cunliffe, B. W., 1968. 'Early pre-Roman iron age communities in eastern England', *Ant. J. 48*: 175–91.
Cunliffe, B. W., 1971. 'Some aspects of hill-forts and their cultural environments', in Hill and Jesson 1971: 53–69.
Cunliffe, B. W., 1974a. *Iron Age Communities in Britain* (1974; rev.edn 1978).

Cunliffe, B. W., 1974b. 'The iron age', in Renfrew 1974: 233–62.
Cunliffe, B. W., 1976a. *Iron Age Sites in Central Southern England* (CBA Research Report 16).
Cunliffe, B. W., 1976b. 'Hill-forts and oppida in Britain', in *Problems in Economic and Social Archaeology*, ed. G. de G. Sieveking, I. H. Longworth and K. E. Wilson: 343–58.
Cunliffe, B. W., 1976c. 'The origins of urbanisation in Britain', in Cunliffe and Rowley 1976: 135–61.
Cunliffe, B. W., 1976d. 'Danebury, Hampshire: second interim report on the excavations 1971–5', *Ant. J.* 56: 198–216.
Cunliffe, B. W., 1977. 'The iron age: a viewpoint', in Collis 1977a: 62.
Cunliffe, B. W., 1978. 'Settlement and population in the British iron age: some facts, figures and fantasies', in *Lowland Iron Age Communities in Europe*, ed. B. W. Cunliffe and T. Rowley, BAR S48: 3–24.
Cunliffe, B. W. and Phillipson, D. W., 1968. 'Excavations at Eldon's Seat, Encombe, Dorset, England', *PPS* 34: 191–237.
Cunliffe, B. W. and Rowley, T. (eds.), 1976. *Oppida in Barbarian Europe*, BAR S11.
Cunnington, M. E., 1911. 'Knap Hill Camp', *WAM* 37: 42–65.
Cunnington, M. E., 1917. 'Lidbury Camp', *WAM* 40: 12–36.
Cunnington, M. E., 1923. *The Early Iron Age Inhabited Site at All Cannings Cross Farm, Wiltshire.*
Cunnington, M. E., 1929. *Woodhenge.*
Cunnington, M. E. and Goddard, E. H., 1934. *Catalogue of Antiquities in the Museum . . . at Devizes* (Wiltshire Archaeological Society, 2nd edn 1934).
Curle, A. O., 1914. 'Report on the excavations . . . of . . . the Mote of Mark', *PSAS* 48: 125–68.
Curwen, E. and Hawkes, C. F. C., 1931. 'Prehistoric remains from Kingston Buci', *SAC* 72: 185–217.
Curwen, E. C., 1929. 'Excavations in the Trundle, Goodwood, 1928', *SAC* 70: 33–85.
Curwen, E. C., 1931. 'Excavations in the Trundle', *SAC* 72: 100–50.
Curwen, E. C., 1932. 'Excavations at Hollingbury Camp, Sussex', *Ant. J.* 12: 1–16.
Curwen, E. C., 1934. 'Excavations in Whitehawk neolithic camp, Brighton, 1932–3', *Ant. J.* 14: 99–133.
Curwen, E. C., 1954. *The Archaeology of Sussex* (2nd edn.).
Damon, P. E., Ferguson, C. W., Long, A. and Wallick, E. I., 1974. 'Dendrochronologic calibration of the radiocarbon time-scale', *American Antiquity* 39: 350–66.
Daubrée, A., 1881. 'Examen minéralogique et chimique de matériaux provenant de quelques forts vitrifiés de la France, conclusions qui en résulte', *RA*, 2nd ser., 41: 18–28.
Daubrée, A., 1882. 'Examen des matériaux des forts vitrifiés de Château-Meignan (Mayenne) et de Puy-de-Gaudy (Creuse), *RA*, 2nd ser., 43: 275–8.
Daugas, J.-P. and Pétrequin, P., 1970. 'Nouvelles considérations sur la céramique à cannelures en Franche-Comté à l'âge du bronze final', *RAECE* 21: 393–410.
Davies, H., 1936. 'The shale industries at Kimmeridge, Dorset', *Arch. J.* 93: 200–19.
Dayet, M., 1967. 'Recherches archéologiques au "Camp du Château", Salins, 1955–9', *RAECE* 18: 52–106.
Déchelette, J., 1902. 'Note sur l'oppidum de Bibracte et les principales stations gauloises contemporaines', *L'Anthropologie* 13: 74–83.
Déchelette, J., 1913. *Manuel d'archéologie préhistorique, celtique et gallo-romaine*, II pt 2: *Premier âge du fer ou époque de Hallstatt* (Paris).
Dehn, W., 1960. 'Einige Bemerkungen zum Murus Gallicus', *Germania* 38: 43–55.
Dehn, W., 1969. 'Noch einmal zum Murus Gallicus', *Germania* 47: 165–8.
Dehn, W. and Frey, O.-H., 1962. 'Die Absolute Chronologie der Hallstatt-und-Frühlatenezeit Mitteleuropas auf Gründ des Südimports', *Atti dèl 6 Congr. Internat. Sci. Prehist. e Protohist.* (Rome), I.

Delage, F., 1935. 'Le Camp de Cornouin, Vienne', *BSPF 32*: 386–97.

Delage, F. and Gorceix, C., 1923. 'L'Oppidum de Villejoubert, commune de Saint-Denis-des-Murs, Haute-Vienne', *BSPF 20*: 208–28.

Denyer, S., 1978. *African Traditional Architecture*.

Desittere, M., 1968. *De Urnenveldenkultuur in het Gebied tussen Nieder-Rijn en Noordzee* (Dissertationes Archaeologicae Gandenses, XI).

Desmazières, O., 1933. 'La Grosse Motte de Sainte-Hilaire-du-Bois et son enceinte calcinée', *BSPF 30*: 114–15.

Dixon, P. W., 1973. *Crickley Hill. Fifth Report* (Gloucestershire College of Art and Design).

Drewett, P., 1977. 'The excavation of a neolithic causewayed enclosure at Offham Hill, East Sussex, 1976', *PPS 43*: 201–42.

Drioton, C., 1905. 'Contribution à l'étude de la fortification antique dans l'arrondissement de Dijon', *Revue préhistorique illustrée de l'Est de la France 1*: 4–8 and 50–6.

Dubois, J., 1900. 'Monographie du Canton d'Eymoutiers', *Bull. Soc. Archéologique et Historique de Limousin 46*: 299–300.

Dumoutet, J., 1863. *Fouilles des caves du palais du Duc Jean de Berry* (Paris).

Dumville, D. N., 1977. 'On the North British section of the *Historia Brittonum*', *Welsh History Rev. 8*: 345–54.

Dumville, D. N., 1978. 'Palaeographical considerations in the dating of early Welsh verse', *Bull. Board of Celtic Studies 27*: 246–51.

Duncan, A. A. M., 1975. *Scotland, the Making of the Kingdom* (Edinburgh History of Scotland, I).

Durvin, P., 1962. 'A propos de quelques oppida du pays des Bellovaques', *Celticum 3*: 37–55.

Duval, A., 1970. 'Les pointes de flèche d'Alésia au Musée des Antiquités Nationales', *Antiquités Nationales 2*: 35–51.

Duval, P.-M., 1959. 'Une enquête sur les enceintes gauloises de l'Ouest et du Nord', *Gallia 17*: 37–62.

Duval, P.-M. and Kruta, V. (eds), 1975. *L'Habitat et la nécropole à l'âge du fer en Europe occidentale et centrale* (Paris).

Dyer, J. F., 1976. 'Ravensburgh Castle, Hertfordshire', in Harding 1976a: 153–61 and 421–3.

Earle, J. and Plummer, C. (eds), 1892, 1899. *Two of the Saxon Chronicles Parallel* (2 vols.)

Edeine, B., 1966. 'Le rempart de l'éperon barré de la Brèche-au-Diable (dit aussi du Mont-Joly) commune de Soumont-Saint-Quentin (Calvados)', *Gallia préhistoire 10*: 247–62.

Ellison, A., 1972. 'The bronze age pottery', in Holden 1972: 104–13.

Ellison, A. and Drewett, P., 1971. 'Pits and post-holes in the British early iron age: some alternative explanations', *PPS 37.i*: 183–94.

Fairhurst, H., 1939. 'The galleried dùn at Kildonan Bay, Kintyre', *PSAS 73*: 185–228.

Favret, P.-M., 1936. 'Les nécropoles des Jogasses à Chouilly (Marne)', *Préhistoire 5*: 24–119.

Feachem, R. W., 1955. 'Fortifications', in Wainwright F.T. 1955a: 66–86.

Feachem, R. W., 1956. 'The fortifications of Traprain Law', *PSAS 89*: 284–9.

Feachem, R. W., 1961. 'Unenclosed platform settlements', *PSAS 94*: 79–85.

Feachem, R. W., 1966. 'The hill-forts of northern Britain', in Rivet 1966: 59–87.

Fell, C. I., 1952. 'An early iron age settlement at Linton, Cambs.', *Procs Cambridge Ant. Soc. 46*: 31–42.

Feuvrier, J., 1913. 'Les enceintes et défenses préhistoriques et anhistoriques de la région de Dole', *Compte-rendu, Congrès Préhistorique de France 9*: 686–768.

Forde, C. D., Griffiths, W. E., Hogg, A. H. A. and Houlder, C. H., 1963. 'Excavations at Pen Dinas, Aberystwyth', *Arch. Camb. 112*: 125–53.

Forde-Johnston, J., 1976. *Hillforts of the Iron Age in England and Wales: a survey of the surface evidence*.

Fournier, G., 1961. 'Les enceintes en terre en Auvergne', *Bull. historique et scientifique de l'Auvergne 81*: 89–110.

Fowler, P. J., 1967. 'The archaeology of Fyfield and Overton Downs, Wiltshire: third interim report', *WAM 62*: 16–33.

Fowler, P. J., 1971. 'Hill-forts, AD 400–700', in Hill and Jesson 1971: 203–13.

Fowler, P. J., Gardner, K. S. and Rahtz, P. A., 1970. *Cadbury Congresbury, Somerset, 1968* (Dept of Extra-Mural Studies, University of Bristol).

Fox, A., 1961. 'South-western hill-forts', in Frere 1961: 35–60.

Fox, A. and Fox, C., 1960. 'Wansdyke reconsidered', *Arch. J. 115*: 1–48.

Fox, C., 1923. *The Archaeology of the Cambridge Region.*

Fox, C., 1955. *Offa's Dyke.*

Frere, S. S. (ed.), 1961. *Problems of the Iron Age in Southern Britain* (University of London Institute of Archaeology, Occasional Paper no. 11).

Gardner, W. and Savory, H. N., 1964. *Dinorben. A hill-fort occupied in early iron age and Roman times.*

Gates, T., 1975. *The Middle Thames Valley – an Archaeological Survey of the River Gravels.*

Giot, P. R. and Briard, J., 1969. 'Les retranchements du Cap d'Erquy: fouilles de 1968 au Fossé de Pleine-Garenne', *Annales de Bretagne 76*: 21–36.

Giot, P. R., Briard, J. and Avery, M., 1968. 'Les retranchements du Cap d'Erquy: fouilles de 1967 du Fossé Catuélan', *Annales de Bretagne 75*: 67–84.

Gourvest, J., 1961. 'L'Oppidum de Castillon, Calvados: première campagne de fouilles', *Annales de Normandie 11*: 99–103.

Goury, G., 1911. *L'Enceinte d'Haulzy et sa nécropole* (Nancy; Les Étapes de l'Humanité, 1, fasc. 2).

Graff, Y., 1963. 'Oppida et castella du pays des Belges', *Celticum 8*.

Graham, A., 1951. 'Archaeological gleanings from dark-age records', *PSAS 85*: 64–91.

Graham, A., 1959. 'Giudi', *Antiquity 33*: 63–5.

Graham-Campbell, J. A., 1976. 'The Viking-age silver and gold hoards of Scandinavian character from Scotland', *PSAS 107*: 114–35.

Gransden, A., 1974. *Historical Writing in England c. 550–c. 1307.*

Gray, H. St G., 1930. 'Excavations at Kingsdown Camp, near Mells, Somerset', *Archaeologia 80*: 59–96.

Green, H. S., 1974. 'Early bronze age burial, territory and population in Milton Keynes, Buckinghamshire, and the Great Ouse Valley', *Arch. J. 131*: 75–139.

Guilaine, J. (ed.), 1976. *La Préhistoire française* (Paris; Centre National de la Recherche Scientifique; 2 vols).

Guilbert, G. C., 1975a. 'Planned hillfort interiors', *PPS 41*: 203–21.

Guilbert, G. C., 1975b. 'Moel y Gaer, 1973: an area excavation on the defences', *Antiquity 49*: 109–17.

Guilbert, G. C., 1976. 'Moel y Gaer (Rhosesmor) 1972–1973: an area excavation in the interior', in Harding 1976a: 303–17 and 465–73.

Guilbert, G. C., 1977. 'The northern Welsh Marches: some recent developments', in Collis 1977a: 41–50.

Guilbert, G. C., 1978. 'Dinorben 1977–8', *Current Archaeol. 6*: 182–8.

Guyot, E., 1964. 'Découverte des époques d'édification et de transformation d'un éperon en Côte d'Or', *Celticum 9*: 95–102.

Harbison, P., 1971. 'Wooden and stone chevaux-de-frise in central and western Europe', *PPS 37.i*: 195–225.

Harden, D. B. (ed.), 1956a. *Dark-Age Britain.*

Harden, D. B., 1956b. 'Glass vessels in Britain and Ireland, AD 400–1000', in Harden 1956a: 132–67.

Harding, D. W., 1966. 'The pottery from Kirtlington, and its implications for the chronology of the earliest iron age in the Upper Thames Basin', *Oxoniensia 31*: 157–61.

Harding, D. W., 1972. *The Iron Age in the Upper Thames Basin.*

Harding, D. W., 1974. *The Iron Age in Lowland Britain.*

Harding, D. W. (ed.), 1976a. *Hillforts: later prehistoric earthworks in Britain and Ireland.*

Harding, D. W., 1976b. 'Blewburton Hill, Berkshire: re-excavation and reappraisal', in Harding 1976a: 133–46 and 408–13.

Harding, D. W. and Blake, I. M., 1963. 'An early iron age settlement in Dorset', *Antiquity 37*: 63–4.

Hardy, M., 1882. 'Le Camp-refuge à murailles vitrifiées de Castel-Sarrazi (Dordogne)', *Bull. de la Soc. Historique et Archéologique du Périgord 9*: 101–11.

Harris, M., 1975. *Culture, People, Nature* (New York).

Hartley, B. R., 1957. 'The Wandlebury iron age hill-fort, excavations of 1955–6', *Procs Cambridge Ant. Soc. 50*: 1–27.

Hatt, J.-J., 1941. 'Quelques objets de La Tène III trouvés au Puy-du-Tour près d'Argentat (Corrèze)', *Bull. de la Soc. Scientifique, Historique et Archéologique de la Corrèze 83*: 13–27.

Hatt, J.-J., 1955a. 'Chronique de protohistoire I', *BSPF 52*: 96–100.

Hatt, J.-J., 1955b. 'Chronique de protohistoire II', *BSPF 52*: 397–400.

Hatt, J.-J., 1956. 'Chronique de protohistoire III', *BSPF 53*: 434–45.

Hatt, J.-J., 1959. 'Chronique de protohistoire IV', *BSPF 55*: 304–6.

Hatt, J.-J., 1961. 'Chronique de protohistoire V', *BSPF 58*: 184–95.

Hatt, J.-J., 1976. 'Les fouilles du Pègue (Drome) de 1957 à 1975', *Gallia 34*: 31–56.

Hatt, J.-J. and Roualet, P., 1976. 'Le cimetière des Jogasses en Champagne et les origines de la civilisation de La Tène', *RAECE 27*: 421–48 and pls 1–57.

Hatt, J.-J. and Roualet, P., 1977. 'La chronologie de La Tène en Champagne', *RAECE 28*: 7–36.

Hawkes, C. F. C., 1931. 'Hillforts', *Antiquity 5*: 60–97.

Hawkes, C. F. C., 1934. 'The pottery', in Stevens 1934: 598–606.

Hawkes, C. F. C., 1940. 'The Marnian pottery and La Tène I brooch from Worth, Kent', *Ant. J. 20*: 115–21.

Hawkes, C. F. C., 1947. 'Britons, Romans and Saxons round Salisbury and in Cranborne Chase', *Arch. J. 104*: 27–81.

Hawkes, C. F. C., 1948. 'From bronze age to iron age: Middle Europe, Italy, the North and West', *PPS 14*: 196–218.

Hawkes, C. F. C., 1961. 'The ABC of the British iron age', in Frere 1961: 1–16.

Hawkes, C. F. C., 1962. 'Early iron age pottery from Linford, Essex', in Barton 1962: 83–7.

Hawkes, C. F. C., 1971. 'Fence, wall, dump, from Troy to Hod', in Hill and Jesson 1971: 5–18.

Hawkes, C. F. C., 1973a. '"Cumulative Celticity" in pre-Roman Britain', *Études celtiques 13*: 607–28.

Hawkes, C. F. C., 1973b. 'Innocence retrieval in archaeology', *Antiquity 47*: 176–8.

Hawkes, C. F. C. and Fell, C. I., 1943. 'The early iron age settlement at Fengate, Peterborough', *Arch. J. 100*: 188–223.

Hawkes, C. F. C., Myres, J. N. L. and Stevens, C. G., 1930. 'Saint Catharine's Hill, Winchester', *PHFCAS 11*.

Hawkes, C. F. C. and Smith, M. A., 1957. 'On some buckets and cauldrons of the bronze and early iron ages', *Ant. J. 37*: 131–98.

Hawkes, S. C. and Gray, M., 1969. 'Preliminary note on the early Anglo-Saxon settlement at New Wintles Farm, Eynsham', *Oxoniensia 34*: 1–4.

Hayes, J. W., 1972. *Late Roman Pottery.*

Hedges, J. and Buckley, D., 1978. 'Excavations at a neolithic causewayed enclosure, Orsett, Essex, 1975', *PPS 44*: 219–308.

Henderson, I., 1975. 'Inverness, a Pictish capital', in *The Hub of the Highlands, the Book of Inverness and District* (Inverness Field Club).

Henry, F., 1933. *Les Tumulus du Département de la Côte d'Or* (Paris).

Herrmann, F.-R., 1966. *Die Funde der Urnenfelderkultur in Mittel-und-Südhessen* (Römisch-Germanische Forschungen, Bd 27).

Hill, D. and Jesson, M. (eds), 1971. *The Iron Age and its Hill-Forts*.

Hodges, R., 1977. 'Some early medieval French wares in the British Isles: an archaeological assessment of the early French wine trade with Britain', in *Pottery and Early Commerce, Characterization and Trade in Roman and Later Ceramics*, ed. D. P. S. Peacock: 239–55.

Hodson, F. R., 1962. 'Some pottery from Eastbourne, the "Marnians" and the pre-Roman iron age in southern Britain', *PPS 28*: 140–55.

Hodson, F. R., 1964. 'Cultural grouping within the British pre-Roman iron age', *PPS 30*: 99–110.

Hodson, F. R., 1971. 'Three iron age brooches from Hammersmith', *British Museum Q. 35*: 50–7.

Hodson, F. R., 1975. Review of Harding 1974, *Ant. J. 55*: 430–2.

Hodson, F. R. and Rowlett, R. M., 1974. 'From 600 BC to the Roman Conquest', in Piggott *et al.* 1974: 157–91.

Hogg, A. H. A., 1945. 'Roman fragments from . . . St Abb's Head', *PSAS 79*: 172–3.

Hogg, A. H. A., 1960. 'Garn Boduan and Tre'r Ceiri, excavations at two Caernarvonshire hill-forts', *Arch. J. 117*: 1–39.

Hogg, A. H. A., 1969. 'A sample of French hill-forts', *Antiquity 43*: 260–73.

Hogg, A. H. A., 1971. 'Some applications of surface fieldwork', in Hill and Jesson 1971: 105–25.

Hogg, A. H. A., 1972a. 'Hill-forts in the coastal area of Wales', in *The Iron Age in the Irish Sea Province*, ed. C. Thomas (CBA Research Report 9): 11–23.

Hogg, A. H. A., 1972b. 'The size-distribution of hill-forts in Wales and the Marches', in Lynch and Burgess 1972: 293–306.

Hogg, A. H. A., 1973. 'Hill-forts and Herefordshire', *Trans. Woolhope Nat. Field Club 41*: 14–21.

Hogg, A. H. A., 1975. *Hill-Forts of Britain*.

Hogg, A. H. A., 1976. 'Hill-forts and settlements', in RCAHMW, *An Inventory of the Ancient Monuments in Glamorgan*, I: *Pre-Norman*, pt 2 *The Iron Age and Roman Occupation*: 5–79.

Hogg, A. H. A., 1978. 'Sample excavation', *Current Archaeol. 6*: 125–7.

Hogg, A. H. A., 1979. *British Hill-Forts: an index*, BAR 62.

Holden, E. W., 1972. 'A bronze age cemetery-barrow on Itford Hill, Beddingham, Sussex', *SAC 110*: 70–117.

Holste, F., 1953. *Die Bronze-zeit in Süd-und-Westdeutschland* (Handbuch der Urgeschichte Deutschlands, Bd 1; Berlin).

Hope-Taylor, B., 1966. 'Dunbar, Doon Hill', *Medieval Archaeol. 10*: 175–6.

Houlder, C., 1968. 'The henge monuments at Llandegai', *Antiquity 42*: 216–21.

Hugoniot, E. and Gourvest, J., 1961. 'L'oppidum de Mediolanum: Châteaumeillant, Cher. Fouilles de 1956–60', *Celticum 1*: 193–206.

Hugoniot, E. and Vannier, B., 1971. 'Fouille du rempart du camp de la Groutte', *Cahiers d'archéologie et d'histoire du Berry 24–5*: 22–3.

Hunter Blair, P., 1954. 'The Bernicians and their northern frontier', in *Studies in Early British History*, ed. N. K. Chadwick: 137–72.

Jackson, D. A. and Ambrose, T. M., 1978. 'Excavations at Wakerley, Northants., 1972–5', *Britannia 9*: 115–242.

Jackson, K., 1953. *Language and History in Early Britain*.

Jackson, K. H., 1959a. 'Edinburgh and the Anglian occupation of Lothian', in *The Anglo-Saxons*, ed. P. Clemoes: 34–42.

Jackson, K. H., 1959b. 'Arthur in early Welsh verse', in *Arthurian Literature in the Middle Ages*, ed. R. S. Loomis: 12–19.

Jackson, K. H., 1963. 'On the Northern Britain section in Nennius', in *Celt and Saxon, Studies in the Early British Border*, ed. N. K. Chadwick: 20–62.

Jackson, K. H., 1965. 'The Ogam inscription at Dunadd', *Antiquity 39*: 300–2.

Jackson, K. H., 1969. *The Gododdin.*

Jackson, K. H., 1973. 'Some questions in dispute about early Welsh literature and language', *Studia Celtic 8*: 1–32.

Joachim, H.-E., 1968. 'Die Hünsruck-Eifel-Kultur am Mittelrhein', *29. Beiheft der Bonner Jahrbücher.*

Jobey, G., 1965. 'Hill-forts and settlements in Northumberland', *Arch. Ael.*, 4th ser., *43*: 21–64.

Jobey, G., 1974. 'Notes on some population problems in the area between the two Roman walls', *Arch. Ael.*, 5th ser., *2*: 17–26.

Jobey, G., 1976. 'Traprain Law: a summary', in Harding 1976a: 191–204 and 436–8.

Jockenhövel, A., 1971. *Die Rasiermesser in Mitteleuropa* (Munich; Prähistorische Bronzefunde VIII, 1).

Joffroy, R., 1958. *Les Sépultures à char du premier âge du fer en France* (Paris).

Joffroy, R., 1960. *L'Oppidum de Vix et la civilisation hallstattienne finale dans l'Est de la France* (Paris; Publications de l'Université de Dijon, XX).

Joffroy, R., 1975. 'Vix: habitats et nécropoles', in Duval and Kruta 1975: 71–4.

Jope, E. M., 1961. 'Daggers of the early iron age in Britain', *PPS 27*: 307–43.

Jope, E. M., 1963. 'The regional cultures of medieval Britain', in *Culture and Environment: essays in honour of Sir Cyril Fox*, ed. I. L. Foster and L. Alcock: 327–50.

Kendrick, T. D., and Hawkes, C. F. C., 1932. *Archaeology in England and Wales 1914–1931.*

Kenyon, K. M., 1952. 'A survey of the evidence concerning the chronology and origins of iron age A in southern and midland Britain', *8th Ann. Rep. London Univ. Inst. Archaeol.*: 29–78.

Kimmig, W., 1940. *Die Urnenfelderkultur in Baden* (Römisch-Germanische Forschungen, Bd 14).

Kimmig, W., 1951. 'Où en est l'étude de la civilisation des champs d'urnes en France, principalement dans l'Est?', *RAECE 2*: 65–81.

Kimmig, W., 1952. 'Où en est l'étude de la civilisation des champs d'urnes en France, principalement dans l'Est?', *RAECE 3*: 137–72:

Kimmig, W., 1954a. 'Où en est l'étude de la civilisation des champs d'urnes en France, principalement dans l'Est?' *RAECE 5*: 7–28.

Kimmig, W., 1954b. 'Zur Urnenfelderkultur in Südwesteuropa', in *Festschrift für Peter Goessler* (Stuttgart; Tübinger Beiträge zur Vor-und-Frühgeschichte): 41–98.

Kimmig, W., 1970. 'Zur Frage der Urnenfelderkultur am Niederrhein', *Helinium 10*: 39–51.

Kimmig, W., 1979. Review of Chertier 1976, *Germania 57*: 201–6.

Kinnes, I., 1979. *Round Barrows and Ring Ditches in the British Neolithic.*

Kossack, G., 1957. 'Zur chronologie der alteren Hallstattzeit (Ha C) in bayerischen Alpenvorland', *Germania 35*: 207–23.

Kossack, G., 1959. *Südbayern während der Hallstattzeit* (Römisch-Germanische Forschungen, Bd 24; 2 vols).

De Laet, S. J., 1958. *Contributions a l'étude de la civilisation des champs d'urnes en Flandre* (Dissertationes Archaeologicae Gandenses, IV).

Laing, L., 1973a. 'The Mote of Mark', *Current Archaeol. 4*: 121–5.

Laing, L., 1973b. 'Cooking-pots and the origins of the Scottish medieval pottery industry', *Arch. J. 130*: 183–216.

Laing, L., 1975a. 'The Mote of Mark and the origins of Celtic interlace', *Antiquity 49*: 98–108.

Laing, L., 1975b. *Settlement Types in Post-Roman Scotland*, BAR 13.

Laing, L., 1975c. *The Archaeology of Late Celtic Britain and Ireland c. 400–1200 AD.*

Laing, L., 1977. 'Segontium and the post-Roman occupation of Wales', in *Studies in Celtic Survival*, ed. L. Laing, BAR 37: 57–60.

de Lasteyrie, R., 1883. 'Séance du Comité des Travaux Historiques et Scientifiques du

28 mars 1883', *BA 1*: 13–18.

Lawlor, H. C., 1925. *The Monastery of Saint Mochaoi of Nendrum*.

Lecler, A., 1883. 'Monographie du canton de Saint Mathieu', *Bull. de la Société Archéologique et Historique du Limousin 31*: 5–70.

Leeds, E. T., 1935. 'Recent iron age discoveries in Oxfordshire and north Berkshire', *Ant. J. 15*: 30–41.

Léger, P., 1972. 'Le Camp des Chastres, commune d'Aubusson, campagne de fouilles 1972', *Mémoires de la Soc. des Sciences Naturelles et Archéologiques de la Creuse 38*: 35–9.

Liddell, D. M., 1933. 'Excavations at Meon Hill', *PHFCAS 12*: 126–62.

Liddell, D. M., 1935. 'Report of excavations at Meon Hill, second season, 1933', *PHFCAS 13*: 7–54.

Liddell, D. M., 1936. 'Report on the excavations at Hembury Fort', *Procs Devon Arch. Exploration Soc. 2*: 134–75.

Lièvre, A. F., 1888. 'Le camp de Voeuil', *Bull. de la Soc. Archéologique et Historique de la Charente*.

Lintz, G., 1976. 'L'oppidum du Puy de Sermus, commune de Saint-Geniez-ô-Merle (Corrèze), *Bull. de la Soc. des Lettres, Sciences et Arts de la Corrèze 79*: 41–52.

Lobjois, G., 1965. 'Les fouilles de l'oppidum gaulois "du Vieux Laon" à Saint-Thomas, Aisne', *Celticum 15*: 1–26.

Lynch, F. and Burgess, C. (eds), 1972. *Prehistoric Man in Wales and the West – essays in honour of Lily F. Chitty*.

MacCana, P., 1971. Review of Jackson 1969, *Celtica 9*: 316–29.

MacGibbon, D., and Ross, T., 1896–7. *The Ecclesiastical Architecture of Scotland from the Earliest Christian Times to the Seventeenth Century* (3 vols).

MacKie, E. W., 1976a. *Science and Society in Prehistoric Britain*.

MacKie, E. W., 1976b. 'The vitrified forts of Scotland', in Harding 1976a: 205–35 and 439–45.

MacNair, A. S., 1973. 'History', in *Queen Elizabeth Forest Park, Ben Lomond, Loch Ard and the Trossachs*, ed. H. L. Edlin (Forestry Commission Guide): 1–17.

McNeill, P. and Nicholson, R. (eds), 1975. *An Historical Atlas of Scotland c. 400–c. 1600*.

Mansfeld, G., 1973. *Die Fibeln der Heuneberg, 1950–1966* (Römisch-Germanische Forschungen, Bd 33).

Mariën, M.-E., 1964. *La Nécropole à Tombelles de Saint-Vincent* (Bruxelles; Musées Royaux d'Art et d'Histoire, Monographies d'Archéologie Nationale, 3).

Martin, G., 1905. *Histoire d'une frontière: Aigurande depuis l'époque gauloise jusqu'à nos jours* (Guéret).

Matthews, C. L., 1976. *Occupation Sites on a Chiltern Ridge*, pt 1: *Neolithic, Bronze Age and Early Iron Age*, BAR 29.

Maxe-Werly, L., 1877. 'Notice sur l'oppidum de Boviolles, Meuse', *Mémoires de la Soc. des Antiquaires de France 38*: 276–92.

May, J., 1974. 'British antiquity 1973–4. The iron age', *Arch. J. 131*: 392–8.

Mayaud, S. P., 1881. *Notice sur l'oppidum gaulois de Châteauvieux, Creuse* (Paris).

Mercer, R. J., 1970. 'Metal arrowheads in the European bronze and early iron ages', *PPS 36*: 171–213.

Mercer, R. J., 1975. 'Carn Brea', *Current Archaeol. 4*: 360–5.

von Merhart, G., 1952. 'Studien über einige Gattungen von Bronzegefässen', in *Festschrift des Römisch-Germanischen Zentralmuseums in Mainz*, II: 1–71 and Taf. 1–26.

Meyrick, O., 1947. 'Notes on some early iron age sites in the Marlborough district', *WAM 51*: 256–63.

Miles, D., 1974. 'Abingdon and region: early Anglo-Saxon settlement evidence', in *Anglo-Saxon Settlement and Landscape*, ed. T. Rowley, BAR 6: 36–41.

Miles, H. and Miles, T., 1974. 'Trethurgy', *Current Archaeol. 4*: 142–7.

Millotte, J.-P., 1963. *Le Jura et les plaines de Saône aux âges des métaux* (Paris, 2 vols; Annales Littéraires de l'Université de Besançon 59).

Millotte, J.-P., 1965. *Carte archéologique de la Lorraine* (Paris; Annales Littéraires de l'Université de Besançon 73).

Millotte, J.-P., 1976. 'Les civilisations de l'âge du fer dans l'est de la France', in Guilaine 1976: II, 837–46.

Ministry of Public Building and Works, 1967. *Excavations – Annual Report 1967*.

Mohen, J.-P., 1972. 'Que savons nous de l'âge du bronze dans le nord de la France? (Départements du Nord et du Pas-de-Calais)', *BSPF* 69: 444–64.

Mohen, J.-P. and Coffyn, A., 1970. *Les Nécropoles hallstattiennes de la région d'Arcachon* (Madrid; Bibliotheca Praehistorica Hispana, XI).

Mommèja, J., 1901. 'L'oppidum des Nitiobriges', *Congrès archéologique de France 48*: 167–242 (Agen).

Money, J., 1974. 'Garden Hill', *Current Archaeol. 4*: 185–8.

Mordant, C. and D., 1970. *Le site protohistorique des Gours-aux-Lions, à Marolles-sur-Seine (Seine-et-Marne)* (Mémoires de la Société Préhistorique Française 8).

Müller-Karpe, H., 1948. *Die Urnenfelderkultur im Hanauer Land* (Schriften zur Urgeschichte, Bd 1; Hessisches Landesmuseum Kassel und Hanauer Geschichtsverein).

Müller-Karpe, H., 1959. *Beiträge zur Chronologie der Urnenfelderkultur nördlich und südlich der Alpen* (Römisch-Germanische Forschungen, Bd 22, 2 vols).

Munro, R., 1882. *Ancient Scottish Lake-Dwellings or Crannogs*.

Murat, A. and Murat, J., 1967. 'Cinquante ans de recherches archéologiques à la station du Puy-du-Tour près d'Argentat, Corrèze', *Ogam 19*: 369–96.

Musson, C. R., 1976. 'Excavations at the Breiddin, 1969–1973', in Harding 1976a: 293–302 and 461–4.

Musson, R., 1950. 'An excavation at Combe Hill Camp near Eastbourne, August 1949', *SAC 89*: 105–16.

Myres, J. N. L., 1964. 'Wansdyke and the origin of Wessex', in *Studies in British History*, ed. H. R. Trevor-Roper: 1–27.

Myres, J. N. L., 1969. *Anglo-Saxon Pottery and the Settlement of England*.

Myres, J. N. L., 1977. *A Corpus of Anglo-Saxon Pottery of the Pagan Period* (2 vols).

Naroll, R., 1962. 'Floor area and settlement population', *American Antiquity 27*: 587–9.

Nash, D., 1978. *Settlement and Coinage in Central Gaul, c. 200–50 BC*, BAR S39.

Nicolardot, J.-P., 1973. 'Structures et datations par mesure du radio carbone du rempart et de l'habitat néolithique du Camp de Myard à Vitteaux, Côte d'Or', *BSPF* (CRSM), 8: 68.

Nicolardot, J.-P., 1974. 'Structures d'habitats de hauteur à caractères défensifs dans le Centre-Est de la France', *Antiquités nationales 6*: 32–45.

Nicolardot, J.-P., 1975. 'Nécropoles et habitats de la Côte d'Or aux âges du fer', in Duval and Kruta 1975: 87–93.

Niederlender, A., Lacam, R. and Arnal, J., 1966. 'Le Gisement néolithique de Roucadour (Thémines-Lot)', *Gallia préhistoire*, 3rd suppl.

Nisbet, H., 1974. 'A geological approach to vitrified forts: the archaeological and scientific background', *Science and Archaeol. 12*: 3–12.

Nisbet, H., 1975. 'A geological approach to vitrified forts: bedrock and building stone', *Science and Archaeol. 15*: 3–16.

de la Noë, G.-O., 1887. 'Principes de la fortification antique depuis les temps préhistoriques . . .', *Bull. géographique, historique et descriptive 2*: 201–331.

de la Noë, G.-O., 1892. 'Les enceintes vitrifiées et les enceintes calcinées', *Bull. géographique, historique et descriptive*.

O'Kelly, M. J., 1970. 'Problems of Irish ring-forts', in *The Irish Sea Province in Archaeology and History*, ed. D. Moore: 50–4.

Olivier, L., Olivier, M. and Olivier, G., 1969. 'L'enceinte du Fou de Verdun et son environnement', *RAECE 20*: 107–31.

Oswald, A. (ed.), 1967. 'Excavations for the Avon/Severn Research Committee at Barford, Warwickshire', *Trans. Birmingham Arch. Soc. 83*: 2–64.

Page, J. N. L., 1890. *An Exploration of Exmoor*.

Palmer, R., 1976. 'Interrupted ditch enclosures in Britain: the use of aerial photography ₋or comparative studies', *PPS 42*: 161–86.

Parrington, M., 1978. *The Excavation of an Iron Age Settlement, Bronze Age Ring-Ditches and Roman Features at Ashville Trading Estate, Abingdon, Oxfordshire 1974–76* (CBA Research Report 28).

Passmore, A. D., 1914. 'Liddington Castle (Camp)', *WAM 38*: 576–84.

Pautreau, J.-P., 1976. 'Le Camp Allaric, commune d'Aslonnes (Vienne): premiers résultats', *L'Anthropologie 80*: 389–430.

Perry, B., 1969. 'Iron age enclosures on the Hampshire chalklands', *Arch.J. 126*: 29–43.

Philippe, J., 1936. 'Le Fort-Harrouard', *L'Anthropologie 46*: 257–301.

Philippe, J., 1937. 'Le Fort-Harrouard', *L'Anthropologie 47*: 253–308.

Piggott, C. M., 1943. 'Report on the pottery from Winklebury Camp, Hants.', *PHFCAS 15*: 56–7.

Piggott, S., 1948. 'The excavations at Cairnpapple Hill, West Lothian, 1947–48', *PSAS 82*: 68–123.

Piggott, S., 1959. *Approach to Archaeology*.

Piggott, S., 1965. *Ancient Europe from the Beginnings of Agriculture to Classical Antiquity*.

Piggott, S., 1968. *The Druids*.

Piggott, S., Daniel, G. and McBurney, C. (eds), 1974. *France before the Romans*.

Piggott, S. and Piggott, C. M., 1940. 'Excavations at Rams Hill, Uffington, Berkshire', *Ant.J. 20*: 465–80.

Pilcher, J. R. and Baillie, M. G. L., 1978. 'Implications of a European radiocarbon calibration', *Antiquity 52*: 217–22.

Pintaud, R. C., 1956. 'Camp des Anglais ou de Voeuil ou Fort des Anglais', *Congrès Préhistorique de la France: Compte-rendu de la XV session Poitiers-Angoulême 1956*: 122–6.

Piroutet, M., 1906. 'Note sommaire pour servir d'introduction à l'étude des enceintes du Jura salinois', *Revue préhistorique illustrée de l'Est de la France 2*: 33–53.

Piroutet, M., 1909. 'Une fouille au Mont Guérin, Jura', *RA*, 4th ser., *13*: 39–45.

Piroutet, M., 1913. 'Note sur l'existence et l'âge des retranchements à calcination dans les camps préhistoriques du Jura salinois', *BSPF 10*: 161–6.

Piroutet, M., 1930. 'La citadelle hallstattienne à poteries helléniques de Château-sur-Salins (Jura)', *Ve Congrès International d'Archéologie Alger*: 47–86.

Piroutet, M. and Déchelette, J., 1909. 'Découverte de vases grecs dans un oppidum hallstattien du Jura', *RA*, 4th ser., *13*: 193–202.

Pitt Rivers, A., 1888. *Excavations in Cranborne Chase*, II.

Pollard, S. H. M., 1966. 'Neolithic and dark-age settlements on High Peak, Sidmouth, Devon', *Procs Devon Arch. Exploration Soc. 23*: 35–59.

Powell, T. G. E., 1948. 'A late bronze age hoard from Welby, Leicestershire', *Arch.J. 105*: 27–40.

Powell, T. G. E., 1963. 'The inception of the final bronze age in Middle Europe', *PPS 29*: 214–34.

Preynat, J.-P., 1962. 'Un site de La Tène en Forez: l'oppidum d'Essalois', *Celticum 3*: 287–314.

Radford, C. A. R., 1954. 'The tribes of southern Britain', *PPS 20*: 1–26.

Radford, C. A. R., 1956. 'Imported pottery found at Tintagel, Cornwall', in Harden 1956a: 59–70.

Raftery, B., 1969. 'Freestone Hill, Co. Kilkenny . . .', *Procs Royal Irish Academy 68c*: 1–108.

Rahtz, P. A., 1969. 'Cannington hillfort 1963', *Procs Somerset Arch. and Nat. Soc. 113*: 56–68.

Rahtz, P. A., 1977. 'Late Roman cemeteries and beyond', in *Burial in the Roman World*, ed. R. Reece (CBA Research Report 22): 53–64.

Rahtz, P. A. and ApSimon, A. M., 1962. 'Excavations at Shearplace Hill, Sydling St Nicholas, Dorset, England', *PPS 28*: 289–328.

Rahtz, P. A., and Barton, K. J., 1963. 'Maes Knoll Camp . . .', *Procs Univ. Bristol Spel-*

aeological Soc. 10.i: 9–10.

Rahtz, P. A. and Fowler, P. J., 1972. 'Somerset AD 400–700', in *Archaeology and the Landscape*, ed. P. J. Fowler: 187–221.

Rahtz, P. A. and Musty, J. W. G., 1960. 'Excavations at Old Sarum, 1957', *WAM* 57: 352–70.

Ralston, I. B. M., 1980. 'The Green Castle and the promontory forts of North-East Scotland', *Scottish Arch. Forum* 10: 27–40.

Ralston, I. B. M. and Büchsenschütz, O. E., 1975. 'Late pre-Roman iron age forts in Berry', *Antiquity* 49: 8–18.

Raymond, P., 1910. 'Etude sur les enceintes vitrifiées et calcinées de la Gaule', *Revue préhistorique* 5: 1–32.

RCAHME 1975. *An Inventory of the Historical Monuments in the County of Dorset*, V: *East Dorset*.

RCAHME 1976. *Ancient and Historical Monuments in the County of Gloucester*, I: *Iron Age and Romano-British Monuments in the Gloucestershire Cotswolds*.

RCAHME 1979. *Stonehenge and its Environs: monuments and land use*.

RCAHMS 1951. *An Inventory of the Ancient and Historical Monuments of the City of Edinburgh*.

RCAHMS 1971. *Argyll, an Inventory of the Ancient Monuments*, I: *Kintyre*.

RCAHMW 1956. *An Inventory of the Ancient Monuments in Caernarvonshire*, I: *East*.

Renaud, J., 1962. 'Notes sur l'oppidum d'Essalois (Loire): le tracé et la structure du rempart', *Celticum* 3: 57–67.

Renfrew, C., 1973. *Before Civilization: the radiocarbon revolution and prehistoric Europe*.

Renfrew, C. (ed.), 1974. *British Prehistory: a new outline*.

Renfrew, C., Harkness, D., and Switsur, R., 1976. 'Quanterness, radiocarbon and the Orkney cairns', *Antiquity* 50: 194–204.

Reynolds, N., 1980. 'Dark age timber halls and the background to excavation at Balbridie', *Scottish Arch. Forum* 10: 41–60.

Reynolds, P. J., 1972. 'Experimental archaeology', *Worcs. Arch. Newsletter* 9.

Reynolds, P. J., 1979. *Iron-Age Farm. The Butser experiment*.

Rhodes, P. P., 1948. 'Prehistoric and Roman site at Wittenham Clumps, Berkshire', *Oxoniensia* 13: 18–31.

Richardson, K. M., 1940. 'Excavations at Poundbury, Dorchester, Dorset, 1939', *Ant. J.* 20: 429–48.

Richardson, K. M., 1951. 'The excavation of iron age villages on Boscombe Down West', *WAM* 54: 123–68.

Richardson, K. M. and Young, A., 1951. 'An iron age A site on the Chilterns', *Ant. J.* 31: 132–48.

Rigoir, J., 1968. 'Les sigillées paléochrétiennes grises et orangées', *Gallia* 26: 177–244.

Ritchie, A., 1971. 'Settlement archaeology – methods and problems', in Hill and Jesson 1971: 91–5.

Ritchie, J. N. G., 1976. 'The Stones of Stenness, Orkney', *PSAS* 107: 1–60.

Rivet, A. L. F. (ed.), 1962. Introduction to *Map of Southern Britain in the Iron Age* (Ordnance Survey).

Rivet, A. L. F. (ed.), 1966. *The Iron Age in Northern Britain*.

Rivet, A. L. F., 1971. 'Hill-forts in action', in Hill and Jesson 1971: 189–202.

Rivet, A. L. F. and Jackson, K., 1970. 'The British section of the Antonine Itinerary', *Britannia* 1: 34–82.

Robertson-Mackay, R., 1962. 'The excavation of the causewayed camp at Staines, Middlesex', *Arch. Newsletter* 7: 131–4.

Robertson-Mackay, R., 1977. 'The defences of the iron age hillfort at Winklebury, Basingstoke, Hampshire', *PPS* 43: 131–54.

Rossi, L., 1971. 'Dacian fortifications on Trajan's Column', *Ant .J.* 51: 30–5.

Rowlett, R. M., Rowlett, E. S.-J. and Boureux, M., 1969. 'A rectangular early La Tène

Marnian house at Chassemy (Aisne)', *World Archaeol.* 1: 106–35.

Rupin, E., 1893. 'L'enceinte vitrifiée de Sermus, commune de Saint-Privat (Corrèze)', *Bull. de la Soc. Scientifique, Historique et Archéologique de la Corrèze* 15: 177–98.

Rutherford, A., 1976. 'Giudi revisited', *Bull. Board of Celtic Studies* 26: 440–4.

Salway, P., 1967. 'Excavations at Hockwold cum Wilton, Norfolk, 1961–62', *Procs Cambridge Ant. Soc.* 60: 39–80.

Sancier, R., 1964. 'L'oppidum d'Erquy', *Ogam* 16: 591–8.

Sandars, N. K., 1957. *Bronze Age Cultures in France.*

Sandars, N. K., 1971. 'From bronze age to iron age: a sequel to a sequel', in Boardman *et al.* 1971: 1–29.

Saunders, C., 1971. 'The pre-Belgic iron age in the central and western Chilterns', *Arch. J.* 128: 1–30.

Savory, H. N., 1937. 'An early iron age site at Long Wittenham, Berks.', *Oxoniensia* 2: 1–11.

Savory, H. N., 1939. 'Early Man IV: early iron age', *Victoria County History, Oxfordshire*, I: 251–61 and pls. X–XII.

Savory, H. N., 1960. 'Excavations at Dinas Emrys, Beddgelert (Caerns.), 1954–56', *Arch. Camb.* 109: 13–77.

Savory, H. N., 1971a. *Excavations at Dinorben, 1965–9.*

Savory, H. N., 1971b. 'A Welsh bronze age hillfort', *Antiquity* 45: 251–61.

Savory, H. N., 1976a. *Guide Catalogue of the Early Iron Age Collections* (National Museum of Wales).

Savory, H. N., 1976b. 'Welsh hillforts: a reappraisal of recent research', in Harding 1976a: 237–91 and 446–60.

Sawyer, P. H., 1968. *Anglo-Saxon Charters: an annotated list and bibliography* (Royal Historical Society).

Schauer, P., 1971. *Die Schwerter in Süddeutschland, Österreich und der Schweiz*, I (Munich; Prähistorische Bronzefunde, IV.2).

Simpson, G., 1964. 'The hill-forts of Wales and their relation to Roman Britain: a recension', in Gardner and Savory 1964: 209–20.

Simpson, W. D., 1941. 'The development of Dunnottar Castle', *Arch. J.* 98: 87–98.

Simpson, W. D., 1951. 'Glen Urquhart and its castle', in *Aspects of Archaeology in Britain and Beyond*, ed. W. F. Grimes: 316–31.

Simpson, W. D., 1964. *Urquhart Castle.*

Simpson, W. D., 1968. *Dunnottar Castle, Historical and Descriptive.*

Simpson, W. G., 1967. 'The Welland Valley project'. *Current Archaeol.* 1: 2–4.

Skinner, Rev. J., *Journals* (British Museum Add. MSS. 33646 F10, 33719 F95–98; 1812 and 1830).

Small, A., 1969. 'Burghead', *Scottish Arch. Forum* 1: 61–8.

Small, A. and Cottam, M. B., 1972. *Craig Phadrig* (University of Dundee, Department of Geography, Occasional Papers no. 1).

Small, A., Thomas, C. and Wilson, D. M., 1973. *St Ninian's Isle and its Treasure*, 2 vols.

Smith, C., 1977. 'The valleys of the Tame and Middle Trent – their populations and ecology during the late first millennium BC', in Collis 1977a: 51–61.

Smith, I. F., 1965. *Windmill Hill and Avebury: excavations by Alexander Keiller.*

Smith, K., 1977. 'The excavation of Winklebury Camp, Basingstoke, Hampshire', *PPS* 43: 31–130.

Smith, M. A., 1955. 'The limitations of inference in archaeology', *Arch. Newsletter* 6: 3–7.

Smith, M. A. (ed.), 1957. 'Bronze age hoards and grave-groups from the N.E. Midlands', *Inventaria Archaeologica, Great Britain*, 4th set, cards G.B. 19–24.

Smith, M. A., 1959. 'Some Somerset hoards and their place in the bronze age of southern Britain', *PPS* 25: 144–87.

Smith, R. A. (ed.), 1925. *British Museum Guide to Early Iron Age Antiquities* (2nd edn).

Soutou, A., 1962. 'Le castellum gabale du Roc de la Fare (commune de Laval-du-

Tarn), Lozère', *Gallia 20*: 333–51.

Stanford, S. C., 1970. 'Credenhill Camp, Herefordshire: an iron age hill-fort capital', *Arch. J. 127*: 82–129.

Stanford, S. C., 1971. 'Invention, adoption and imposition – the evidence of the hill-forts', in Hill and Jesson 1971: 41–52.

Stanford, S. C., 1972. 'The function and population of hill-forts in the central Marches', in Lynch and Burgess 1972: 307–19.

Stanford, S. C., 1974a. *Croft Ambrey.*

Stanford, S. C., 1974b. 'Native and Roman in the central Welsh borderland', in Birley *et al.* 1974: 44–60.

Stead, I. M., 1967. 'A la Tène III burial at Welwyn Garden City', *Archaeologia 101*: 1–62.

Stead, I. M., 1968. 'An iron age hill-fort at Grimthorpe, Yorkshire, England', *PPS 34*: 148–90.

Stevens, F., 1934. ' "The Highfield Pit Dwellings", Fisherton, Salisbury', *WAM 46*: 579–624.

Stevenson, R. B. K., 1949. 'The nuclear fort of Dalmahoy, Midlothian, and other dark age capitals', *PSAS 83*: 186–98.

Stevenson, R. B. K., 1976. 'The earlier metalwork of Pictland', in *To Illustrate the Monuments. Essays on archaeology presented to Stuart Piggott*, ed. J. V. S. Megaw: 246–51.

Stone, J. F. S., 1935. 'Trial excavations at Hayes Wood Enclosure, Freshford, Som.', *Procs Somerset Arch. and Nat. Soc. 81*: 133–48.

Stuart, J. D. M. and Birkbeck, J. M., 1937. 'A Celtic village on Twyford Down, excavated 1933–1934', *PHFCAS 13*: 188–207.

Swan, V. G., 1975. 'Oare reconsidered and the origins of Savernake ware in Wiltshire', *Britannia 6*: 36–61.

Tauvel, D., 1973. 'Le premier âge du fer dans la Vienne', *Revue archéologique du Centre de la France 12*: 227–42.

Thénot, A., 1976. 'Les civilisations de l'âge du fer en Champagne', in Guilaine 1976: II, 826–36.

Thomas, C., 1959. 'Imported pottery in dark-age western Britain', *Medieval Archaeol. 3*: 89–111.

Thomas, C., 1971. *The Early Christian Archaeology of North Britain.*

Thomas, C., 1976. 'Imported late-Roman Mediterranean pottery in Ireland and western Britain: chronologies and implications', *Procs Royal Irish Academy 76c*: 245–55.

Thomas, F. W.L., 1879. 'Dunadd, Glassary, Argyllshire; the place of inauguration of the Dalriadic kings', *PSAS 13*: 28–47.

Thomas, I., 1960. 'The excavations at Kynance 1953–1960', *The Lizard* (The Lizard Field Club, Marazion, Cornwall), *n.s. 1.iv*: 5–16.

Toms, H., 1925. 'Bronze age or earlier lynchets', *PDNHAS 46*: 89–100.

Tratman, E. K., 1963. 'The iron age defences and Wansdyke', *Procs Univ. Bristol Spelaeological Soc. 10.i*: 11–15.

Tratman, E. K., 1970. 'The Glastonbury Lake Village: a reconsideration', *Procs Univ. Bristol Spelaeological Soc. 12.ii*: 143–67.

Triger, R., 1907. *Sainte-Suzanne (Mayenne): son histoire et ses fortifications* (Paris).

Tronquart, G., 1976. 'Le camp celtique de la Bure (Vosges)', *Gallia 34*: 201–14.

Unz, C., 1973. 'Die spätbronzezeitliche Keramik in Sudwestdeutschland, in der Schweiz und in Ostfrankreich', *Prähistorische Zeitschrift 48*: 1–124, plus 49 plates and 5 maps.

Varley, W. J., 1964. *Cheshire before the Romans.*

Varley, W. J., 1968. 'Barmston and the Holderness crannogs', *East Riding Archaeologist 1.i*: 12–26.

Vazeilles, M., 1936. *La très vieille histoire locale (part 3): archéologie préhistorique, celtique et gallo-romaine de la Montagne Limousine* (Bourges).

Vazeilles, M., 1938. 'Les bracelets en or du Bois de Train, commune de Saint-

Pardoux-le-Vieux', *Bull. de la Soc. Scientifique, Historique et Archéologique de la Corrèze* 60: 102.

Verron, G., 1976. 'Les civilisations de l'âge du bronze en Normandie', in Guilaine 1976: II, 585–600.

Vimont, E. and Pommerol, F., 1884. 'Présentation d'un échantillon de muraille vitrifiée provenant des environs du Châteauneuf-les-Bains', *Revue d'Auvergne* 1: 68–72.

Viré, A., 1913. 'Les fouilles protohistoriques de Luzech, du Puits d'Issolud, et d'Uzerche', *BSPF* 10: 687–713.

Vogt, E., 1950. 'Der Beginn der Hallstattzeit in der Schweiz', *Jahrbücher der Schweizerischen Gesellschaft für Urgeschichte* 40: 209–31.

Wade-Evans, A. W., 1938. *Nennius's 'History of the Britons'*.

Wailes, B., 1976. 'Dún Ailinne: an interim report', in Harding 1976a: 319–38 and 474–7.

Wainwright, F. T., 1948. 'Nechtansmere', *Antiquity* 32: 82–97.

Wainwright, F. T. (ed.), 1955a. *The Problem of the Picts*.

Wainwright, F. T., 1955b. 'The Picts and the problem', in Wainwright 1955a: 1–53.

Wainwright, F. T., 1963. *The Souterrains of Southern Pictland*.

Wainwright, G. J., 1962. 'The excavation of an earthwork at Castell Bryn-Gwyn, Llanidan parish, Anglesey', *Arch. Camb.* 111: 25–58.

Wainwright, G. J., 1967. 'The excavation of an iron age hillfort on Bathampton Down, Somerset', *Trans Bristol and Glos. Arch. Soc.* 86: 42–59.

Wainwright, G. J., 1968. 'The excavation of a Durotrigian farmstead near Tollard Royal in Cranborne Chase, southern England', *PPS* 34: 102–47.

Wainwright, G. J., 1970. 'An iron age promontory fort at Budbury, Bradford-on-Avon, Wilts.', *WAM* 65: 108–66.

Wainwright, G. J., 1971. 'The excavation of a fortified settlement at Walesland Rath, Pembrokeshire', *Britannia* 2: 48–108.

Wainwright, G. J., 1979a. *Mount Pleasant, Dorset: Excavations 1970–71* (Society of Antiquaries of London, Research Report 37).

Wainwright, G. J., 1979b. *Gussage All Saints. An iron age settlement in Dorset.* (Department of the Environment, Archaeological Report 10).

Wainwright, G. J. and Longworth, I. H., 1971. *Durrington Walls: Excavations 1966–68* (Society of Antiquaries of London, Research Report 29).

Wamser, G., 1975. 'Zur Hallstattkultur in Ostfrankreich. Die Fundgruppen im Jura und in Burgund', *56. Bericht der Römisch-Germanischen Kommission*: 1–179.

Ward Perkins, J. B., 1938. 'An early iron age site at Crayford, Kent', *PPS* 4: 151–68.

Waterbolk, H. T., 1977. 'Walled enclosures of the iron age in the north of the Netherlands', *Palaeohistoria* 19: 97–172.

Watkins, T., 1979. 'Dalladies: the excavation of an iron age settlement in Kincardineshire', *PSAS* 110.

Watson, W. J., 1926. *The History of the Celtic Place-Names of Scotland* (Edinburgh 1926; reprinted Shannon 1973).

Wendland, W. M. and Donley, D. L., 1971. 'Radiocarbon-calendar age relationship', *Earth and Planetary Science Letters* 11: 135–9.

Wheeler, R. E. M., 1926. 'The Roman Fort near Brecon', *Y Cymmrodor 37*.

Wheeler, R. E. M., 1943. *Maiden Castle, Dorset* (Society of Antiquaries of London, Research Report 12).

Wheeler, R. E. M., 1953. 'An early iron age "beach-head" at Lulworth, Dorset', *Ant. J. 33*: 1–13.

Wheeler, R. E. M., 1954. *Archaeology from the Earth*.

Wheeler, R. E. M. and Richardson, K. M., 1957. *Hill-Forts of Northern France* (Society of Antiquaries of London, Research Report 19).

Wheeler, R. E. M. and Wheeler, T. V., 1932. *Report on the Excavation of the Prehistoric, Roman and Post-Roman Site in Lydney Park, Gloucester* (Society of Antiquaries of London, Research Report 9).

Whitelock, D. (ed.), 1955. *English Historical Documents c. 500–1042*.

Williams, A., 1950. 'Excavations at Allard's Quarry, Marnhull', *PDNHAS* 72: 20–75.

Williams, I., 1938. *Canu Aneirin*.

Williams-Freeman, J. P., 1940. 'Field archaeology, 1938–39', *PHFCAS* 14: 270.

Worsfold, F. H., 1943. 'A report on the late bronze age site excavated at Minnis Bay, Birchington, Kent, 1938–40', *PPS* 9: 28–47.

Young, A., 1966. 'The sequence of Hebridean pottery', in Rivet 1966: 45–58.

Young, H. W., 1891. 'Notes on the ramparts of Burghead, as revealed by recent excavations', *PSAS* 25: 435–47.

Young, H. W., 1893. 'Notes on further excavations at Burghead', *PSAS* 27: 86–91.

Youngblood, E., Fredriksson, B. J., Kraut, F. and Fredriksson, K., 1978. 'Celtic vitrified forts; implications of a chemical-petrological study of glasses and source rocks', *J. Arch. Science* 5: 99–115.

Ziegert, H., 1963. *Zur Chronologie und Gruppengliederung der westlichen Hügelgräberkultur* (Berliner Beiträge zur Vor-und-Frühgeschichte, Bd 7).

Zumstein, H., 1964. 'L'âge du bronze dans le département du Haut-Rhin', *RAECE* 15: 7–66 and 161–213.

Zumstein, H., 1965. 'L'âge du bronze dans le département du Haut-Rhin (suite et fin)', *RAECE* 16: 7–56.

Zumstein, H., 1976. 'Les civilisations de l'âge du bronze dans l'Est de la France. A: les civilisations de l'âge du bronze en Alsace', in Guilaine 1976: II, 630–9.

Index

GEOGRAPHICAL

SUBJECT